David L
and the Amer

David Lynch and the American West

Essays on Regionalism and Indigeneity in Twin Peaks *and the* Films

Edited by ROB E. KING, CHRISTINE SELF *and* ROBERT G. WEAVER

Foreword by John Thorne

McFarland & Company, Inc., Publishers
Jefferson, North Carolina

This book has undergone peer review.

ISBN (print) 978-1-4766-8208-2
ISBN (ebook) 978-1-4766-4705-0

LIBRARY OF CONGRESS AND BRITISH LIBRARY
CATALOGUING DATA ARE AVAILABLE

Library of Congress Control Number 2022057336

Front cover image: David Lynch on the set of *Mulholland Dr.,* 1999
(Imagine Television/Photofest); *background*: Washington State
(© Jose Luis Stephens/Shutterstock)

Printed in the United States of America

*McFarland & Company, Inc., Publishers
Box 611, Jefferson, North Carolina 28640
www.mcfarlandpub.com*

Acknowledgments

We would like to thank Andrés Halskov, Freedonia Paschall, Andrew Hinton, Elizabeth Massengale, and Monica Montelongo Flores for their encouragement and appreciated support of this project. The existence of this collection also owes a special thanks to the editors of *25YL* and *Blue Rose Magazine*, as well as the hosts of the *Twin Peaks Unwrapped* and *Diane* podcasts, for their years of encouragement, intellectual curiosity, and engagement with David Lynch fandom. Without the mentorship and confidence of our colleagues Robert G. Weiner, Joy Perrin, Shelley Barba, and Matt McEniry, this book would not have been possible. Kristin Loyd must be thanked for the time she shared of a valued editor to this collection as well as support and patience with our process. Finally, a notable contributor to this collection's proposal, selection process, and early edits, we would like to acknowledge valued colleague Austin Allison for his belief that we could manifest something wonderful, western, and strange.

Table of Contents

Foreword

A Long Way from the World:
David Lynch and the American West

John Thorne

Here's something you already know: David Lynch's films defy labels. Despite scholarly insistence that Lynch's films be categorized as horror, noir, mystery, the truth is no label satisfactorily encompasses the whole of Lynch's work. His themes, moods, and style elude genre. He is an artist sui generis. You know this.

Still, Lynch's films exhibit patterns and repetitions. Again and again David Lynch returns to familiar tropes. Fractured protagonists, blurred thresholds, ominous landscapes—all are part and parcel of Lynch's work. If you stand far enough back, you see these commonalities.

And there's something else. Migration. Look at the films from the second half of Lynch's career and it's indisputable. Like David Lynch himself, the settings of Lynch's movies shift inexorably from the claustrophobic cityscapes of the industrial East to the wide-open spaces of the American West.

David Lynch's formative years in places such as Philadelphia and New York left indelible psychic scars on the young artist. "Everything in New York made me fearful," Lynch says of his childhood visits to the city.[1] Philadelphia was no better. As a young man (and young father) studying and living in a rundown tenement, Lynch describes the city as a place of "violence and hate and filth."[2] These oppressive city-life experiences stayed with Lynch and permeated the worlds of his early films, *Eraserhead, The Elephant Man*, and the Harkonnen environs of *Dune*. But after Lynch moved west and settled in Los Angeles ("I couldn't believe how beautiful the light was!"), his films explored striking new territories.[3] From *Wild at Heart* to *Twin Peaks* Season 3, also known as *The Return*, the American West informs and envelops Lynch's later work.

To be clear, Lynch is not interested in the generic trappings of the classic "Western." Only once has he ventured into this tricky territory. In his 1988 short film *The Cowboy and the Frenchman*, Lynch leans heavily into clichés and stereotypes ("Dude ranches," "Indians," "Cowboys") to make a broad point about cultural misconception, and to make finer points about language and miscommunication. Lynch is not probing the "Western" to deconstruct it or to comment on the genre. He has larger ideas in mind.

David Lynch explores a different kind of West. His West embodies the East. Not the geographic east—the east of big cities, industry and European heritage—but the philosophical East, the east as found in Hindu teachings.

Lynch's interest in Hindu philosophy is well known. He quotes liberally from Hindu texts in his short memoir, *Catching the Big Fish*, and he has long been a proponent of Transcendental Meditation, a meditative process developed by the Hindu sage, Maharishi Mahesh Yogi. The inspiration Lynch finds in Hindu belief is reflected in the works he creates. Not surprisingly, David Lynch's Western aesthetic is rooted in the philosophical soil of Eastern belief.

Cyclical time, infinite consciousness, the search for spiritual stability—these Eastern concepts manifest in Lynch's depictions of wildernesses, indigenous spirituality, journeys through shifting landscapes. Time and again the American West provides a venue for Lynch to explore ancient ideas.

To be sure, Lynch's West is not all peace and harmony. His West requires careful navigation, a wariness of lures and mirages that might lead one astray. Threats lurk in the vast dark spaces of David Lynch's films, and man's trespasses into natural and supernatural realms often lead to desolation.

In *Twin Peaks*, Dale Cooper, an agent of a structured, orderly eastern government, travels west to solve a murder and to restore order to a shaken community. But he's also there for ulterior motives. Cooper is an unsettled soul in search of identity. Sheriff Harry Truman tells Cooper Twin Peaks is "a long way from the world," describing the remote physical location of the town but also conveying the spiritual distance of Twin Peaks from the frenzy of civilization. Indeed, the otherworldly environs of Twin Peaks work their magic on Cooper, and he decides to make the town his home. But Cooper falls into a trap, stumbling into a supernatural snare waiting in the dark woods. Ultimately, the West of *Twin Peaks* is a place of promise and of portent, but one needs fortitude (and perfect courage) to negotiate its terrain.

In *Wild at Heart*, two young lovers, Sailor and Lula, flee west to escape the threat of an angry matriarch. The West beckons, promising individualism and liberation. Sailor and Lula race into the sunset hoping to leave both physical and psychic pain behind. Like so many Lynch protagonists, however, Sailor and Lula carry burdens with them, and these self-inflicted wounds detour the couple and ultimately interrupt their momentum. But all is not lost. In a rare happy ending, Sailor and Lula shed their burdens and reunite under the bright light of Los Angeles sunshine. The West has delivered them to each other's arms.

In *The Straight Story*, Alvin Straight journeys west, leaving the shelter of home to visit his ailing, estranged brother, Lyle. Alvin does not have means to travel swiftly, but he does the best he can. Riding a lawn mower, Alvin passes through pastoral landscapes and rural communities. As he travels inexorably west, Alvin atones for past sins and seeds hard-won wisdom among all who will receive him. Eventually, Alvin crosses a definitive Western boundary—the Mississippi River—before reuniting with Lyle. Once across this crucial threshold, Alvin exchanges one life for another, finding peace and comfort in a probable afterlife. The West absolves Alvin.

In *Mulholland Drive*, Betty Elms seeks fame and fortune when she moves from Deep River, Ontario, to Hollywood, California. But Betty isn't really Betty. She's the alter ego of failed actress Diane Selwyn, whose success requires navigating the West's tricky mazes. When Diane fails to do so, she slips into nightmares both real and imagined. The West may promise hope but, as Diane tragically learns, delusions lurk just one wrong step away.

For David Lynch, the West always beckons. Perhaps it's only coincidence, but in Lynch's most recent work, *Twin Peaks: The Return*, elements of the narrative begin in Philadelphia and New York (Lynch's nightmare cities) before moving rapidly, permanently west. Answers (and more questions) linger in the deserts and the forests and the vast dark skies of Lynch's American West, a place where a story decades in the making at last achieves consummation.

Clearly, there are many ways the "American West" informs and inflects Lynch's films. Now, with *David Lynch and the American West*, we can dig deeper into this fascinating area of study. Essays here examine Lynch's work in terms of setting (Regionalism), social and historical context (Indigeneity), and style (Road Narrative and Genre). These kinds of analyses are important. They delve into previously unexplored territory and chart new paths in the field of David Lynch scholarship. Each essay in this book opens a door to new ideas. Each reframes Lynch's work in crucial ways.

* * *

Journeys west proffer hazards and rewards, and so it is for the films of David Lynch. Both Lynch and the West entice, hypnotize, and challenge, and if you're not careful you can easily lose your way. But you can also find revelation.

Neither the West nor Lynch's art is for everyone; it takes an intrepid soul to forge into these fraught spaces. But risk the journey and turn toward the setting sun; there are treasures to be found, endless landscapes to explore, and visions shimmering in the perfect light.

NOTES

1. David Lynch and Kristine McKenna, *Room to Dream* (Random House, 2018), 18.
2. Chris Rodley, ed., *Lynch on Lynch* (Faber and Faber, 1997), 43.
3. Lynch and McKenna, *Room to Dream*, 119.

Introduction

ROB E. KING, CHRISTINE SELF
and ROBERT G. WEAVER

Studies of the American West may not seem the most obvious access point when reading a book on David Lynch's films. Compiling a book on Eastern rather than Western mythology and Vedic traditions in his art would on the surface provide for a more evident volume with ample one-to-one correspondence, given his statements on Transcendental Meditation and personal interests. Martha P. Nochimson provides some clear examples of that analysis in her University of Texas Press books *The Passion of David Lynch: Wild at Heart in Hollywood* (1997) and *David Lynch Swerves: Uncertainty from* Lost Highway *to* Inland Empire (2014). Yet to ignore the American West and its influences on Lynch would be short-sighted and resistant to the larger mysteries in his art. To that point, this is the first book of essays to collect dedicated studies on American western regionalism as well as elements of the Western genre across Lynch's filmography.

For readers who come to this collection for Lynch studies but who may be new to studies of the American West, there are some perspectives worth noting—those of regionalism versus genre; historical versus contemporary; myth and narrative. The key is to remember the distinction between western regionalism and the Western as a genre. As an example, while the character of The Cowboy is an on-the-nose representation of a regional time and Western archetype in *Mulholland Drive*, the neo-noir film's statements on Hollywood and disillusionment reflect a larger heritage of regional California fiction from the 1920s and 1930s, which evolved out of western genre tropes. As Peter C. Rollins states in his introduction to *Hollywood's West: The American Frontier in Film, Television, and History*, "[P]rior to cinema, painting, works of sculpture, and literary representations conveyed the myths of the West. But in our media age, by far the most influential forces in shaping images of the American West have been entertainment films and television programs."[1] One can ask how the larger myth of the American West as represented in traditional Westerns is furthered and present in the contemporary American West. How is it communicated today in films and media, particularly in that of Lynch?

While the notion of the West evokes "enduring visions in the popular imagination: wagon trains of pioneers snaking across the prairie, the suffering of and near-desolation of indigenous peoples, the surveying and mapping of vast and alien landscapes," Mark Frost and David Lynch engage unexpected yet nonetheless existing narratives of the region—UFOs; Theosophy and occultism on the plains; oil and industrialization; and homage to the pulp fiction of the region.[2] Without claiming Lynch as a director of contemporary or neo-westerns—though that reading is included here— his works as regional products, which engage the majestic rural and urban shadow are influenced by the existing identity of the region. An access point to a study of Lynch and the West is an idea of the mythic west and its people seen through the lens of a re-imagined frontier in genre and in a historical context. To open the western landscape even more, we acknowledge Neil Campbell's argument that "To examine the West in the twenty-first century is to think of it as always already transnational, a more routed and complex rendition, a traveling concept whose meanings move between cultures, crossing, bridging, and intruding simultaneously." Before the American West was "imagineered"—as Josh Garrett-Davis would phrase in *What is a Western?: Region, Genre, Imagination*—to embody a Manifest Destiny through a conquest of American exceptionalism, the land had experienced real native travel, cultural settlement, and farming that has persisted in the culture despite any efforts to erase its existence.[3] The essays in this volume acknowledge this history in their arguments.

Beyond well-mythologized nineteenth-century westward expansionism, migration in the twentieth century originated from different, even spiritual motivations. As stated in *Enchanted Modernities: Theosophy, the Arts and the American West*, "Imaginings of the American West (including the modern states of New Mexico, Arizona, Utah, Nevada, and California) spawned not only powerful mythologies of American nationhood but also … new terrain for spiritual evolution."[4] As spirituality figures into the works of David Lynch, this spiritual migration must figure into a reading of David Lynch and the West. An additional notion of travel in the West comes from Campbell that can ground our understanding of western regionalism in film and narrative studies.

> All of the "routes" by which we might travel are, of course, no longer tied to physical movement, to bourgeois privileges of a white middle class, since every billboard, every commodity purchased, every radio, iPod, CD player, TV, and PC permits "travel" to some extent, however virtual, creating a movement that

affects the local and interferes with perceptions of where and what we are. Traversing the West as tourist site, website, advertising imagery, fiction, theme park, film, or immigrant experience—all of these are continuations of the processes that constructed the American West like those described in a novel that in many ways has come to encapsulate a myth of settlement, *The Virginian* [1902].[5]

The twelve essays in this collection examine the region as it is communicated and portrayed in Lynch's films. The volume is divided into three parts: Regionalism; Indigeneity and Representation; and Road Narrative and Genre. Readers will also note that six of the twelve essays are focused on *Twin Peaks*.

The retrospective nature of *Twin Peaks* Season 3, regarding Lynch's oeuvre with its inclusion of western settings in Las Vegas, New Mexico, and Odessa, Texas, inspired me to propose a collection that locates western elements across most of his full-length films. It was *Twin Peaks* Season 3 that led to my research for a special issue of *New American Notes Online* (*NANO*), where I came across a McFarland book of essays titled *A Fistful of Icons: Essays on Frontier Fixtures of the American Western* (2017) that included an essay by Monica Montelongo Flores titled "Cowboy Accommodations: Plotting the Hotel in Western Film and Television." In that essay, she presents an examination of iconic hotels across a chronology of Western films and their changing significance in communicating social mores, including the Great Northern Hotel of *Twin Peaks*. Many of the authors in this collection acknowledge Geoff Bil's seminal 2016 essay, "Tensions in the World of Moon: *Twin Peaks*, Indigeneity and Territoriality," where he argues that "...*Twin Peaks*' use of indigenous iconography fits generally in a longer Western televisual, filmic and cultural tradition of making symbols of indigeneity serve patently non-indigenous ends."[6] I also discovered Bil's essay in my research along with David Titterington's studies on Indigenous art in *Twin Peaks* for *25YL*, "Jumping Kokopelli" and "Garmonbozia and The United States' Demonic Show." All three of these authors—Flores, Bil, and Titterington—appear in this volume—two in interview and one in essay. Ultimately, this book was proposed as a space to collect the ideas of like-minded researchers, who were already identifying Western elements and tensions in the works of David Lynch. Additionally, given the constraints of space on my *NANO* essay, I was left convinced that a monograph could be written by widening the regional scope to the larger West (U.S.) and by incorporating Lynch's entire filmography.

As Josh Garrett-Davis contextualizes, "Sometimes distortion results from viewing western regional culture and Westerns together.... There is no denying the region and genre—at least as framed in terms of the West or Western—are more peripheral than they were a generation ago...."[7]

Across the essays, the elements of the West in Lynch's films, Lynch's western distortions, are leveraged to advance our understanding of the region and its mythology as imagineered—that is engineered in the imagination to a purpose. Indigenous voices of the West are shown to speak through the mise-en-scène of Lynch's films, road narratives to reveal American instability, and inclusions of industrialization, petroculture, and forestry to portray states of the Anthropocene.

Regionalism

This portion of essays begins with an interview with Andréas Halskov, whose most recent book is *Beyond Television: TV Production in the Multiplatform Era*. As a film and television scholar at Aarhus University, he brings an international perspective to a regionalist view of Lynch's works. He shares that "[A]s a foreigner I am only a visitor of the American West…. So, I suppose the American West to me is in part a figment of a televisual and cinematic fantasy in a way, and it is interesting how David Lynch exploits and does something to that televisual and cinematic fantasy." Just as the myth of the West was romanticized and promulgated following nineteenth-century expansionism through art and literature, as noted in Rollins's earlier quote, it continues to be communicated through televisual and cinematic representations beyond the region. This is what makes a study of Lynch's unique inclusion of the contemporary West essential to an international understanding of the region and its influences in his filmography.

To further open the exploration of regionalism, another international scholar, Fernando Gabriel Pagnoni Berns, follows his interview with an essay titled "'To the hellhole it is now': The Pastoral and Industrialization in *Eraserhead*." The editors were pleased to be able to open this volume with an essay examining David Lynch's first full-length film, *Eraserhead*, in the context of what it conveys regarding industrialization and a disappearing pastoral, which felt a proper start in an exploration of the west. With the influence of industrialization and its corruptive effects on the land presented, Rebecca Heimel provides a historical understanding of the American West in her essay "Watch and Listen to the Dream of Time and Space: Historiography, Geography and *Twin Peaks*." She establishes a background for this study through a context of New Western History, arguing that commonalities in scholarship following the formation of New Western History in 1987 helped to retire worn frontier narratives that persisted since Frederick Jackson Turner's Frontier Thesis, allowing such a collection as this to be possible.

The study of the region is then expanded upon in Andy Hageman's "The Wood for the Trees: Regional and Anthropocene Signals in the Pacific Northwest Forests of *Twin Peaks*." With a focus on the Pacific Northwest, Hageman's essay accompanies Berns's essay as one of two in this collection to incorporate an ecological perspective on the region. Hageman invites readers to note with an ecological lens a larger message of sustainability in the regional forestry of *Twin Peaks*. "While *Twin Peaks* may seem, on the surface, an odd choice to identify as possessing a productive ecological aesthetic ... its exceptionally surreal twists and turns provide a sophisticated invitation to, as well as a map and model for, sustaining life and love in uncertain times." Regionalism is then further explored in Marko Lukić's "Dark Americana: Identity, Frontiers and Heterotopias in David Lynch's Dreams," which examines our understanding of regional space through Foucault's discourse on heterotopias in *The Order of Things*. Given Lynch's surrealism and dream-logic, Lukić's exploration of space adds to a contextualization on liminality, borders, and frontier.

Indigeneity and Representation

Geoff Bil's interview begins this collection's section on indigeneity. He reminds readers that we cannot relegate native existence to a past, to the American frontier.

> In general, for fans of *Twin Peaks*, or of any media representation of settler colonialism, it's tremendously important to remember that Indigenous peoples are still here, and that the struggles faced by Indigenous peoples are essentially continuous over the longue durée of settler colonialism. That might seem self-evident, but it's not what dominant media representations tend to show, nor has it been common in many settler colonial education systems—whether in Canada, the US or elsewhere. It's still very commonplace to speak about Native peoples as if they do not exist, and to speak about settler colonialism as something that happened in the distant past. Even academics frequently write about what they call the "colonial era" as if it's something that happened a hundred years ago.

The editors would like to highlight that, upon the call for papers for this collection, it was announced that the Snoqualmie Tribe recovered its rights to the land upon which the Salish Lodge, setting for The Great Northern, and Snoqualmie Falls are located. Speaking to native survivance and persistence, David Titterington, an art instructor at the Haskell Indian Nations University, explores the heritage of native arts in "'It has something to do with your heritage': Indigenous Arts in *Twin Peaks*," bestowing on long silent background characters—paintings on walls, weavings, and baskets—their traditional heritage, an honor to those people reclaiming their own rightful heritages. This is followed by Garrett Wayne Wright's "'Very old, but always current': Indigenous Geographies in *Twin Peaks*." While key native imagery in Lynch films is remarked upon throughout the Essays in this collection, the combination of Titterington's and Wright's essays in this collection convey the most thorough investigations of indigeneity in respect to *Twin Peaks*. Still, this section is concluded with the topics of American identity and native representation in Molly O'Gorman's "'I am the FBI': American Identity in *Twin Peaks*" a survey of Lynch's use of American identity. O'Gorman articulates a key tension teased throughout this collection, that "White American identity is constructed … as Cooper and the FBI's repeated venturing into other worlds can be read as a form of imperial imposition of settler law."

Road Narrative and Genre

Monica Montelongo Flores's interview serves to pivot this collection's focus from regionalism and indigenous representations to that of narrative and genre. As she states of her teaching approach, "I've taught courses that focus specifically on the Western, a genre that mythologizes the American West, but I've also taught courses that surround the literature and creative productions that deal with the American West. And oftentimes we get really differing perspectives when we start to think about it outside of the genre-specific Western film, for example." As a follow-up, genre is skillfully explored with a return to *Twin Peaks* Season 3 in long-time Lynch writers and researchers, Franck Boulègue and Marisa C. Hayes's "Once Upon a Time in Rancho Rosa: Reading *Twin Peaks* Season 3 as a Neo-Western." The authors argue that "Various tropes of the genre intersect with the spiritual preoccupations of the show's creators, while generationally, both Frost and Lynch witnessed the golden era of Western cinema, leaving its mark on their respective writing and visual practices." By extrapolating the Western genre in *Twin Peaks*, the authors perfectly set the stage for Andrew T. Burt's research on the masculinity of the traditional cowboy of this film era in "I'm Going West, Diane: Masculinity and the Cowboy Archetype in the Works of David Lynch." It is worth noting that no volume can completely or sufficiently cover the entirety of a subject such as American Western Studies, and the editors believe there is much more to mine in a study of gender in a context of the West through Lynch's filmography.

The western precedent for this message on genre and narrative transitions to the byways that crisscross the nation in an examination of road narratives, liminality, desert horror, frontiers, and heterotopias from *Blue Velvet* to *Lost Highway* in Thomas Britt's "David Lynch's Desert Frontier: Road Movie, Desert Horror and Western Liminality" and Mark Henderson's "The Western Road as Metaphor for American Instability in *Lost Highway*." Each essay contextualizes such tensions and reframes our understanding of Lynch's use of the West to show an evolved American Dream, one Rob E. King explores as traumatized in "Re-Imagined West in the L.A. Trilogy: A Heritage of California Fiction and American Trauma." The essays can be read in any order, though we have delineated the collection's intentional structure.

The book is largely aimed at researchers and general Lynch fandom as readers interested in how regionalism can be related and explored through the works of auteurs and modern popular culture mythologies as seen through the scope of David Lynch's filmography and the collaborative narrative of *Twin Peaks*. Furthermore, this book adds a much-needed contemporary investigation of the American West that acknowledges Hollywood's deeply ingrained portrayals of the West in determining how worldwide audiences perceive the land, the people, and economy.

Released more than seventy-five years after the Trinity Test at New Mexico's White Sands Missile Range, more than thirty years since Dale Cooper was locked in the Black Lodge, and more than four years following the premiere of Season 3, this volume also anticipates Lynch's tentatively titled *Unrecorded Night*. It is the hope of the editors that readers will find among these essays encouragement to continue Western regionalist studies of Lynch's films with each contribution as an integral starting point as we continue engaging with his thought-provoking mysteries.

NOTES

1. Peter C. Rollins and John E. O'Connor, *Hollywood's West: The American Frontier in Film, Television, and History* (Louisville: University of Kentucky, 2009), 1.

2. Christopher Scheer, Sarah Victoria Turner, and James G. Mansell, *Enchanted Modernities: Theosophy, the Arts, and the American West* (Logan: Nora Eccles Harrison Museum of Art, Utah State University, 2019), 1.

3. Josh Garrett-Davis, *What Is a Western? Region, Genre, Imagination* (Norman: University of Oklahoma Press, 2019). Kindle.

4. Scheer, 1.

5. Neil Campbell, *The Rhizomatic West: Representing the American West in a Transnational, Global, Media Age* (Lincoln: University of Nebraska Press, 2008), 5.

6. Geoff Bil, "Tensions in the World of Moon: *Twin Peaks* Indigeneity and Territoriality," *Senses of Cinema* 79 (2016).

7. Garrett-Davis, *What Is a Western?*, introduction, para. 3–4.

PART I

Regionalism

Considering Regionalism
in the Films of David Lynch

An Interview with Andréas Halskov

Rob E. King

RK: You have thoroughly researched and published on Twin Peaks *and other Lynch films. When you look at American television and film, what kind of messages about the American West do you get? And is the way that Lynch portrayed the West somehow different?*

AH: That's a major and quite interesting question. I think it is interesting for a foreigner to ponder this question because as a foreigner, I am only a visitor of the American West. I have traveled to America, but, of course, much of what I know of the American West is in fact informed by what I've seen in popular Hollywood films and TV series. So, I suppose the American West to me is in part a figment of a televisual and cinematic fantasy in a way, and it is interesting how David Lynch exploits and does something to that televisual and cinematic fantasy. It's as if he plays around with it.

Depending on what part of the American West we're dealing with, there are many typical tropes and cinematic or televisual depictions. Of course, we have the Mid–West as one major region that we have seen covered in whole genres, and the Western in and of itself gives you this idea of a vast inexplicable landscape with an ever-expanding horizon where you can continually move to new frontiers, and it seems you can walk forever. You would see that also in modern renditions, the "Bagman" episode, for example, of *Better Call Saul* gives you that almost Western-like feel, that sense of the vast, endlessly expansive landscape. Other parts of the American West are subject to other types of depictions and visions. Los Angeles or California as a broader concept, for example, has become very central to foreigners' perception through film and television of what the U.S. also is.

15

And I'd say that, for example, Lynch exploits the noir to create a new conception of that particular part of America.

It's interesting that when doing his Sunshine Noir Trilogy, or whatever you call it, his L.A. Noir Trilogy, the landscape becomes strangely abstract and very concrete at the same time. It's as if the road and that landscape become everything and nothing in *Lost Highway* because it's not as if you can really, clearly identify the places—of course, if you've been to Senalda, you'd know that there is this actual house and Lynch actually works there—but *Lost Highway* still seems to be taking place in a sort of "nowhere" or in an ever-expanding "nowhere" and "everywhere" at the same time. You have the road, the traditional Lynchian motif of the road as seen from the front window of a car, and you can see that this is in a way indelibly American, but it is not as if it's that easy to locate. We have the scenes with the Mystery Man's small cabin in the desert, and that is clearly an image of the American West or one part of the American West. But it's not as if it's easy to place, and the extreme use of low-key lighting and the strange non-chronological plot, I think, help shape a landscape that is also quite abstract, fluid and un-locatable. We still have sequences that feel very California-like—I mean, the party scene, for example, but that's indoors. It is just a matter of it being near a pool and stuff like that. It's as if David Lynch plays around with tropes and elements that we know from noir films that are, in a way, quite intrinsically connected to Los Angeles as a place, but in Lynch's version of Los Angeles the city is envisioned almost as dreamscape and an abstract non-place.

There is a French anthropologist called Marc Augé who has written about "non-places"—places such as airports that are almost the same wherever you go. *Lost Highway*, I think, is a sort of film that takes place in a specific and real part of America while appearing as something of an abstraction. It is so evidently American, indelibly American, and at the same time, it's not as if you can quite clearly place it. So, it is much less immediately connected to a very specific, locatable place than, for example, the original *Twin Peaks*, even if it takes place in a fictional town. You can find Snoqualmie. You can find North Bend, and they look like that *Twin Peaks*, and they seem like that place. *Lost Highway* takes place in a real American city, and you can find the house, but still *Lost Highway* takes place in a noir-ish dreamscape. So, it has become a metascape in a way. I don't know how to phrase it, but it's interesting to me that *Twin Peaks* takes place in a fictional town that still seems quite real, whereas *Lost Highway* and *Mulholland Dr.* take place in a very real city that in both films seems almost unreal or unbounded. *Mulholland Dr.* takes place near a street that we actually know, and we have street names that we know, not just specifically from L.A., but also from other movies. It clearly references

Sunset Boulevard—like Figueroa, for example—when we see these different street names. It's evidently a Los Angeles setting. It is even specifically placed around Hollywood, but Hollywood not just as a landscape, but also as a concept that seems to be beyond place. A phenomenon that stretches beyond geographical limits and locatability. That's what fascinates me about those three films in particular—*Lost Highway*, *Mulholland Drive*, and then, of course, *INLAND EMPIRE*, which not only takes place in one place, but also includes Poland and all of these different locations. But, again, it seems to be located in specific places in different parts of the world but at the same time, thoroughly unlocatable. *INLAND EMPIRE* also alludes to particular places, and when we hear about Pomona it looks like a reference to both a concrete place and Billy Wilder's aforementioned film, *Sunset Boulevard*. At the same time, Lynch's film is set in a strangely, even uncannily dream-like geography. I think that's what's so interesting, that David Lynch can take something so simple as a house or a street, and he can deconstruct that space and make it into an ever-expanding place without any borders.

When Fred moves down the hallway in *Lost Highway*, he is engulfed in eternal darkness, and it is as if it's absolutely impossible to say where he is at that particular point in the movie. Have we in fact moved inside of Fred's imagination? Is he just down a dark hallway which seems endless due to the extreme use of chiaroscuro, or does he, in fact, slip away into another dimension or into the dark abysses of his mind? In *Mulholland Drive*, they also reference specific places in Los Angeles, but it is more Los Angeles as a phenomenon—and even Los Angeles as a cinematic construction—than it is Los Angeles as an actual location. We are far away from the touristy use of locations that we know from TV series such as *Billions* and *Sex in the City* where you are meant to see that, oh, this is the real New York or something to that effect. Here, we are in Los Angeles, but we are not in Los Angeles. We are in the Los Angeles of movies. We are in Hollywood, but Hollywood is one of the fussiest concepts ever used by people. The American media scholar Amanda D. Lotz has written that the word "cable" is used somewhat like the word "Hollywood," something that you use both to reference a very specific thing and to reference a very fluid and fussy concept. So, to most people, Hollywood would represent movies in a broad sense, even if many American films are produced outside Hollywood, but David Lynch's L.A. seems to be a cinematic, dreamy L.A. that in a way deconstructs what Los Angeles really is.

I am interested in places, but at the same time, my geographical sense is very bad. I have no sense of place and direction, and at the same time, I'm quite interested in places and geography. But from watching David Lynch's films—that particular trilogy, at least—I wouldn't be able to follow that map to L.A. I've certainly been on Mulholland Drive, and I've certainly taken some trips to specific parts of those locations. And I can also sometimes get a Lynchian vibe when going there. But at the same time, it seems as if he has chosen to bend that location to make his films about something much vaster than a specific physical place that you can enter in reality. And I think that fits his entire idea about dreams. Lynch's worlds are never physical geographies, but expansive and uncanny "psycho-graphies."

RK: Yeah, I'm glad you said that because that answer in a lot of ways validates about three different essays in the collection. There are two that look at road narratives that will appear in this collection focusing on Lost Highway, *and my essay focuses on the L.A. Trilogy as you were just discussing. What I end up saying is that while Lynch is not a director of contemporary or neo westerns, the traumas that he's engaging with in his regional Western narratives and in his characters communicate Americans' conflicted interiorities following westward expansion. There is another essay I have read that speaks to L.A. as representing a terminus—California's coastline representing a wall at the end of westward expansion. And then we had to, you know—conquest expands to empire or space, etcetera. So, that's interesting, that idea of where do we go from here.*

AH: Yeah, it is interesting. It's hardly coincidental that he would choose Los Angeles in particular, because, I mean, not only is it where you have the major parts of the film industry, but it is a place that you venture to when you want to visit or become part of that shiny, artificial world: the world of cinema. So, it is the land of cinema and it is the mind of dreams, two elements that, of course, naturally seem to interest David Lynch. I think he's both, as you mentioned. He is both clearly an American director and he focuses very much on the American West. Yet at the same time, his stories are beyond place and they very much deal with classically American genres, if you call film noir a genre. That would be one of them, of course. But then again, I think *Lost Highway* and certainly in *INLAND EMPIRE*, but also *Mulholland Drive*, they transcend that genre and they are all about getting lost or about losing oneself. *Lost Highway* is, in fact, a lost highway. It is also about getting lost within the maze of your mind, I suppose. And *Mulholland Drive*, though referencing a physical, actual place, is very much about losing yourself and getting lost inside an artificial world that holds a lot of promises, but most of those promises might be fictitious or only ever real in fictions that take place in those places.

RK: Right, and I was saying—I was thinking about this the other day as I was composing these questions, that there is that novel by Hermann Hesse, The Journey to the East. *That is an allegory on the road to Enlightenment. And I was thinking that feels very in line with Lynch's interests in more*

Eastern belief systems—Transcendental Meditation and Vedic religion. And so maybe we could discuss how Lynch's films paint a larger journey in the contemporary west in the way that maybe Twin Peaks *in particular—a story that begins with the death of a homecoming queen—is an American journey to the east, a kind of spiritual exploration using the region. Do you sense that?*

AH: I think that makes total sense. I think the journey is central to David Lynch and his work in both a concrete and a metaphorical way. I wouldn't know exactly what his own ideas are, but I agree with you that it fits neatly with the Vedic elements and the Transcendental parts. His films are often about journeys, in the double sense of the word. First, many of his films and works are about people physically transporting themselves from one part of America to another. Of course, we have road movies like *The Straight Story*, which is a very concrete example of it, and which almost looks like a deconstruction of the West(ern). And it is also a deconstruction of the biopic in a way, in that it deals with an actual biographical story about a real person.

But in contrast to most traditional biopics, it is not about a famous person. It's about a fairly ordinary man who has just done something that was somewhat extraordinary, right? But it is the closest you come to a John Ford Western deconstructed and set in modern times. It is about a journey in a concrete sense, but it is also essentially about a psychological or relational journey for Alvin Straight, who is on a path to redemption and hoping to rebuild his relationship with his brother after many years of non-communication and estrangement. In a concrete sense, the film as about travelling the American landscape, at a very leisurely pace, as Lynch would have it, but at the same time it is about a man who is trying to redeem himself and patch things up with his brother, Lyle, who has suffered a stroke. Was Alvin an alcoholic, and was it, in fact, his fault that the state took away Rose's children? The film never answers those questions, yet those are the most pivotal questions of the entire movie. It unfolds as one "straight" story and a concrete journey across America, yet the actual story is hidden beneath the straight veneer and beyond the geographical journey. It sort of has that Western-like element to it, but the journey also is more psychological, a metaphorical aspect. And we see that in many of his films. *Lost Highway*, of course, takes place on a highway, but the journey is more about the psychological workings of the mad mind than about a physical trip. It's a journey, perhaps, to understand the repressed part of your psyche or whatever stuff that you might have done. It's an inner journey, but it's also an external journey.

Mulholland Drive—at least one part of the movie—is about a very concrete journey and somebody, you know, coming from Deep River,

Ontario to Los Angeles in order to hopefully become someone. But then it turns into a story about losing oneself in film or perhaps having major psychological issues of trauma, perhaps connected to love life, unrequited love and self-loathing, but again there is a physical, actual journey connected to a much more psychological one. And so—and in *Twin Peaks* in particular—I think it is interesting what you say. Again, the journey becomes a central part of the original *Twin Peaks*—there would never have been the original *Twin Peaks*, had we not had a person travel from one place to another. If Ronette Pulaski had not crossed that border, it would never have become a federal case, and that federal case is what becomes the central or even centrifugal part of the original *Twin Peaks*. Because Ronette Pulaski crosses the border between two states, it becomes a federal case, and Agent Cooper can then, after 30 minutes of the pilot episode—or 40 minutes, I don't know exactly—he enters town. And so, we have somebody who travels from one place to another. Then, the original *Twin Peaks*, mostly, even if it is shot in different places, takes place in Washington.

I don't know that the original *Twin Peaks* was realistic; it had surreal elements, but it was at least borderline or seemingly realistic. You could see it mostly as a realistic story with quirky or uncanny aspects. And those different aspects that were either surreal or perhaps fantastical could, at least to some degree, be described as dreams, visions or figments of Cooper's imagination. In the new *Twin Peaks*, it is much less easy to discount those things. The supernatural elements can hardly be described *only* as figments of somebody's imagination. But it's interesting that as *Twin Peaks* moves beyond the physical location of the American Northwest, and as we move from one place to another, it also becomes much more a story about an inner journey, perhaps much closer to that Transcendental aspect that you mentioned. And physically, we see Cooper journeying through different layers of the mind, almost, as he is physically transporting himself from one place to another and the series, in a way.

It is much less of a return to Twin Peaks, hence the name being kind of strange, and I know that that was a Showtime idea, to call it *Twin Peaks: The Return*, because it is much less a return to Twin Peaks than it is an expansion of *Twin Peaks* and a deconstruction of Twin Peaks as a physical location. I mean, concretely we are in many different places, but at the same time, maybe, almost all of this new *Twin Peaks* is about a journey, an inner journey for Dale Cooper. But we also have other characters, e.g., Audrey Horne, that seem to be going through inner journeys, and it's strange that that American Northwest that seemed very real in the original series, even to those who might never have visited Snoqualmie, seems like a non-place in the new one. I mean, when we are at the Roadhouse, does that seem like a small venue in the state of Washington? Not to me.

It seems like that would be the entire musical scene in Seattle crammed into one place. It certainly doesn't seem like the small bar that we saw in the original series, and even from the very title sequence—I talked with Duwayne Dunham about this. It's interesting, even from that one in the original series, we have the landscape and then we have Angelo Badalamenti's score music. There's no diegetic sound whatsoever. We have images of the waterfalls and The Great Northern, underscored by Badalamenti's leitmotif, but in the new one, those elements have become, in a way, both more physically locatable and real as we actually hear the diegetic sounds of wind and water. At the same time, they become more interconnected with metaphysical or unreal places when intercut with shots of the Red Room or the Black Lodge. So, those surreal aspects, which could be seen as just surreal aspects in the original series, now seem to merge with the physical landscapes and, at the same time, they seem more physically concrete and much more inherently abstract at the same time. There is a strangeness to it, certainly, and especially in Part 8, which seems to take place outside of Twin Peaks concretely and also almost outside of the series—and at the same time, seems to be the point from which everything springs, so perhaps the very origin of *Twin Peaks* in a way. There's something interesting to that, and I'm not sure that I thought this to the very end, but it's interesting at least.

RK: Yeah, you know, I took a journey out to that area of New Mexico, where I went to the site of the Trinity Test, and I know that John Thorne has as well. So, at the very least, it encouraged some of us that have some proximity to it, to visit it. And then you get there, and you feel a little guilty because you are there for a television show and then realize the immensity of what it really means. You know, it is a very powerful place to be. So, this collection covers quite a bit related to those areas, and in the introduction, I say that "Indigenous voices of the West are shown to speak through the mise-en-scène of Lynch's films, road narratives to reveal American instability, and inclusions of industrialization, petroculture, and forestry to portray states of the Anthropocene." How do you think that film and television communicate regionalism in general? And are there particular shows or films that you think leverage region better than others?

AH: Well, there are a few genres in America that I would say really give you a strong sense of place, and I'd say that we even have those elsewhere, too, naturally. We are seeing it even more so these days. I recently talked with TV producer Kelly Luegenbiehl—she's the vice president of Netflix International Originals—and she talked a lot about how much they, when prompting creators to produce non–American content, tried to get the TV creators to be very regional in their approach. Netflix wanted the regional series to be very specific to the different countries and regions. In film and television, we have always seen arenas as being a sort of attraction. A typical arena could be a police station or a courtroom or even a funeral home, as in *Six Feet Under*. But these days, it seems as if different regions are becoming those kinds of attractions in and of themselves.

So, that might be the reason why you watch a show like *Trapped* from Iceland because it seems so indelibly Icelandic that even from the title sequence of it, where you have these aerial shots of the Icelandic landscape superimposed with close-ups of the human skin almost giving you this organic sense of the Icelandic landscape, it is as if that becomes very much a part of what makes the series fascinating. Of course, it's a crime series, but then again, especially because the genres are perhaps universal—crime fiction is a globally popular genre with many universal tropes—then the location itself becomes the interesting and fascinating part. And I think we certainly have American films that showcase the American landscape in different ways. I mean, you could think of numerous series and films that depict New York in a way that would give people from outside of the U.S. a very clear understanding of what New York might be. Well, you could go to virtually any gangster film from *The Godfather* to sort of a modern neo-noir like *Taxi Driver* and you would see one type of New York. New York is sort of almost a hellish, nightmarish place. But you could also see it in a modern show like *Succession* or, as I mentioned, *Sex in the City*, and you would get a very clear and attractive sense of place.

In David Lynch's films—you mentioned two things that I think are so central to him. I remember when I was younger, we thought of him mostly as a director who focused on bucolic settings, and I suppose that was because of *Blue Velvet* and Lumberton and the entire lumber industry as a central element to *Blue Velvet* and then also in *Twin Peaks*. But his films take place in many different places. They are scattered around many parts of America. We have New Orleans and the American South in *Wild at Heart*, for example. We have Lumberton in *Blue Velvet* where you get a very interesting image of America as a vast continent that holds a lot of forests and as a proud lumbering nation that is full of rural towns with friendly fireman, white picket fences and seedy underbellies. But then you also have the industrial reflection of America as seen in *Eraserhead* that—even if it's recorded in L.A., much of it in a studio—seems to be outside any concrete or locatable reality. It might be set in L.A., but it also looks like a beautiful and nightmarish reflection of Philadelphia, a place that Lynch could not wait to escape from. In the end, *Eraserhead* seems to take place in an abstract industrial place that is both anywhere and everywhere in the U.S.

It is an industrial place, but exactly where, we wouldn't know, and then we have these also slightly industrial noir-like landscapes in Los

Angeles and in that trilogy. I'm not sure that that answers your question, but I think that we have specific genres that have existed from the earliest years of film history and that have each their own generic ways of depicting different regions in the U.S. The small-town genre became a central genre in and of itself because it depicted these American small towns that everyone seems to know, even if he/she has not been to the U.S., and we know this genre from Frank Capra. But we also know it from David Lynch with *Blue Velvet*. It harkens back to a traditional American genre. It also seems like something totally new.

And we have the film noir, which is, you know, intrinsically connected to Los Angeles, as a place with beautiful palm trees, illusory promises and winding roads. We see that in David Lynch's work, too. Then we have, of course, the Western genre. We see that in countless films. It has historically been one of the most impressive and massive genres, and it's still exploited to this day, I think. Quentin Tarantino is known for making his slightly counterfactual and revisionist Westerns that play around with the traditional settings and tropes that we know from directors like John Ford, Fred Zinnemann and Howard Hawks. It is almost as if different genres throughout cinema history—even the gangster genre that is often very closely connected to the streets of New York—are associated with different regional places that in a way tell different stories of the U.S.

It is interesting to me that when I look at David Lynch's films, he revisits those different genres—he twists those genres and places, and he makes something else out of it. And in doing so, he also recasts America or changes the map in a way, so it seems recognizable and at the same time, it is uncharted territory for a foreigner, in a way. And sometimes because his towns are fictional but placed in an actual setting, that you can find and locate, sometimes because they take place in an actual environment, but they're mostly shot in the studio, and you can't figure out where in that particular environment it takes place.

RK: Yeah, we've become kind of the Jerry Horne out there, kind of lost.

AH: Yeah, but, you know, what's interesting for me is I don't know that much about the American landscape, of course, mainly given that I'm not American. So, even if I visited America, and I've been to different places in America, it's very different for a tourist. So, there's something very interesting—it's so different from watching *True Detective*. You want to go to Louisiana. You want to see those specific places, and even if some of those places are in fact slightly metaphysical, like Carcosa, in a way, you go to Fort Macomb. I was there, and it's just not at all like with Lynch's work, because it seems as if you can visit those places and you do that—and when doing that, perhaps you can feel as if you are, you are going back into those worlds that he created, but the physical places are jumping-off points, and it's as if the localities transcend the physical area that they seem to depict, perhaps because his stories are both about an actual America and about something else. They are for better or worse, in a sort of a Lynchian understanding of the word, they are abstractions, or as you say, perhaps, mental journeys.

RK: *Did you have any other thoughts on the subject that haven't brought up?*

AH: Well, I do have one thing. Many years ago, a Danish reviewer said that the reason why *Dune* doesn't work—and I'm not sure that I would agree with that totally—is that David Lynch is best when his films take place "two blocks down the street," and *Dune* takes place in an entire galaxy. I'm not sure that I would agree, but I would agree at least to the point where I'd say that what makes Lynch great is that he is able to take something that seems physically very concrete, very real, very placeable, and then transform that into something that seems thoroughly unreal and abstract and unlocatable. Location is central to David Lynch, and America is a central part of his films, but his stories and his films in many ways transgress that. And indeed, they are about transcending borders, of transgressing borders. I said *Wild at Heart* takes place in New Orleans, at least partly, but what we see from the very opening is that it takes place in "Cape Fear, Somewhere Near the Border." In Lynch's work, it is always "somewhere near the border." It is at the border of Twin Peaks, and it's because Ronette Pulaski crosses that border that it starts. We transgress a border at the opening of *Wild at Heart*. And then that is the jumping-off point of the film, and in *Blue Velvet* it becomes interesting, dangerous and nightmarish at the very point when Jeffrey chooses to cross a street that he should not cross: "You're not going down by Lincoln, are you?"

I suppose that is what makes his films seem very American, even when taped or taking place outside of the U.S. *The Elephant Man* is an industrial film that takes place in London, but it could be seen in direct lineage with *Eraserhead* and could potentially have been an industrial scape in America. It is almost as if the Londonness, the Britishness of that film is less important than the industrial scape in and of itself. And I think that plays into part of what you were saying. Lynch is interested in lumber; he's interested in smokestack industry; he's interested in cars and roads; he's interested in vast desert-like landscapes. All those things, to me, rhyme with America or the American West, different parts of it. So, it is as if perhaps together, all of his films, even those that take place in galaxies, London or Poland create an image of America that's both enigmatic and strange—and at the same time, very concrete.

"To the hellhole it is now"

The Pastoral and Industrialization in Eraserhead

Fernando Gabriel Pagnoni Berns

David Lynch's *Eraserhead* (1977), one of the director's most surreal works, illustrates the end of the pastoral era and the poisonous impact of industrialization and urbanization upon human society.[1] The film's main lead, Henry Spencer (Jack Nance), is stuck in a dark industrial wasteland, forced to take care of an illegitimate premature child birthed by his girlfriend, Mary (Charlotte Stewart). Adding to the tension is the fact that the child does not look quite human, but rather like a sick creature covered with slime, a consequence of ill semen.

This essay suggests that *Eraserhead* should be imagined as the uneasy passage from the ideal of a healthy, spiritual Apollonian pastoral landscape—as imagined and projected through the American myth—to a scenario that privileges composted matter to the detriment of the transcendental, the industrial era. This approach to materialism, however, is not entirely negative as the film emphasizes the valor inherent in earthy elemental matter, the latter ignored by the pastoral. Lynch's film takes viewers to the other side—as surrealism does with "shocked eyes embedded in shocked bodies"—of visible things: behind the spirituality-infused pastoral lies purposely ignored ugliness.[2] In the film, industrialization has a double impact. One representation is negative, as it is shown to produce sick environments and subjects. The second representation is more positive as it reveals an intimate connection to dirt, a component of the pastoral. Thus, the industrial era is in opposition to and in continuation of the pastoral.

In a key scene, Mary's father, Bill, evokes the pastoral past. Sick of industrialization, he screams "Printing is your business, huh? Plumbing is mine, thirty years. I've seen this neighborhood change from pasture to the hellhole it is now." This new hell, Lynch tells us, is a surrealist reversal of the Midwestern American myth of Nature-as-garden.

25

From the Transcendent Pastoral to Material Industrialization

Historically, the West was considered as the "most American part of America."[3] This geographical zone is considered the "heartland" of the country, meaning: "a regional label that associates geographical centrality with a defining role in national identity and emotional responses to place."[4] The "defining role" is attached to the pastoral. The geographical localization was conceived and projected as a landscape akin to Eden and, as such, infused with biblical authority and Romantic idealism. Green landscapes, wide prairies, small towns, and healthy, happy people populating the surroundings were the main tropes of this pastoral discourse.

The pastoral image and the spiritual ethos attached to it were keys to understand the history of America after the prairie wilderness was slowly turned into an agricultural heartland. The agro-economic turn was not important solely for the economy of the United States, but also for the way in which pastoralism was imagined. Life-as-civilization begins with the arrival of settlers who group together in a natural area to build a community. To Timothy Morton, the great divide between culture and nature was delimited in this "agrilogistic" moment: the first settlements shaping a set of oppositions regarding culture/nature, and out of which models of humanity emerged. What Morton calls "agrilogistics" refers to a combination of effects such as settlement, economy and technology, and this form of logic—the human/nature divide—is responsible for the Anthropocene.[5] Thanks to the agro-economic turn, nature was definitively conceived as something to be subjected to man's exploitation.

This ethos of exploitation was sustained by two main pillars. First, in the conversion of Nature into something friendly, a gentle Mother who gives freely all her gifts to humankind. Nature lies there, passively waiting to be exploited. The second support is the conversion of nature into something pretty, closer to the spiritual than the material, a simile of the Christian Heaven. This ideal connects with the previous one: Nature is there for us, to make us humans feel better.

Both visions need to suppress or repress other aspects of Nature. Earthquakes, prolonged droughts, tsunamis, famines. These are deemed disasters and aberrations. In this sense, Todd Moffett and Tina Eliopulos argue that the American pastoral was constructed as a "counterforce," a "historical force, a political force, or death."[6] The ideal of beautiful landscapes as the embodiments of a perfect harmony between the human and Nature was not a given image, but a social and cultural construction slowly developed to "counteract" other more frightening realities. What the pastoral has to counterattack is double. Foremost, the materialism lurking behind the spiritual, Christian façade. For Camille Paglia, Western Culture's Apollonian vision (Apollonian in the sense it gives clear Euclidean form and shape to things that have none) regarding Nature is a lie, a myth, a sanitized surface grafted upon the "aggressiveness" of Nature.[7] "Our focus on the pretty is an Apollonian strategy. The leaves and flowers, the birds, the hills are a patchwork pattern by which we map the known." It is a defense strategy to avoid openly saying that Nature is basically indifferent to us—not a giver, not a Mother. "Scratch that skin, and nature's daemonic ugliness will erupt."[8] This ugliness is not just the different ways through which Nature can show its indifference to us, but also includes what lies beneath what our eyes want to see: the Dionysian, meaning; the mud, swamp, the amorphous, bacteria, and fluid shapelessness of primal materialism; the rotting manure that gives life anew every day.

This was the opposite of one of the pillars of the pastoral: transcendentalism, which rejected the reliance on external or sensual experience, or materialism, as the only source of knowledge "and emphasized instead the value of human intuition and extrasensory perception as a route to moral and spiritual truths."[9] Transcendentalism was key for understanding the Midwestern pastoral, particularly in the work of Ralph Waldo Emerson, as contemporary theories of holism and ecological preservationist philosophies are rooted "in the western pastoral tradition."[10] As such, bucolic Nature was embodied with divinity rather than with the material. It is Paglia, "daemonic" nature, that transcendentalism discarded, thus creating the pastoral myth.

The second motive that made the pastoral a counterforce was industrialization. The pastoral was slowly erected as part of the American myth precisely after the green landscapes of the prairies began to feel the effects of industrialization worming its way into America and especially the West. Facing the first signs of industrialization, Nature was deemed the locus of spiritual enterprise and health, a place for melancholic escape from the dangers of modernity and urbanization.[11] The unyielding processes of acculturation and transformation brought about by the economic forces of urbanization and industrialization were troublesome, as the rapidly changing landscapes were increasingly filled with smoke, smog, and the destruction of the green. Within this scenario, human health was seriously affected, both in psychological as well as in physical terms. Additionally, industrialization was deemed responsible for male "emasculation," due to the effects of "overcivilized domesticity" in contrast with the prior healthy state of primitiveness.[12] The pastoral was dead, now crystallized into myth and melancholy, and buried deep into gray landscapes framed by new concerns, such as over-population, pollution, mass alcoholism, and rising criminality.

Newspapers from the first half of the twentieth century circulated discourses about the many social illness of industrialization. *The Evening Independent*, dated January 20, 1936, explains the power residing within vitamins so necessary to battle rickets. Doctor Morris Fishbein tells readers: "At one time—before there was such a thing as a window glass and before people began herding together in sunless slums—rickets were not a common disease." Now, however, thanks to ills of "overcrowding and industrialization," people were more liable to get weak and sick.[13] Besides health, industrialization and urbanism also affected human relationships. In 1912 a report in *The Evening Tribune* mentioned the Rev. Doctor Frank Crowder, who criticized "the industrialization of women" as one of the many "evil influences against the conservation of the home." Women working in factories, according the reverend, led to lack of desire "for home keeping," child-bearing, and nurturing, leaving behind "discontent husbands."[14]

David Lynch's *Eraserhead* mirrors this uneasy shift from the Midwestern pastoral to a new landscape where everything is ill. This illustration, however, is not univocal, as Lynch seems to follow Camille Paglia and her notion of the daemonic: humble, ugly-looking materialism lives at the roots of both Romanticism and Enlightenment. Proposing a critique of the brutalizing effects of industrialization upon the human psyche and culture, Lynch, through a dialectic oscillation, highlights modest, dirty forms of materialism as the continuation of the pastoral.

The Material World Around Eraserhead

What this essay calls "modest materialism" is the emphasis made on the existence of humble examples of the "material," such as mud, dirty waters, rocks, grains, living microorganisms, and compost, each important components of human life but neglected by humanism, either as disgusting or marginal to human life. This modest materialism is best represented both by Lynch's *Eraserhead* and industrialization itself, as people mostly learn how to cohabit with the dirtiness of the new social order in order to make unbearable life bearable. *Eraserhead* begins with Henry's spirit or subconscious floating in space above an orb that represents Earth. Thus, Lynch starts with a transcendental image that is immediately downplayed as a human figure is superimposed on a globe which does not resemble its common representation in photos or drawings. Rather than being a perfect blue sphere speckled by beautiful white clouds, this rendition of our planet is an ugly, simple mud piled up until it took the form of a ball or rock. Lynch's Earth is basically soil and water. This follows Paglia's warnings about the "beautification" exerted upon Nature as a way to legit-imatize forms of dominion.[15]

Henry's mind/spirit views through horrified eyes an albino lam-prey resembling a spermatozoon growing larger and larger beside him and a man (Henry himself?) covered with pustules, weakly sitting beside a broken window. The lamprey signifies the first organism giving life to Earth, producing a disruption of the biblical Genesis. Man has not come from God. His origins reside in tiny, incredibly ugly creatures swim-ming in muddy waters. This Darwinian nightmare of remembering that we humans descend from animals is called "a supernaturalist or Gothic one" by Kelly Hurley, who observes that evolution theory described the body as containing within it the "mark of the beast" as humans, derived from beasts, "might still be abhuman entities."[16] The body becomes a site of tension, rendered unstable and abnormal in cohabitation with dirt-iness and amorphous creatures such as the lamprey. Part of the human body is structured through the massive presence of scary-looking crea-tures viewed through a microscopic lens residing in our skins and organs. "There are upwards of ten times as many such organisms as there are cells in the entire human body."[17] To remind viewers that life is inextricably linked to modest materiality, the opening scene ends when the ugly crea-ture falls into liquid, the chthonic swamp where life was originated at the dawn of Earth.

With this opening, Lynch unites the images of the sick body and poverty linked to the working classes in the most marginal urban areas (imagery oppositional to the pastoral myth) with monstrous tiny crea-tures sharing life with us (continuation of the pastoral, but in "negative photo.") To accentuate this linkage, the man sitting at the window pushes and pulls levers possibly to create life on Earth? The concrete function of the levers remains unexplored. This evokes the image of a man working as an automaton at any of the Henry Ford factories. Through this image, God is a blue-collar worker. Mass production was found in many parts of America through the twentieth century, "but as a technical and social sys-tem Fordism had originated in the Midwest and remained there well after World War II."[18] Like the pastoral, mass production is inextricably linked to Midwestern America and the overcrowded environments that would become a springboard for western expansion as people fled its conditions.

The film cuts to Henry arriving home. His surroundings are com-prised of dilapidated buildings and what look like abandoned factories, while the streets are filled with mud and piles of trash. Everything seems unhygienic, an image that mirrors realities through the first years of industrialization, especially after World War I: "Poor housing and health, unemployment, crime, and a generalized culture of violence dramatically highlighted the plight of those who lived in poverty in the overcrowded cities in America's industrializing Northeast and Midwest."[19] Henry lives in an industrial wasteland, where tubes and holes in the mud exist alongside broken windows and oily, polluted waters. The camera frames in close-up the dirty waters running through the place, creating a parallel between the primordial waters where the human was nurtured and these new waters that are equally disgusting, thus connecting the ugliness of the cradle of life with industrialism.

The ethnographic, social, and cultural mapping after industrialization changed to accommodate new ways of community that privileged, in one hand, overcrowding and in the other, anonymity. Industrial overcrowding is illustrated in the relationship Henry has with his neighbor (Judith Roberts). She is billed in the final credits only as "Beautiful Girl Across the Hall." She has no name. Nobody in the building where Henry lives seems to know each other. Other characters are billed anonymously as well: "the boss" (T. Max Graham), "the boy" (Thomas Coulson), or "pencil machine operator" (Hal Landon, Jr.), the latter bearing a name solely based on his role as a factory worker. Mary's family surname is just an X. City saturation means higher personal anonymity, which leads to lower social control and therefore the increase of jobs outside the law. It is implied that "Beautiful Girl Across the Hall" may be a sex worker, an instigator of seedy crimes taking place under an umbrella of anonymity within a family residence.

The worst effect of industrialization, however, is marked by the destruction of the pastoral. Railroad building and factories have displaced non-human life, the latter only surviving in sad forms: a weird mound of dying grass on top of Henry's dresser, a mat of the same material beneath the radiator, and on his bedside table, a stack of dirt from which juts a leafless dry twig. The other "green" is a garden in front of the X's house, filled with steams drifting from railway yards containing withered flowers and shrubs. The last aspect of nature resides in a dog, who viciously barks at Henry. Even further, there is no glimpse of sun throughout the whole film, only dirtiness.

Illnesses were more common during the first years of industrialization, to the point that "mortality did rise with city size."[20] Fitting within this image of industrialization as the locus of corporeal illness and mental weakening, the majority of the film's characters are sick. When Henry meets Mary's parents, the girl starts to suffer an attack that prompts fits of choking that can only be calmed when her mother brushes her hair. The attack ends as suddenly as it started. Bill, Mary's father (Allen Joseph), babbles mostly incoherently and has an arm that is all but paralyzed. The grandmother (Jean Lange), sitting silently in the kitchen, seems catatonic, smoking cigarettes her only action. Mary's mother (Jeanne Bates) suffers from fits of hysteria and must retire from dinner. After a discussion, Henry starts to bleed from his nose. Even the roasted chicken looks unhealthy. Bill says the chicken is man-made, insinuating that the animal had been mass-produced in a factory rather than being completely "real." Indeed, the desiccated chicken moves when pierced by the fork, a dark liquid oozing from its cavities.

The unhealthy chicken is a blueprint for the sickest creature in *Eraserhead*, Mary and Henry's baby. It has no limbs, only a bundled, fragile body wrapped in bandages with its head sticking out. The unhealthy creature rejects food and cries incessantly. Disgusted by the sight of the perpetually ill creature, Henry stabs his offspring. After the stabbing, a strange white substance begins to ooze from the baby, evoking the liquid that came out of the roasted chicken. Both are tiny, sickly, and fragile things churned out from the smoke and dirtiness of industrialism.

The impact of industrialization is illustrated through a negative lens. The intimate relationship with the material face of Nature, on the other hand, is a continuation—not an opposition—of the pastoral era. In a key scene, what seems to be a little white worm escapes from Henry's closet. In close-up, the worm looks like a seed. Following this logic, the animal/plant hybrid creature buries itself into the soil to reappear larger later in the film, as the result of an accelerated process of growth. This image returns viewers to Paglia's idea of the chthonic, a Greek term, "khthonios," meaning "of the earth," used in reference to that which is beneath the surface of the Earth. Seeds and worms exist under the soil, both sustaining life on the surface of the planet, both passing mostly invisible to human eyes, as humanity is hopelessly disconnected from what exists underground. Without that life, however, the pastoral would not exist.

Eraserhead is a triumph of the material. Microorganisms, mud, brown waters, and the disgusting are recurrently framed through close-ups to engage with the viewer through a haptic lens.[21] Bill states he has worked in the prairies, laying plumbing pipe for thirty years, resulting in the transformation from natural landscape into the industrial hell it has become. Through Biblical exegesis, this hell may be read as the antagonist of the pastoral. However, this man-made hell is the continuation of the pastoral via the daemonic. In his landmark 1964 text *The Machine in the Garden*, Leo Marx points to the sharply contradictory readings of America through the era of colonialism and Elizabethan travel: savage American Nature was a "virgin land" and "paradise regained."[22] In other words, America was a garden. For others, "America might be made to seem the very opposite of a bountiful garden," a chthonic landscape dominated by "hideous wilderness."[23] Amidst these contradictions, the pastoral was born—one image superimposed upon the other, one obliterating the other:

What is most revealing about these contrasting ideas of landscape is not, need-
less to say, their relative accuracy in picturing the actual topography. They are
not representational images. America was neither Eden nor a howling desert.
These are poetic metaphors, imaginative constructions which heighten meaning far beyond the limits of fact. And yet, like all effective metaphors, each had
a basis in fact. In a sense, America was both Eden and a howling desert.[24]

Like Paglia, Marx advocates for an understanding of the pastoral as the
container of both the beautiful and the ugly, as well as the suffering associated with the new factory system. As argued by Paglia, the Apollonian
won in its battle against the material, as nature was transformed into a
form or continuation of traditional depictions of human Motherhood—
self-sacrificing and nurturing instincts—as a necessary way to secure the
exploitation of the Natural by human hand.

Eraserhead (re)connects viewers with the experience of haptic sensu-
ality framed by unhealthy conditions of life. Myth and American history
meet through the elemental qualities of industrialization. Lynch's film
attempts to fill the void left when the landscape lost its mystical qualities
through depictions of excluded dirt.

Conclusions: Cultural Materialism

Eraserhead highlights the ugly surface of the purely material after the
romantic lens is stripped away. The exaggerated hideousness of Mary and
Henry's son can be seen as a statement on new parents' anxieties and the
effects of industrial pollution. The soil that gives its fruits in the shape of,
say, apples or oranges is infested with worms. Humankind's cradle con-
sisted of muddy waters filled with microorganisms and life-givers such
as spermatozoids and worm-like beings. Part of the human body is composed of tiny creatures such as parasites or symbiotic bacteria and miner-
als and, if one looks closely, Earth itself is a pile of rocks, grains, heath, and
organisms piled up.

The dirty is life and vice versa, but contradictorily and in part due
to the Midwestern pastoral myth, this truth has been rejected as abject.
Dirt was conceived through negative, Apollonian ontology as "matter out
of place," because things such as brown waters (the color not necessarily
implying pollution) or soil is not so much a threat to health but to the "idea
or order," the latter part of the transcendental acculturation that privileged the intangible.[25]

In a key hallucination, Henry sees the Lady in the Radiator (Laurel Near) stepping on spermatozoon-like creatures and, thus, destroy-
ing unborn life even as she sings about afterlife in Christian Heaven. The

Lady, her face disfigured by sickness, her cheeks resembling testicles or ovaries (both imageries attached to birth and life), is the perfect communication between on one hand the pastoral and the image of "heaven" it carries, and on the other industrialization and the image of corruption attached to it. Both are sides of the same coin, as ugliness was a constitutive (but neglected) part of the Midwestern myth of pastoral Nature. What industrialization brought was the realization that life, with its beautiful green leaves or humanity, is sustained in material forms. Assessing the fundamental role of materiality in shaping humanity, *Eraserhead* unpacks the passage from the pastoral to industrialization not so much as opposites but as reversals of each other, an idea that only surrealism, pledged to reverse the contents of life, can successfully depict.

NOTES

1. Emanuel Levy, *Cinema of Outsiders: The Rise of American Independent Film* (New York: New York University Press, 1999), 68.

2. Adam Lowenstein, "Feminine Horror: The Embodied Surrealism of In My Skin," in *The Dread of Difference: Gender and the Horror Film*, ed. Barry Keith Grant (Austin, TX: University of Texas Press, 2015), 476.

3. Golden Tyler, "Across the Wide Missouri: The Adventure Narrative from Lewis and Clark to Powell," in *A Literary History of the American West*, ed. Western Literature Association (Fort Worth: Texas Christian University Press, 1987), 90.

4. William Barillas, *The Midwestern Pastoral: Place and Landscape in Literature of the American Heartland* (Athens: Ohio University Press, 2006), 4.

5. Timothy Morton, *Dark Ecology: For a Logic of Future Coexistence* (New York: Columbia University Press, 2016).

6. Todd Moffett and Tina Eliopulos, "The Paths of Unjust Profit: John Keeble's Portrait of the American West," in *Science, Values, and the American West*, ed. Stephen Tchudi (Reno: Nevada Humanities Committee, 1997), 57.

7. Camille Paglia, *Sexual Personae: Art and Decadence from Nefertiti to Emily Dickinson* (New York: Vintage Books, 1991), 2.

8. *Ibid.*, 5.

9. Tiffany Wayne, *Encyclopedia of Transcendentalism* (New York: Facts on File, 2006), 153.

10. Anne Raine, "Embodied Geographies: Subjectivity and Materiality in the Work of Ana Mendieta," in *Generations and Geographies in the Visual Arts: Feminist Readings*, ed. Griselda Pollock (Routledge, 1996), 231.

11. Leo Marx, *The Machine in the Garden: Technology and the Pastoral Ideal in America*, 2000 edition (New York: Routledge, 2000), 26.

12. Catherine Cavanaugh, "No Place for a Woman: Engendering Western Canadian Settlement," in *Women and Gender in the American West*, ed. Mary Ann Irwin and James Brooks (Albuquerque: University of New Mexico Press, 2004), 187.

13. Morris Fishbein, "'Sunshine Vitamin' D Strengthens Bones of 'Sun-Starved' Waifs," *Evening Independent* (Massillon, Ohio), January 20, 1936, 5.

14. Rev. Dr. Frank Crowder, "untitled," *The Evening Tribune* (unspecified location), 1912, 3.

15. Paglia, *Sexual Personae*.

16. Kelly Hurley, *The Gothic Body: Sexuality, Materialism, and Degeneration at the Fin de Siècle* (Cambridge: Cambridge University Press, 2004), 56.

17. Wesley Wildman, "Distributed Identity: Human Beings as Walking, Thinking Ecologies in the Microbial World," in *Human Identity at the Intersection of Science, Technology, and Religion*, ed. Nancey Murphy and Christopher Knight (New York: Routledge, 2016), 174.

18. Joshua Freeman, *American Empire: The Rise of Global Power, the Democratic Revolution at Home, 1945–2000* (New York: Penguin, 2012), 15–16.

19. Michael Ryan and Les Switzer, *God in the Corridors of Power: Christian Conservatives, the Media, and Politics in America* (Santa Barbara, CA: Praeger, 2009), 39.

20. Dora Costa and Richard Steckel, "Long-term Trends in Health, Welfare and Economic Growth in the United States," in *Health and Welfare during Industrialization*, eds. Richard Steckel and Roderick Floud (Chicago: University of Chicago Press, 1997), 65.

21. Haptic refers to the connection between the "skin" of the film and that of viewers.

22. Marx, *The Machine*, 36.

23. *Ibid.*, 40, 43.

24. *Ibid.*, 43.

25. Marvin Harris, *Cultural Materialism: The Struggle for a Science of Culture* (Walnut Creek, CA: Altamira Press, 1991), 196.

Works Cited

Barillas, William. 2006. *The Midwestern Pastoral: Place and Landscape in Literature of the American Heartland*. Athens: Ohio University Press.

Cavanaugh, Catherine. 2004. "No Place for a Woman: Engendering Western Canadian Settlement." In *Women and Gender in the American West*, edited by Mary Ann Irwin and James Brooks, 183–209. Albuquerque: University of New Mexico Press.

Costa, Dora, and Richard Steckel. 1997. "Long-Term Trends in Health, Welfare and Economic Growth in the United States." In *Health and Welfare during Industrialization*, edited by Richard H. Steckel and Roderick Floud, 47–90. Chicago: The University of Chicago Press.

Fishbein, Morris. 1936. "'Sunshine Vitamin' D Strengthens Bones of 'Sun-Starved' Waifs." *The Evening Independent*, January 20, 1936.

Freeman, Joshua. 2012. *American Empire: The Rise of a Global Power, the Democratic Revolution at Home, 1945–2000*. New York: Penguin.

Harris, Marvin. 1991. *Cultural Materialism: The Struggle for a Science of Culture*. Walnut Creek, CA: Altamira Press.

Hurley, Kelly. 2004. *The Gothic Body: Sexuality, Materialism, and Degeneration at the fin de siècle*. Cambridge: Cambridge University Press.

Levy, Emanuel. 1999. *Cinema of Outsiders: The Rise of American Independent Film*. New York: New York University Press.

Lowenstein, Adam. 2015. "Feminine Horror: The Embodied Surrealism of *In My Skin*." In *The Dread of Difference: Gender and the Horror Film*, edited by Barry Keith Grant, 470, 487. Austin: University of Texas Press.

Marx, Leo. 2000. *The Machine in the Garden: Technology and the Pastoral Ideal in America*. New York: Routledge.

"Modern Tendencies in Home Decried." 1912. *The Evening Tribune*, February 26, 1912.

Moffett, Todd, and Tina Eliopulos. 1997. "The Paths of Unjust Profit: John Keeble's Portrait of the American West." In *Science, Values, and the American West*, edited by Stephen Tchudi, 55–80. Reno: Nevada Humanities Committee.

Morton, Timothy. 2016. *Dark Ecology: For a Logic of Future Coexistence*. New York: Columbia University Press.

Paglia, Camille. 1991. *Sexual Personae: Art and Decadence from Nefertiti to Emily Dickinson*. New York: Vintage Books.

Raine, Anne. 1996. "Embodied Geographies: Subjectivity and Materiality in the Work of Ana Mendieta." In *Generations and Geographies in the Visual Arts: Feminist Readings*, edited by Griselda Pollock, 228–250.

Ryan, Michael, and Les Switzer. 2009. *God in the Corridors of Power: Christian Conservatives, the Media, and Politics in America*. Santa Barbara, CA: Praeger.

Tyler, Golden. 1987. "Across the Wide Missouri: The Adventure Narrative from Lewis and Clark to Powell." In *A Literary History of the American West*, edited by the Western Literature Association. Fort Worth: Texas Christian University Press.

Wayne, Tiffany. 2006. *Encyclopedia of Transcendentalism*. New York: Facts On File.

Wildman, Wesley. 2016. "Distributed Identity: Human Beings as Walking, Thinking Ecologies in the Microbial World." In *Human Identity at the Intersection of Science, Technology and Religion*, edited by Nancey Murphy and Christopher Knight, 165–178. New York: Routledge.

Watch and Listen to the Dream of Time and Space

Historiography, Geography and Twin Peaks

REBECCA HEIMEL

History does not capture our emotions without stories, nor does geography. When Frederick Jackson Turner delivered his now-famous paper at the 1893 Chicago World's Fair, it was received with enthusiasm because it confirmed the prevailing story that America had long told about itself. In the subsequent decades in which the thesis was incorporated into both popular and academic understandings of the United States, it continued to resonate with existing images, narratives, and cultural ideologies about the West and its role in American exceptionalism.[1] Turner's thesis, that "[t]he existence of an area of free land, its continuous recession, and the advance of American settlement westward, explain American development," laid the foundation for historical thinking that stubbornly persists.[2]

In 1991 the National Museum of American Art curated a show titled "The West as America: Reinterpreting Images of the Frontier, 1820–1920." The exhibit was received by the public with controversy because it presented ideas from a small group of historians who had only recently begun to substantially challenge Turner's frontier thesis. The sensation of this distinctly academic paradigm shift, quickly known as New Western History, briefly crossed over into the cultural mainstream with coverage in *The New York Times*, *USA Today*, and *U.S. News and World Report*, among others.[3] New Western Historians interpreted the West as a place of conflict and convergence with a lasting legacy. Rather than use the West to justify the "creation myth" of America or to see the region as disconnected by one hundred years from the realities of the present, the scholars understood the West as a real place where indigenous erasure, immigrant convergence, and boom-and-bust economics were the center of the story.[4]

36

The vast gap between academic and popular understandings of the West produced contradictory frontier narratives. New Western History "did much to finally retire the uncritically triumphant frontier process— at least within academic circles."[5] As a result of New Western Historians and those that preceded them, critical Asian studies, postcolonial and area studies, feminist studies, borderland studies, immigration studies, and critical feminist studies took up the mantle of study of the West. Western historians did the same with renewed energy and focus. This scholarship had commonalities beyond the region in question. Barely anyone outside academia was listening. The bridge between the academy and the public still had to be crossed.

The timing of New Western History, beginning roughly in 1987 with the publication of Patricia Nelson Limerick's synthesis *A Legacy of Conquest*, coincides with the 1990 premier of *Twin Peaks*. That these two seemingly disparate events shared a similar timeframe is one significant thing that they have in common, but timing is not their only commonality.

Twin Peaks invites its viewers to consider a different, more complex understanding of the West. As a popular story in a popular medium, it succeeds where academic scholarship often falls short—it bridges the gap between a persistent, Turnerian understanding of the West and the understandings brought about by New Western History in the late 1980s and early 1990s. Just as twenty-first-century academic understandings of the West defy simple readings, so too does *Twin Peaks* present us with complexity. This is the case not only in complex places and convergence of people, but also in the series' treatment of the West. Physical location— place—is key in the series, but the metaphysical, dreams, and visions are just as significant to our understanding. The treatment of time and place in the series write back to indigenous understandings of history, in which place is paramount, and undermine a progressive, linear history on which past interpretations of the West relied.

Home on the Range

Popular conceptions of the West require a disconnected region that escapes complexity, with simple ideas of good and bad and clear-cut winners and losers. New Western History went beyond just a critique of Turner. Since the 1960s and the Vietnam War, American scholars had begun to take a less optimistic, more tragic view of the American past. Many New Western Historians sought to examine the realities of the West using what were then new tools of race, gender, and environment. But their scholarship also pointed out a certain anti-intellectualism in past writing of Western history, and to a distrust of work grounded in a larger theoretical framework.[6]

Many fans of *Twin Peaks* appreciate David Lynch's adherence to an intelligent and sophisticated vision, despite pressure to simplify for a mass audience. "For viewers, what made the program so exceptional was the demands *Twin Peaks* made upon the spectator, the justification its narrative complexity offered."[7] *Twin Peaks* continues to delight fans without spoon-feeding viewers or offering easy answers. Rather than treat *Twin Peaks* as a stable object, viewers extend it and produce from its language further meaning, generating seemingly never-ending intellectual responses and discourses.

Lynch and Frost do not just create characters, establish setting, or communicate experience. Through intertextuality they reflect upon history, geography, and the language of the text they are creating. *Twin Peaks* is carefully and purposefully framed by references—names, music, and historical events—as well as a grounding in the visual reality of the Pacific Northwest, all of which move outside of the text in order to illustrate the social realties of New Western History.

Music is a significant geographical reference, particularly through the songs sung by characters. At Ben Horne's party for the Icelandic investors, the scene opens with a group singing "Home on the Range." As Windom Earle and Leo Johnson approach Major Briggs in the woods dressed in a horse costume in Season 2, Windom Earle again sings "Home on the Range." Leland Palmer sings "Surrey with the Fringe on Top" from *Oklahoma!* while driving to dispose of the body of Madeleine Ferguson, and at an outdoor picnic, John Wheeler sings "Bury Me Not on the Lone Prairie," otherwise known as the "Cowboy's Lament." In Season 3, Carl Rodd accompanies himself on the guitar singing "Red River Valley."

Names are used to reference social realities. Agent Dale Cooper suggests the American author James Fenimore Cooper and his 1820s–1840s Leatherstocking Tales of Natty Bumppo. The Great Northern Hotel references the Great Northern Railway, completed in 1889. The brothel that features heavily in Season 1, One Eyed Jacks, is also the name of a 1961 Western film featuring Marlon Brando. The most overt of name references belongs to Sheriff Harry S. Truman, a character literally named for the thirty-third President of the United States. Significant for our understanding of a Western reading is the role that Western locations played in nuclear history. President Truman's administration was responsible for the testing and eventual use of the atom bomb, and atomic testing and warfare figures prominently in the series' plot, particularly in that of Season 3.

In Season 3, Part 8, a great deal of screen time is used to show the Trinity Test in White Sands, New Mexico, in 1945, the first detonation of a nuclear device. Part 8 seems to reveal that BOB was born of nuclear power, or "the evil that men do" according to Albert Rosenfield. This reference is reinforced by the huge photographic image in Gordon Cole's Philadelphia office of the 1957 Nevada nuclear test.

The year 1945 is significant to consider in the history of the West, and using it as a basis for the major conflict of the series is a clear historical marker. The era of the New Deal and World War II made the West's economic growth and independence possible while enlarging the financial and regulatory role of the federal government. The West emerged from World War II a different region entirely. New Western History insisted in positioning the West as America's leading source of resources rather than a region whose story had ended. From the gold rush and fur trade to uranium, oil shale, and timber, New Western Historians read reckless exploitation as a serious and strong undercurrent of the West's identity. That BOB is born of this atomic energy mirrors New Western History's analysis of the West.

In treating the West as a region, Patricia Nelson Limerick argues for recognition of the boom and bust economies of extractive industries—oil, uranium, logging, and gold.[8] Uranium was essential to the story of the West and is emphasized through these atomic references, but no other resource is as heavily referenced throughout the series as is timber. *Twin Peaks* is grounded in the visual reality of trees and woods. Repeated images of the woods and references to the woods are constant. There are visuals of trees and logs between and within scenes. The Bookhouse Boys patch features a Douglas fir, and the Twin Peaks Sheriff's office conference room has timber-framed historical photographs of loggers with springboards and crosscut saws. In the pilot Agent Cooper tells Diane by way of his recorder, "Never seen so many trees in my life," and later says, "I've got to find out what kind of trees these are. They're really something special." The Great Northern is paneled in pine in every room, and the Timber Room features heavily in Seasons 1 and 2. Images of the mill at work, including saw blades in logs, and long-haul trucks of logs rolling past the Double R Diner, are repeated elements in the opening credits and the transition scenes of the show. This imagery echoes the significance of timber in New Western Historians' approach to the region.

The Dream of Time and Space

In Season 3 the character Freddie Sykes says that he was given a message from a "bloke in the sky" who told him, "once you've got the glove on, go to Twin Peaks, Washington, United States of America, and there you will find your destiny." Place is destiny in *Twin Peaks*, and not just for Freddie. In the Pilot episode, Agent Cooper's tape-recording reports that he is "entering the town of Twin Peaks, five miles south of the Canadian border, twelve miles west of the state line." Place is established from the start as a critical reality.

Limerick notes that Turner's frontier was a process, not a place. "When civilization had conquered savagery at any one location, the process—and the historian's attention—moved on. In rethinking Western history, we gain the freedom to think of the West as a place."[9] Sheriff Truman describes the town of Twin Peaks as "different" and "a long way from the world." Judge Sternwood asks Agent Cooper, "how do you find our little corner of this world?," to which Cooper answers, "Heaven, sir." Sternwood returns, "this week, heaven includes arson, multiple homicides, and the attempt on the life of a federal agent," to which Cooper says, "Heaven is a large and interesting place."

Locations take on extreme significance in Season 3, in which Mr. C is searching for geographical coordinates. In Season 3, Part 11, Maggie, the dispatcher at the Twin Peaks Sheriff's department, repeats "What's your location?" over and over again on the phone. A few parts later, Mr. C says to Richard Horne, "I'm looking for a place. Do you understand, a place?" The coordinates that Mr. C searches for are finally found in the town of Twin Peaks, underlining that the series is as much about characters and events as it is about the geographical reality of the town and the surrounding Pacific Northwest. In the teaser trailer for Season 3, Michael Horse, speaking as himself rather than his character Deputy Hawk, claims, "location sometimes becomes a character." Specificity underscores location to make this possible. Though the town is fictional, details of its reality are used to connect to viewers. The traffic light at Sparkwood and 21 and the ceiling fan in the Palmer house take on presence and intention that seem as real as the human presence that surrounds them.

Maps, specifically ledger maps, figure prominently into the plot of each season, and serve to focus the narrative on concepts of place. Deputy Hawk's elk skin map is a key point in Season 3 and acts as both a way to find a location as well as a way to understand unfolding events. The petroglyph on the wall of Owl Cave, later drawn on the chalkboard in the Sheriff's office by Deputy Andy Brennan, gives the time and place of the Black and White Lodges. While using the chalkboard map to figure out how to access the Black Lodge in Season 2, Agent Cooper says to Sheriff Truman, "An object like a door normally exists at a point in space and time. By way of contrast, a shooting star exists for us at a point in time over a continuum in space … looking at it from the star's point of view might be an entirely different experience."

Time and place are elements that cannot be separated from either New Western History or *Twin Peaks*. The plot of Season 2 and *Fire Walk with Me* moved forward by moving backward. Instead of further advancing the plot from the moment of Laura Palmer's murder, both filled in backstory to show the ways in which the past continues to affect the present.[10] In Season 3, Part 10, the Log Lady calls Deputy Hawk and advises him to "Watch and listen to the dream of time and space." Both time and place are essential to reading the series and respond to the central themes of New Western History's emphasis on place over process. Not only does the "past dictate the future," as the title of Season 3, Part 17, announces, but also the continual reliance on both of these elements taken together are key to reading and understanding the series.

A preoccupation with time never leaves the foreground of the narrative. More than once a character asks the question, "Is it future or is it past?" In the ultimate part of Season 3, Agent Cooper asks Carrie Page: "What year is this?" With the exception of the faint sound of Sarah Palmer calling Laura's name, this is the last piece of dialog a character utters; the question ends the series. Throughout the series and especially in Season 3, linear time is difficult and complicated to follow using traditional Western notions of narrative structure.

Significant to this aspect of *Twin Peaks* is the convergence of time and place in American Indian histories and narrative traditions, which many scholars have read as forms of resistance. Joseph Bauerkemper has characterized the treatment of time and place in American Indian literatures as "the primacy of spatiality in relation to temporality."[11] Paula Gunn Allen explains that traditional tribal narratives "possess a circular structure, incorporating event within event, piling meaning upon meaning, until the accretion finally results in a story."[12]

Progressive, linear history supports an ideology of progress, precisely that of the mythic frontier refuted by New Western History. American Indian activist and scholar Vine Deloria writes that "the very essence of Western European identity involves the assumption that time proceeds in a linear fashion" and argues that this identity assumes that the peoples of Western Europe become the "guardians of the world."[13] The story of triumph over an "uncivilized" West presupposes a timeline that is not only linear but also permanent.

Peter Nabokov, a scholar of American Indian studies, spent decades among the Navajo, Lakota, Crow, Penobscot, and Alabama-Coushatta Indian nations. Careful not to paint tribes as conforming to a single tradition, Nabokov explains the commonality of multiple pasts in Indian histories. He writes that American Indian history is not preoccupied with dates and historical periods. A displacement of narrative elements features heavily in many American Indian historicities, and present and past experience frequently merge. Nabokov writes of the integral bonds between culture, history, and landscape among the Yaqui, Pima-Papago, and Navajo communities. "Whether in physical reality or cultural memory, language, religion, and history always 'took place.'"[14] Here Nabokov quotes Deloria, who points out "the preeminence of topography over chronology" that "remains a key diagnostic of Indian historicity in general."[15] Nabokov explains that non-built environments (mountains, springs, rivers, trees, etc.) in Indian historicity often take on intentionality and volition and are full players in passages through time.[16]

So it is for *Twin Peaks*. Place is paramount throughout the series, and despite our attempts to understand timing, the constant the viewer is offered to hold on to is the town of Twin Peaks. Its elements—the Double R Diner, Glastonbury Grove, the Sheriff's station, the Palmer house—have intentionality and volition throughout the story. As Nabokov points out about many Indian historicities, the past, present, and future of *Twin Peaks* have "no meaning apart from where they occur."[17]

Michael Carroll and Geoff Bil have both appropriately criticized Seasons 1 and 2 for relying on indigenous traditions that "serve patently non-indigenous ends."[18] Intentionally creating a narrative that defies linear, progressive history could be regarded as similarly problematic when considering American Indian literature and histories. But in writing back to the tradition of circular and non-linear, place-based historicities, *Twin Peaks* provides the viewer an opportunity to approach the West from another tradition, destabilizing Turner's progressive, linear history so refused by New Western Historians.

Playing Indian

Johnny Horne, wearing a Sioux headdress and banging his head against a dollhouse, is a classic image from the pilot of *Twin Peaks*. Less noticeable, many episodes later, viewers see the same character "playing Indian" by using a suction cup bow and arrow to hunt wooden cutouts of buffalo. Modern audiences would likely see this as problematic, and there is no shortage of these types of images in any season of *Twin Peaks*. The interior of the Great Northern hotel is rampant with totem poles and murals. Catherine Spooner posits that the use of American Indian textiles in the series "perform[s] regionality and authenticity while simultaneously trading on a fake ethnicity" and explains that the show "draws on a number of different indigenous traditions in order to create a composite pastiche of Native American identity that informs and enables its invented 'local' mythology."[19] Geoff Bil argues that despite these numerous allusions, indigenous individuals largely remain absent.[20] How are viewers to read *Twin Peaks* in light of indigenous representation, a key component of New Western History?

Sheer, et al., conducted a mixed-methods study of K-12 state standards to uncover the representation of Indigenous histories and cultures within state curricula. Their research revealed that on the whole, despite years of academic understanding and activism on the part of American Indians and allies, standards persist in presenting American Indians without tribal or geographical differences and only within a pre–1900s context.[21] In light of this one could argue that presenting a modern Nez Perce, in the character of Deputy Hawk, overtly challenges the persistent belief in the myth of the vanishing race.

Deputy Hawk is modern, but his character is complicated. His dialog and actions frequently communicate expected tropes of indigenous people. In Season 1, Hawk says of Ronette Pulaski that "body and spirit are still far apart." Hawk is tracking Phillip Gerard, the One-Armed Man. Sheriff Truman says, "If anyone can find him, Hawk can." When Cooper asks if Hawk is a tracker, Truman replies, "The best." When Sheriff Truman and Agent Cooper are in trouble at One Eyed Jacks, Hawk shows up to save them by throwing a Bowie knife. It is Hawk who explains the White and Black Lodges to Agent Cooper, saying: "Cooper, you may be fearless in this world. But there are other worlds." He goes on to explain what "his people" believe about the White and Black Lodges. Early in Season 1, Cooper asks Hawk, "Do you believe in the soul?" Hawk answers, "several" and describes a Blackfeet legend related to "waking souls that give life to mind and body."

In each of these examples, Hawk displays an archetype of an Indian, filtered through the cultural priorities of settler colonialism rather than an actualized character in his own right.[22] But much like the rest of *Twin Peaks*, Hawk is complex. When Agent Cooper asks Hawk if Laura Palmer is in "The Land of the Dead" of the Blackfoot legend, Hawk replies "Laura's in the ground … that's all I know for sure." Hawk recites a poem written for his girlfriend, full of stereotypical allusions to nature. "One woman can make you fly like the eagle, another can give you the strength of a lion." When asked if his girlfriend is a "Local gal," Hawk replies "Diane Shapiro, PhD, Brandeis." Hawk further subverts archetypical indigenous portrayals in Season 1. Lucy's sister says to Hawk, "God, after all we've done to you, how you must hate us white people." Hawk replies, "Some of my best friends are white people." Hawk's subtle humor defies some—though not all—American Indian stereotypes. *Twin Peaks* provides an indigenous character that is not rendered as a relic of the past but is instead a contentious and relevant presence in the present day.

However, as much as viewers long for it, there is little progress in *Twin*

Peaks. Though Season 3 allowed viewers to see beloved characters and settings again, the narrative refused to neatly wrap itself up. With very few
exceptions, characters are shown living with the consequences of their collective past, seemingly destined to keep repeating what has already taken
place for themselves and for others. Turner believed in progress and in an
intelligible world—that we could see progress as a line that moved successfully and clearly through successive frontiers. Though it was often accused
of pessimism, New Western History grappled with the concept of progress and came up short, preferring instead to consider the West as a place
rich with complexity and living with the consequences of conquest. Current scholarship frames Western history as one of settler colonialism, seeing
what was once a frontier history as connected to a global, colonial relationship among indigenous people, settlers, and nation-states.[23] That we share
stark similarities with colonial Africa or India continues to escape popular
understandings of American history and specifically of the West. We need
narratives—stories—to continue to complicate our own national ideologies.

Addressing the Western History Association (WHA) in 2017, the same
year that Season 3 of *Twin Peaks* premiered, then-President Stephen Aron
examined the twenty-five-year legacy of New Western History. Of the controversy brought by New Western Historians, he concluded that "Twenty-five
years later, all has mostly quieted on the Western front."[24] Aron nonetheless
noted that membership in the WHA had fallen by half and that sessions of
the annual conference were increasingly segregated by "scholarly" and "popular" concerns. The WHA is less publicly-minded and publicly-focused than
it should be. A re-opening focused on deliberate conversing outside of academic circles and academic comfort zones is sorely needed.[25]

Twin Peaks answers Aron's call—not always perfectly, and not always
well—but it answers nonetheless. The series' intertextuality insists on the
real place of the West. Time and place are complex and contradictory, and
they converge to provide a treatment of the West that doesn't give the full
picture but does invite other possibilities to complicate dominant, linear,
historical understanding. Indigenous presence is mostly absent, yet Deputy Hawk's character complicates expected representations of American
Indians. Popular histories circulate at a scale with which counter-histories
cannot compete, but *Twin Peaks* offers a West that captures the emotions
and prepares us to accept what might otherwise not be possible.

NOTES

1. Richard White, Patricia Nelson Limerick, and James R. Grossman, *The Frontier in American Culture: An Exhibition at the Newberry Library, August 26, 1994-January 7, 1995* (Chicago: The Library; Berkeley: University of California Press, 1994).

2. Frederick J. Turner, "The Significance of the Frontier in American History," *Annual Report of the American Historical Association for the Year 1893* (1894), 199.

3. James R. Allison, "Beyond It All: Surveying the Intersections of Modern American Indian, Environmental, and Western Histories," *History Compass* 16, no. 4 (2018): e12447.

4. Richard Slotkin, *Regeneration through Violence: The Mythology of the American Frontier, 1600–1860* (Norman: University of Oklahoma Press, 2000).

5. Allison, "Beyond It All," 3.

6. William G. Robbins, "Laying Siege to Western History: The Emergence of New Paradigms," in *Trails: Toward a New Western History*, eds. Patricia Nelson Limerick, Clyde A. Milner, and Charles E. Rankin (Lawrence: University Press of Kansas, 1991), 182–214.

7. Henry Jenkins, "'Do You Enjoy Making the Rest of Us Feel Stupid?': alt.tv.twinpeaks, the Trickster Author and Viewer Mastery," in *Full of Secrets: Critical Approaches to* Twin Peaks, ed. David Lavery (Detroit: Wayne State University Press, 1995), 65.

8. Patricia Nelson Limerick, *Something in the Soil: Legacies and Reckonings in the New West* (New York: Norton, 2001).

9. Patricia Nelson Limerick, *The Legacy of Conquest: The Unbroken Past of the American West* (New York: W.W. Norton, 1987), 26.

10. Marc Dolan, "The Peaks and Valleys of Serial Creativity: What Happened to/on Twin Peaks," in *Full of Secrets: Critical Approaches to* Twin Peaks, ed. David Lavery (Detroit: Wayne State University Press, 1995).

11. Joseph Baurkemper, "Narrating Nationhood: Indian Time and Ideologies of Progress," *Studies in American Indian Literatures* 19, no. 3 (2007): 41.

12. Paula Gunn Allen, *The Sacred Hoop: Recovering the Feminine in American Indian Traditions: With a New Preface* (Boston: Beacon Press, 1992), 79.

13. Vine Deloria, *God Is Red: A Native View of Religion*, 2nd ed. (Golden, Colorado: Fulcrum Publishing, 1994), 63.

14. Peter Nabokov, *A Forest of Time: American Indian Ways of History* (New York: Cambridge University Press, 2002), 131.

15. Deloria, *God Is Red*.

16. Nabokov, *A Forest of Time*.

17. *Ibid.*, 132.

18. Michael Carroll, "Agent Cooper's Errand in the Wilderness: 'Twin Peaks' and American Mythology," *Literature/Film Quarterly* 21, no. 4 (1993): 287–295; Geoff Bil, "Tensions in the World of Moon: *Twin Peaks*, Indigeneity and Territoriality," *Senses of Cinema* no. 79 (July 2016), http://sensesofcinema.com/2016/twin-peaks/twin-peaks-indigeneity-territoriality/.

19. Catherine Spooner, "'Wrapped in Plastic': David Lynch's Material Girls," in *Return to* Twin Peaks: *New Approaches to Materiality, Theory, and Genre on Television*, eds. Jeffrey Andrew Weinstock and Catherine Spooner (New York: Palgrave Macmillan, 2016), 108.

20. Bil, "Tensions."

21. Sarah B. Shear, Ryan T. Knowles, Gregory J. Soden, and Antonio J. Castro, "Manifesting Destiny: Re/Presentations of Indigenous Peoples in K–12 U.S. History Standards," *Theory & Research in Social Education* 43, no. 1 (2015): 68–101.

22. Bil, "Tensions."

23. John Mack Faragher, "'And the Lonely Voice of Youth Cries "What Is Truth?"': Western History and the National Narrative," *Western Historical Quarterly* 48, no. 1 (2017): 1–21.

24. Stephen Aron, "The We in West." *Western Historical Quarterly* 49, no. 1 (2017): 3.

25. *Ibid.*

WORKS CITED

Allen, Paula Gunn. 1992. *The Sacred Hoop: Recovering the Feminine in American Indian Traditions: With a New Preface*. Boston: Beacon Press.

Allison, James R. 2018. "Beyond It All: Surveying the Intersections of Modern American Indian, Environmental, and Western Histories." *History Compass* 16 (4): e12447.

Aron, Stephen. 2017. "The We in West." *Western Historical Quarterly* 49 (1): 1–15.

Bauerkemper, Joseph. 2007. "Narrating Nationhood: Indian Time and Ideologies of Progress." *Studies in American Indian Literatures* 19 (3): 27–53.

Bil, Geoff. 2016. "Tensions in the World of Moon: *Twin Peaks*, Indigeneity and Territoriality." *Senses of Cinema*, no. 79 (July). http://sensesofcinema.com/2016/twin-peaks/twin-peaks-indigeneity-territoriality/.

Carroll, Michael. 1993. "Agent Cooper's Errand in the Wilderness: 'Twin Peaks' and American Mythology." *Literature/Film Quarterly* 21 (4): 287–95.

Deloria, Vine. 1994. *God Is Red: A Native View of Religion*. 2nd ed. Golden, CO: Fulcrum Publishing.

Dolan, Marc. 1995. "The Peaks and Valleys of Serial Creativity: What Happened to/on Twin Peaks." In *Full of Secrets: Critical Approaches to* Twin Peaks, edited by David Lavery, 30–50. Detroit: Wayne State University Press.

Faragher, John Mack. 2017. "'And the Lonely Voice of Youth Cries "What Is Truth?"'": Western History and the National Narrative." *Western Historical Quarterly* 48 (1): 1–21.

Jenkins, Henry. 1995. "'Do You Enjoy Making the Rest of Us Feel Stupid?': alt.tv.twinpeaks, the Trickster Author and Viewer Mastery." In *Full of Secrets: Critical Approaches to* Twin Peaks, edited by David Lavery, 51–69. Detroit: Wayne State University Press.

Limerick, Patricia Nelson. 1987. *The Legacy of Conquest: The Unbroken Past of the American West*. New York: W.W. Norton.

———. 2001. *Something in the Soil: Legacies and Reckonings in the New West*. New York: Norton.

Nabokov, Peter. 2002. *A Forest of Time: American Indian Ways of History*. New York: Cambridge University Press.

Robbins, William G. 1991. "Laying Siege to Western History: The Emergence of New Paradigms." In *Trails: Toward a New Western History*, edited by Patricia Nelson Limerick, Clyde A. Milner, and Charles E. Rankin, 182–214. Lawrence: University Press of Kansas.

Shear, Sarah B., Ryan T. Knowles, Gregory J. Soden, and Antonio J. Castro. 2015. "Manifesting Destiny: Re/Presentations of Indigenous Peoples in K–12 U.S. History Standards." *Theory & Research in Social Education* 43 (1): 68–101.

Slotkin, Richard. 2000. *Regeneration through Violence: The Mythology of the American Frontier, 1600–1860*. Norman: University of Oklahoma Press.

Spooner, Catherine. 2016. "'Wrapped in Plastic': David Lynch's Material Girls." In *Return to* Twin Peaks: *New Approaches to Materiality, Theory, and Genre on Television*, edited by Jeffrey Andrew Weinstock and Catherine Spooner, 105–20. New York: Palgrave Macmillan.

Turner, Frederick Jackson. 1894. "The Significance of the Frontier in American History." *Annual Report of the American Historical Association for the Year 1893*. Washington, DC: Government Printing Office, 199–227.

White, Richard, Patricia Nelson Limerick, and James R. Grossman. 1994. *The Frontier in American Culture: An Exhibition at the Newberry Library, August 26, 1994–January 7, 1995*. Chicago: The Library; Berkeley: University of California Press.

The Wood for the Trees

Regional and Anthropocene Signals in the Pacific Northwest Forests of Twin Peaks

ANDY HAGEMAN

Introduction

David Lynch and the associated makers of *Twin Peaks* shaped the Pacific Northwestern regionalism of the series through myriad shots of and songs about trees. From the Pilot (1990) through the finale of Season 3 (2017), the Douglas firs, Western red cedars, and other trees play a wide and sometimes wild range of cinematic narrative roles. Yet across that range they consistently root *Twin Peaks* in the Pacific Northwest. This essay analyzes the rootedness and diverse roles of trees and wood to argue that they embody core contradictions within *Twin Peaks*. Furthermore, in identifying these wood-related contradictions, this essay decodes ecocritical signals in the series that point both to regional ecological challenges and to the vast scale of the Anthropocene. While *Twin Peaks* may seem, on the surface, an odd choice to identify as possessing a productive ecological aesthetic, this essay argues that its exceptionally surreal twists and turns provide a sophisticated invitation to, as well as a map and model for, sustaining life and love in uncertain times. The trees and wood in *Twin Peaks* can help us approach the bewildering geological and chronological scales of the Anthropocene by drawing the audience into this rooted, textured Pacific Northwest region that is also a portal to other massive and weird dimensions that limn the borders of what people can imagine.

It is vital to articulate at the start the concepts this essay explores. The trees, living or dead, that are actively enmeshed in the forest ecosystems of *Twin Peaks* gesture at the nonhuman aspects of the narrative. These trees inspire wonder in Agent Cooper within the diegesis. The trees are also capable of provoking audience wonder both vicariously through Cooper and through the speculative conjecture their periodic appearances on screen as non-narrative transitions between human, plot-driven scenes provoke. In both cases, these nonhuman beings of the Pacific Northwest signal agencies, networks, and objectives that are alien from and yet connected to human ones. The plot focus in the first two seasons on the Packard Sawmill and Ghostwood Development, the lavish wood interiors of the Great Northern Hotel, and the omnipresence of pictures of early loggers displayed in the Sheriff's Department all frame the woods as the resource on which the regional extractivist economy is built. The town of Twin Peaks fundamentally exists through a long history of people, from the European settler colonists who founded the town after displacing the indigenous inhabitants of the region through acts of cultural barbarism onward, treating the trees as a resource at their disposal for transmuting into capital. Mark Frost's supplemental novel, *The Secret History of Twin Peaks*, reveals this attitude towards the woods and repeats the silent erasure of indigenous peoples via a town history solicited by the Twin Peaks town council in 1984:

> James Packard arrived first, eldest son of a Boston shipping family, alerted by his Harvard roommate—one of the Weyerhaeuser boys—about the wealth of natural resources that lay west of the Rockies and north of the Columbia River. Inspired by a vision, Packard traveled west and, loved by its natural beauty and untouched trees, laid claim to ten thousand acres around White Tail Falls in 1890 ... the Packard Timber Company became the economic engine for the town that sprang up around his burgeoning business: the town of Twin Peaks.
>
> When Friedrich Weyerhaeuser purchased a million acres in the state of Washington from the railway interests in 1900, he organized the "Weyerhaeuser Syndicate," a confederation of lumber companies that took dominion over his new kingdom. James Packard became one of those partners and the Packard Timber Company grew along with the Syndicate, a beacon of industry attracting waves of northwestward pioneers to seek their own fortunes in the Northwest.[1]

These aspects of the series highlight the capacity for human beings to displace or repress ecological others and focus on their dramas as if detached from and not dependent upon those same ecological others. In cursory viewings, *Twin Peaks* does not explicitly espouse a particular political stance on the wood and the trees. This essay approaches Lynch's apparent apolitical mode as opening a powerful space for critical spectators to analyze the latent messages regarding ecology that the series inherently produces. Since Lynch doesn't invoke what Slavoj Žižek calls a constituted ideology (explicit messaging at the level of content), the signals of *Twin Peaks*' constitutive ideology (the latent structures of the world and events depicted) are particularly accessible for locating and decoding.[2]

Finally, the argument at the center of this essay builds upon ecocritical explorations of *Twin Peaks* by Sherryl Vint and Martha P. Nochimson among others. They have both written about nature/culture and interior/exterior dynamics, with Vint presenting ecocritical analyses and Nochimson delivering broad perspectives on Lynch's cinema style.[3] Other critics and commentators have discussed the regionalism and/or the forests of the series, including Jeva Lange, who focuses on the gothic, nightmarish darkness of the Pacific Northwest.[4] Karra Shimabukuro, Michael Carroll, and others have approached the forests of *Twin Peaks* as a space of folkloric archetypes and/or as American wilderness.[5] This essay connects these insightful conversations by synchronizing—via the trees and wood—regional and broader ecological concerns, and it builds upon them by incorporating the new material of Season 3 while also dilating the scale of ecocritique to the Anthropocene.

Agent Cooper's Whittling in the Dark

The most pervasive and persuasive perspective on the wood and trees in *Twin Peaks* is Agent Cooper's. As other Lynch scholars, following David Lavery in his introduction to the first academic collection on *Twin Peaks*, have noted, Cooper functions as a figure of audience identification.[6] Just like us, Cooper is an outsider newly arrived in the town of Twin Peaks, and his curiosities and questions cue the need to dig into the mystery of who killed Laura Palmer and all the mysteries that unfold once that case is closed. Since we enter *Twin Peaks* through Cooper, our maps of the economies and ecologies of the town are heavily influenced by his own, though it is easy to forget just how subjective his perspective can be. To underscore this point, note how the first time Cooper appears on screen in the Pilot, he is driving a car along a highway that cuts through a forest. He marvels at the trees through screens of glass that mediate the experience through visual framing and proximity separation parallel to watching on a television or computer. To put it analogically: the trees are to Cooper what *Twin Peaks* is to the television spectator. What's more, Cooper makes a note in this same scene to Diane via dictaphone that the gas tank is nearly empty. The memo should also remind us that this mediated enjoyment of Pacific Northwest flora is doubly fueled by the extracted petroleum both in the car's engine and poured into the roadway tarmac. Long before the narrative brings in the smell of scorched engine oil as a sensory association with the Black Lodge, *Twin Peaks* introduces the audience-avatar protagonist by linking a highly mediated fascination with the trees to petroculture.

Once the FBI agent arrives in the town of Twin Peaks, he meets Sheriff

Harry S. Truman. Within a quick debriefing on Laura Palmer and Ronette Pulaski, Cooper makes the non-sequitur inquiry, "What kind of fantastic trees have you got growing around here? Big, majestic." Truman gives the direct reply, "Douglas firs," and Cooper exudes a sense of awe as he repeats (as if to memorize) the name, "Douglas firs." Then, with the shortest of beats, Cooper returns the conversation to the women who've been assaulted. This micro-blip in his train of thought contributes to what is often labeled the quirkiness of Cooper's characterization. However, it produces an alternate latent meaning, too. As audience avatar in the diegesis, Cooper simultaneously reflects and/or instigates audience wonder at the regional landscape on display, akin to how laugh tracks hail us to laugh at the appropriate prompts. In the act of registering and directing audience experience, the agent's side of the dialogue treats the trees as objects of human fantasy and taxonomy. As such, Cooper pulls us along down a path of aestheticizing and classifying the trees and wood for human purposes of projecting a potent combination of fantasy and systems of knowledge and power.

The ideological implications of this combined response to the trees are complicated. There's something laudable about Cooper's capacity to balance aesthetic awe and rational investigation. Yet it's unclear whether the rapid return of his attention to the crimes indicates, on the one hand, an acknowledgment that the rational road of taxonomy will only take him so far into encountering the trees because they are radical others, or, on the other hand, that his dendrological curiosity has been satiated so he can keep consuming this element of the Pacific Northwest ecosystems from a comfortable distance. After all, in this exchange he and Truman are in a windowless hospital corridor from which Cooper can savor only a fantasy of trees he was already observing from the screened remove of a car. Put in terms of established American approaches to the Western frontier, Cooper's wonder, mixed with an impulse to catalogue, runs perilously close to treating this region as a place to be promoted and subjugated by those who explore it. His reaction to this place resonates with the settler colonist ideology of Packard and Weyerhaeuser quoted above such that 1990 seems a lot like 1890, prompting us to ask: is it future or is it past?

In the Pilot episode, there's another scene where Cooper invokes wood explicitly, and he's interacting directly with a harvested piece of it. Cooper and Truman are anticipating trouble since Bobby Briggs was overheard during his release from jail telling his friend Mike Nelson that they are going to exact physical vengeance on James Hurley. As the two law officers sit in a Sheriff's SUV staking out the Roadhouse, a local live-music bar that continues to act as a key location throughout the series, the agent asks the sheriff, "You know why I'm whittling?" Truman replies, "Okay,

I'll bite again. Why are you whittling?" Cooper concludes the exchange by explaining, "Because that's what you do in a town where a yellow light still means slow down, not speed up." The figure of an urban outsider being initially enamored by a small town's values is in itself generic, but by framing this brief city-meets-country exchange through whittling, Lynch codes the scene with regional specificity. The stakeout turns into an SUV-chasing-motorcycle pursuit along a road through dense forest in a nighttime parallel of Cooper's first cut through the woods. Suggestively, Joey Paulson and Donna Hayward elude the law officers by making a rapid turn onto an old logging road, an infrastructure of local extractivism. Enmeshed by visuals of trees and the spoken allusion to the lumber industry, the familiar city/country antagonism is firmly situated in the Pacific Northwest.

What's more, during the stakeout Cooper completes his whittling project sufficiently to reveal the end product, a whistle. He toots it when Bobby and Mike pull into the Roadhouse and asks Truman to "whistle for a little backup." The ideology at work is complicated. In working the wood with his hands and a low-tech tool, Cooper is getting more intimate with and connected to Western timber. Yet he perceives whittling as a leisure activity, a perspective detached from labor connections to wood that determine many of the local citizens' lives via the Packard Sawmill. For Cooper, wood is pure enjoyment. This underscores the limits of Cooper's, and therefore the audience's, perspectives on the role of wood in the region. It's also significant that Cooper decides to handcraft a tool of police work. He asserts control over wood by shaping it into a device for hailing criminals, an Althusserian gesture that points out Cooper's unconscious attitude to wood that elides the unsustainable symbiosis of human-tree coexistence in the Pacific Northwest and as synecdoche of a more general Anthropocene attitude.

Spectres of Lumber Labor

While Cooper's relationship to wood helps establish the audience's own explicit relationship to it, the elision of lumber labor noted above implicitly shapes the ecological ideology of *Twin Peaks*. The opening credits montage of the series, which was minimally modified between the Pilot version and the one for subsequent episodes of Seasons 1 and 2, has rightfully received analysis across a lot of *Twin Peaks* scholarship. Critics have largely read the montage as perturbing a binary of nature and culture. Martha Nochimson's early analysis exemplifies the trend:

Its lap dissolves among sharp images to the strains of the slow, mournful, but somewhat romantic theme music composed by Angelo Badalamenti suggest, according to Lynch, an enigmatic interpenetration of opposites as robins and cascading waterfalls dissolve into the artifacts of an industrialized logging industry, which spews thick smoke from its smokestacks and generates spearlike golden sparks with its gears.[7]

Indeed, the montage produces an intriguing dialectic via juxtaposition and association, one that seems to call directly for an ecocritical interpretation of the series. But to extend Nochimson's analysis, one must also consider the absence of human beings in the sawmill shots. To focus exclusively on the elements of a supposed nature-culture opposition without connecting them to the eerily absent people of the industry depicted is, to borrow a Lynchism, to let the eye wander from the donut to the hole. The act of drawing audience attention to the lumber industry as central to this Western community is figured only through the architecture and mechanical infrastructure of the industry, as if it runs autonomously. In this way, the montage initiates a style that largely spans the series of bracketing lumber laborers to offscreen or the occasional, but very marginal, edges of the screen. *Twin Peaks* thereby conjures a Pacific Northwest lumber town with a deep lacuna regarding the majority of people who live and work there. The resulting portrayal of the town of Twin Peaks hews closer to a fantasy of this part of the American West. And yet a productive byproduct of this omission of lumber labor is the potential for the audience to contemplate broader structures of extractivist capitalism. If the audience can't get caught up in the individual life stories of lumber laborers, they have the opportunity (whether taken or not) to explore the forms and structures of trees and wood extracted, commodified, and consumed.

To circle back to Nochimson's remark on the opening, her reference to the mill's objects on display as "artifacts" was proleptic and poignant if we underline the historical aspect of that term.[8] The original two seasons of *Twin Peaks* are set in February and March 1989. That's the same year Weyerhaeuser shuttered its mill near Snoqualmie, where principal photography was shot. The planing plants and dry kilns were shuttered approximately thirteen years later. These dates are specific to the filming locations that exist in a doppelgänger state of real and reel Twin Peaks, and they're a more general synecdoche of the economic crisis the lumber industry in the West was confronting when the series was filmed and enjoying popular cultural influence. In an eerie way, then, the opening montage shows what was then the near future of people being erased from the wood and the mill. Appropriately enough, the industrial decline of lumber labor in the 1980s reaches apotheosis in the opening credits montage of the Season 3 premiere. Gone are the sparks and smoke, and all that remains is a spectral shot of the shuttered mill slipping through disrepair towards ruin.

On the rare occasions in the original two seasons when lumber laborers are on screen, the texture of their livelihood is nearly as spectral as towns-folk's memories of Laura Palmer. There are really only three such labor-ers identified in these seasons. Janek and Suburbis Pulaski, the parents of Laura's friend and BOB's victim, Ronette Pulaski, get screen time chiefly to deliver a joke. The third is Fred Truax, the Packard Sawmill employee who is fired in an act of wrath by Catherine Martell. Otherwise, the residents of Twin Peaks who work at the town's main industry are visible mostly as back-ground figures in the Double R Diner. Although the series mostly excludes these residents, it is illuminating to consider what was happening in the actual towns of North Bend and Snoqualmie at the time.

A convergence appears in the March 2, 1989, edition of the *Sno-qualmie Valley Record*, a local newspaper to the filming region. This edi-tion includes an article, "'Northwest Passage' Turns Valley into a Movie Set," by Paul Weideman that captures a range of mixed reactions to the filming. Some locals were thrilled about a celebrity director and actors coming to the region, and about local people and businesses being immortalized. However, Weideman also states, "But there's bound to be a negative impression or two left by the invaders from, really, another culture."[9] The article goes on to say that several business owners felt pressured to concede too many future rights to the use of their establish-ments' images. All told, the article documents local anxieties over eco-nomic stresses and the way their home and society will be portrayed on screen. In a telling coincidence, this local response to the making of *Twin Peaks* appears in an edition of the *Record* with a front-page article about a massive mill fire in nearby Preston, the second major mill fire in two months at a time when employment at Weyerhaeuser was already increas-ingly precarious.[10]

A reinforcing coincidence appears in the April 19, 1990, edition of the same newspaper—the next edition to contain any stories on *Twin Peaks*. In another article by Weideman called "The Pies Behind 'Twin Peaks,'" he opens on a local eco-relevant economics note: "It looked like the contro-versial land-use decisions behind Snoqualmie Ridge, and the planned PGA Tour golf course, were going to put the town of Snoqualmie 'on the map' around the country. Then came 'Twin Peaks' and a story in a grocery store tabloid, beating Weyerhaeuser to the punch."[11] At stake is a proposal to sell off lands formerly connected with lumber to corporate interests planning to build a golf course and a for-profit prison. This actual storyline reso-nates uncannily with the early seasons' plotline of *Twin Peaks*, where the likes of Benjamin Horne, Catherine Martell, and Josie Packard all scheme to destroy the mill, and by extension the economic stability of many resi-dents, and sell the land to outside investors for high-end development. On a Mark Frost side note, the prospect of developing a private-run prison was an actually existing harbinger of the Ghostwood development, including just such a prison in Twin Peaks according to his book, *The Final Dossier*.

To pull on a thread that connects the Pulaskis, Fred Truax, and the other implied lumber laborers at the periphery, the flannel they frequently wear in the series signals the ideological milieu of the late 1980s and early 1990s Pacific Northwest as well as perceptions of the region from outside. While the costume design of *Twin Peaks* has garnered attention, from academic arguments about 1950s signals to Tumblr sites obsessed with the 1990s sweaters, the multivalent coding of the flannel has gone largely unremarked. Recall that at the same time the lumber laborers who were central to Twin Peaks, yet marginal to *Twin Peaks*, were wearing flannel as an unofficial uniform of the industry, members of bands such as Screaming Trees, Mudhoney, Green River, and more famously, Nirvana and Pearl Jam, were recoding flannel in music venues and on MTV as the generic uniform for grunge music. In large part due to the marketing strategies of the SubPop record label, the Seattle area became known as a hotbed of grunge music, a proliferation of bands who inherited and innovated upon much of the musical aesthetic of punk. The conventions of grunge emerged conterminously with the aesthetics of *Twin Peaks*, and these flannel-clad bands would rise to cultural dominance through the 1990s. These performers were repurposing a style associated with the regional, then-waning lumber industry into a style still associated with the Pacific Northwest but tied anew to an emerging music culture. And as a revealing temporal turn in style and commodification, as of 2014, the once alternative SubPop now has a storefront in the Seattle-Tacoma International Airport, where travelers can buy high-end flannel shirts and a variety of *Twin Peaks* books in addition to the classic grunge and new albums produced by the label.

The flannels at edges of, and largely off, the screen in the series were hovering between two contradictory styles, and as such they create a space and a prompt for critical thought. Because the people wearing flannel in *Twin Peaks* are fundamentally tied to an extractivist industry experiencing a crisis, class antagonism is unconsciously in play. The imbrication of human-wood entanglements reframes the late 1980s lumber labor conditions, corporate globalization of the industry, and regional environmental pressures as much vaster ecological, anthropocene-scale concerns.[12] For example, the series ran at the same time that the endangerment of the Northern Spotted Owl was circulating widely and in a discourse of environmentalists vs. laborers. As the Giant in the series popularly announces, "The owls are not what they seem." Again, flannel-clad characters in the series can direct audience speculation beyond local and regional economies and ecosystems.

This connection of the ghostly-status flannel with the vaster ecological scale of the Anthropocene is reinforced by the costume design of the Woodsmen who join the series in a sustained way in Season 3 after possible, early versions appeared briefly in the 1992 prequel film, *Twin Peaks: Fire Walk with Me*. At this point in the series, flannel has truly become the style of beings who move through spatial and temporal scales beyond the grasp of most human beings—scales that synchronize with Timothy Morton's definition of a hyperobject, a class of objects that includes global warming and the Anthropocene.[13] What's more, the faces of the Woodsmen in Season 3 appear to be smeared with scorched engine oil, the substance that marks the threshold to the Black Lodge, reminding audiences that *Twin Peaks* links a fascination with forest extractivism and lumber industries to petroculture. The carbon-coated faces, which reiterate the petrocultural forest extractivist fascination attached to Agent Cooper in his first appearances in the series above, double down here on the flannel's symbolism of extractivism in the American West as encompassed within the Anthropocene.

The Plane Story of Exchange Value

After the wood is harvested, processed, and cut, the Packard Sawmill sells it on the market. Across all of *Twin Peaks*, there is only a single scene that features a point-of-sale lumber transaction. Though the scene may seem minor, and originally it was left like sawdust on the cutting-room floor, it captures some of the most forceful critical potential that Lynch's *Twin Peaks* world contains. In *Twin Peaks: The Missing Pieces*, a feature-length film of scenes deleted from the theatrical release of *Twin Peaks: Fire Walk with Me*, Dell Mibbler, the Assistant Manager of Twin Peaks Savings and Loan who was killed by Andrew Packard's revenge bomb late in Season 2, confronts both Josie Packard and Pete Martell because the wood he bought from the mill does not actually measure an exact two inches by four inches, despite being labeled that way. The scene opens with Josie escorting Dell to get answers from Pete. It is significant that the owner by marriage and inheritance of the mill, Josie, and an executive from the local bank are baffled by what is for Pete—and those who labor with lumber—a plain matter. The people at or near the top of the organizations where capital flows through the town, the mill and the bank, are fundamentally detached from the economic activity that they determine, activity that itself determines whether the region-specific industry struggles or thrives, lives or dies. Only Pete, who began his life in the lumber labor class and married into the capitalist owner class after catching Catherine's eye (through his acumen with wood, by the way), has the perspective to resolve Dell's complaint. By highlighting the division, this scene complements Cooper's enthusiastic yet distant attitude to the trees and wood as well as to the lumber laborers of the town who haunt the series through their absent presence.

In the scene Pete translates the dimensions of lumber for sale into the discourse of finance capital. After all, Dell's original misunderstanding was driven by his approaching wood through use value alone. Would the wood meet his construction needs? Pete begins by trying to explain the situation in use value terms when he says that the dimensions are industry uniform across the U.S. and that you couldn't build a decent doghouse with lumber that actually measured two by four, implying that construction designs presume the actual dimensions of the pieces. When the use value approach fails to convince Dell, Pete pivots to exchange value, asking if a dollar at the bank today is still what a dollar used to be worth some time ago. The analogy persuades Dell, and he apologizes and accepts the lumber he has bought. Yet, the analogy should strike the audience as odd, an index of how strange and deceptive capitalist exchange value can be. It is only the abstraction of the rooted regional resource into circulating capital that smooths out the rough edges of the original misunderstanding in the transaction that Dell Mibbler, the banker, and Josie Packard, the owner of the mill—the means of production, are placated by the scene's end. By contrast, for laborers feeling the precarity of the industry and/or environmentalists concerned about the regional ecosystems, Pete's abstraction into capitalist exchange value further roughs up the already splintery edges of the wood being labored into lumber. The once-living, fibrous forest beings have dissolved into financial formulation and speculation, and it's this magic trick that puts the top tier capitalists of the Pacific Northwest town at ease.

To dilate the scale of analysis, this point-of-sale scene calls to mind Deleuze's assertion in *Cinema 1: The Movement-Image*:

> The cinema image is always dividual. This is because, in the final analysis, the screen, as the frame of frames, gives a common standard of measurement to things which do not have one—long shots of countryside and close-ups of the face, an astronomical system and a single drop of water—parts which do not have the same denominator of distance, relief, or light. In all these senses the frame ensures a deterritorialisation of the image.[14]

The specific content of this scene deploys exchange value framing through dialogue. Trees and wood are deterritorialized through the analogy of money across time. It's vital to then apply this act of framing to the cinematic media form itself. The screen creates the illusion of equivalence across the different visual signatures of the Pacific Northwest. One might extrapolate further to claim that this region of the American West is also presented as equivalent to every other cinematic setting on the screen, including not only other series but also all the advertisements so far as the original two seasons are concerned. Perhaps the restoration of this scene in the Missing Pieces compilation is one more instance of a return of the repressed in the trees and wood of *Twin Peaks*. It points not to a casual or unconscious acceptance of the logic of capitalist extractivism in the Pacific Northwest by Lynch, but to the critical potential *Twin Peaks* contains for analytical spectators who tangle with its form and content in the context of the Anthropocene.

The Painting on the Walls

After the wood has left the sawmill, it continues to conjure a dual Pacific Northwest/Anthropocene resonance in *Twin Peaks* through the interiors of the Great Northern, the hotel owned by the Horne family and where Cooper resides while in Twin Peaks. The beautiful wood floors, walls, and beams of the Great Northern's rooms, offices, common spaces, and corridors situate the diverse scenes and situations that take place inside this habitat built through the regional form of extractivism. The hotel is literally built of regional wood, and abstractly the lavish design, quality of wood, and architectural grandeur all point to the accumulation of capital connected with local extractivism. This symbolic complexity of wood itself and wood-based capital is further deepened by the distinctive indigenous-style paintings that adorn Ben Horne's office and the reception lobby of the Great Northern. These murals are a literal and figurative marking (or, writing, if you will) on the wall that connects the modern culture of lumber extractivism in the Pacific Northwest with the history of settler colonialism in the area.

To read these walls through a lens of combined regional and Anthropocene register extends other environmental analyses. In an essay that broadly explores various aspects of the series, Martha Nochimson notes, "Richard Hoover, the production designer of all the series except the pilot, created a look for the show in which the concepts of inside and outside were conflated. A massive use of wood gives an outside feeling to the interiors."[15] More recently and with a more dedicatedly ecocritical approach to *Twin Peaks*, Sherryl Vint developed the nature-culture deconstruction that Nochimson noted and complemented with interpretations of other nonhuman beings in the series.[16] As this essay introduces the regional-Anthropocene resonance it tries to reframe, rather than challenge, Nochimson's and Vint's astute insights into the ecological scale that people on Earth are currently working to comprehend and engage.

As scholars continue theorizing the concept of the Anthropocene, a key historical focal point has been European settler colonialism in the Americas.[17] This development in the geological and ecological arena casts a new light on the Great Northern's walls. The iconic paintings atop the finished-wood canvas represent both the ecological and economic dynamics of the late 1980s as the mills were being shuttered and public environmental discourse was shifting. Also worth noting is the long history of colonial devastation of people and ecosystems who'd long resided in the West. Recall that explicit attention to the multi-century scale of settler colonialism appears in Mark Frost's 2016 book, *The Secret History of Twin Peaks*. Although the novel bears the hallmarks of Frost, he was writing this during the phase of collaborative preparation with Lynch for Season 3. Recall as well that one of the most discussed parts of Season 3 centers around the Trinity Test of an atomic weapon, and innovations to this form of weaponry and energy are among the other key historical focal points for conceptualizing the Anthropocene.[18]

Frost's novel concentrates extensively on the Lewis and Clark expedition as an alien invasion of the Pacific Northwest region where Twin Peaks would later be founded. He features other unsanctioned gold prospectors in the area to draw a line across a long history of extractivist exploitation ideology in this zone that the European settlers fantasized as frontier. The iconic paintings on the Great Northern's wood walls act as a spectral index of the people and other coexistent beings who've been practically erased from the Pacific Northwest ecosystems. They parallel, albeit not exactly, the lumber laborers erased from much of the series, with the vital but nearly singular exception of Deputy (later, Deputy Chief) Hawk. To note these absences is to connect Anthropocene ecocriticism with the widespread approach to eliding racial and ethnic identity in *Twin Peaks* that Melanie McFarland has brilliantly assessed. McFarland points out the deep absence of people of color across the iterations of *Twin Peaks*, and she persuasively argues that the few inclusions, such as the African American sex worker named Jade in Season 3, are themselves structurally problematic: "It's often said that as bizarre and inscrutable as some of Lynch's works can be, even the misfires have solid intent about them. This does not make me more forgiving of Jade or Lynch's other storytelling sculptures masquerading as human characters. Indeed, it gives me less of a reason to embrace and defend Lynch's vision. It tells me that women like me are polished objects, shapes in space."[19]

To extend McFarland's analysis to the intersection of race, gender, political economy, and ecology, consider that the woman of color who arguably possesses the most agency and power across the series, Josie Packard, departed from the narrative in a weird act of what I will call "becoming wood" inside the Great Northern. At the moment of her human death, Josie's face appears to have transferred into the wood of a nightstand drawer pull. That is where the story of Josie, a rare woman of color and ultimate noir character of the original seasons, the mastermind capable of outwitting cunning competitors who even got the drop on Agent Cooper at final moments of Season 1, was left by the series creators. Josie did not reappear in Season 3, but I will suggest that she does haunt this recent season sonically via Naido. As the prominent Asian woman of Season 3, and one who is objectified reasonably akin to Josie in the originals, Naido's incomprehensible voice may be read as the squeaky sound of a tight wooden drawer being pulled out and pushed in.[20] Read this way, Naido sounds like Josie trying to escape and/or communicate. The fact that the voice is encrypted is appropriate to a broad concluding thought: the people missing across the series haunt it through an absent presence that is inscribed in the wood and trees.

Jack Rabbit's Palace of Decay

Jack Rabbit's Palace in Season 3 is an evocative remainder of a long-dead Western Red Cedar that haunts the series in two key registers of Pacific Northwest regionalism and Anthropocene ecology. In regional place-based terms, this figure of a decomposing conifer surrounded by other living conifers, from the very young to the very old, is deeply Pacific Northwest. Along with Douglas fir, these conifers are among the most iconic flora of the region's forests and their aesthetic rendering into landscapes of frontier. In Anthropocene ecological terms, this tableau points to non-human lifespans and temporalities that are being rapidly and radically changed through human activities that affect climate, hydrology, and soils. Both regional and planetary scales are at play as the narrative of *Twin Peaks* highlights this small forest zone as a center of energy and opening between the Earth dimension and that of the Lodges. Furthermore, this woody node is an ultimate testing place at the climax of the season when central characters cross paths.

The two people challenged to their cores in the arboreal zone of Jack Rabbit's Palace are Deputy Andy and Mr. C. When Andy, in the company of Sheriff Truman, Deputy Chief Hawk, and Deputy Briggs, enters this mysterious place of wood, he is the single privileged human being to pass through the vortex to be with the Fireman. The text is not explicit about how, why, or by whom Andy was selected to have this dimensional crossing, but what is clear is Andy's concern and care for Naido in the moments before the vortex spins up and upon returning to his colleagues in the woods. Naido is an Asian woman with her face altered through what comes across as a crude, and likely cruel, surgery so that her eyes are covered by flesh. She is lying nude and unconscious at the location where the vortex portal exists, and Andy is the first officer to react as he reaches out to see if she is okay and to reassure her. He is then whisked up through the vortex to the Fireman. After the chosen deputy has received key knowledge from the Fireman's dimension, the vortex disappears. The other law officers return to material presence, and Andy walks out from behind the decaying remains of Jack Rabbit's Palace carrying Naido. He exhibits uncharacteristic assertiveness. Unlike his usual rambling approach to sharing information, he authoritatively declares that Naido is very important before personally carrying her back to the Sheriff's Department vehicle.

In this forested zone of power and border openings, Andy is a law officer, a partner, and a parent who puts his instructions from the Lodge into play in a way that blends confidence with empathy and commitment to a common good. As such, the experience at this weird wooded zone makes Andy's character arc a productive alternative to that of Agent Cooper and his flawed attempt at white-knight masculinity concerning Laura Palmer and Carrie Page.

In closing, the wood of Jack Rabbit's Palace at the end of *Twin Peaks*— at least for now and the foreseeable future—embodies the Anthropocene contradictions and complexities featured in this essay. The decomposing stump is not a nurse log with saplings rising out of its rich mulch. Nurse logs are all over the woods around Snoqualmie and North Bend, but Lynch chose the less obviously regenerative tree in decay to stand as the Palace. For audience members to be fascinated with this particular collapsed tree is to embrace the dark and the dead on its own terms. No tender tree life is sprouting up to point to a future of continuity already unfolding—no next generation of the same cedars. Instead, these woods will take new shapes in a transforming ecosystem within a warming planet. To love this wood, then, is to love the contradictions and mysteries and ecological signals within *Twin Peaks* without rushing into thoughtless desire for a future Season 4 or other expansions of this fictional universe. To love this decaying mass of wood is to love a node in a local ecosystem that is decaying each day between the ecological history of people in the Pacific Northwest and a future that will be differently wooded. Jack Rabbit's Palace is the fiber of an Anthropocene future that is dictated by the past, inside the series and out. A future of certain tragedies but also unpredictable mysteries in the challenges it holds for those who will inhabit the timelines being shaped by economic, political, and cultural forces, including David Lynch's amazing cinema and these very words printed on woody fibers.

NOTES

1. Mark Frost, *The Secret History of Twin Peaks* (New York: Flatiron Books, 2016), 157.
2. Slavoj Žižek, *Living in the End Times* (New York: Verso, 2010), 55.
3. Martha Nochimson, "Desire under the Douglas Firs: Entering the Body of Reality in *Twin Peaks*," in *Full of Secrets: Cultural Approaches to* Twin Peaks, ed. David Lavery (Detroit: Wayne State University Press, 1995), 144–159; Sherryl Vint, "'The Owls are not What They Seem': Animals and Nature in *Twin Peaks*," in *Return to* Twin Peaks: *New Approaches to Materiality, Theory, and Genre on Television*, ed. Jeffrey Andrew Weinstock and Catherine Spooner (New York: Palgrave Macmillan, 2016), 71–86.
4. Jeva Lange, "The Scariest Thing about *Twin Peaks* is the Pacific Northwest," *The Week*, May 18, 2017, accessed May 20, 2020, https://theweek.com/articles/699012/scariest-thing-about-twin-peaks-pacific-northwest.
5. Karra Shimabukuro, "The Mystery of the Woods: 'Twin Peaks' and the Folkloric Forest," *Cinema Journal* 55, no. 3 (Spring 2016): 121–125; Michael Carroll, "Agent Cooper's Errand in the Wilderness: *Twin Peaks* and American Mythology," *Literature/Film Quarterly* 21, no. 4 (1993): 287–295.
6. David Lavery, "Introduction: The Semiotics of Cobbler: *Twin Peaks*' Interpretive Community," in *Full of Secrets: Cultural Approaches to* Twin Peaks, ed. David Lavery (Detroit: Wayne State University Press, 1995), 13.
7. Nochimson, "Desire under the Douglas Firs," 148.
8. *Ibid.*, np.
9. Paul Weideman, "'Northwest Passage' Turns Valley into a Movie Set," *Snoqualmie Valley Record* (North Bend, WA), March 2, 1989.
10. "Untitled," *Snoqualmie Valley Record*, March 2, 1989, 1.
11. Paul Weideman, "The Pies Behind 'Twin Peaks,'" *Snoqualmie Valley Record* (North Bend, WA), April 19, 1990.
12. Andrew Hageman, "Dale Cooper and the Mouthfeel of *Twin Peaks*," in *Food on Film: Bringing Something New to the Table*, ed. Thomas J. Hertweck (New York: Scarecrow Press, 2014), 141–156.
13. Timothy Morton, *Hyperobjects: Philosophy and Ecology After the End of the World* (Minneapolis: University of Minnesota Press, 2013).
14. Gilles Deleuze, *Cinema 1: The Movement-Image*, trans. Hugh Tomlinson and Barbara Habberjam (Minneapolis: University of Minnesota Press, 1986), 14–15.
15. Nochimson, "Desire under the Douglas Firs," 148.
16. Vint, "'The Owls.'"
17. Simon L. Lewis and Mark A. Maslin, "Defining the Anthropocene," *Nature* 519 (2015): 171–180, accessed May 20, 2020, https://doi.org/10.1038/nature14258.
18. *Ibid.*
19. Melanie McFarland, "A Colorless Sky: On the Whiteness of Twin Peaks," in *The Women of David Lynch: A Collection of Essays*, ed. Scott Ryan and David Bushman (Columbus, OH: Fayetteville Mafia Press, 2019), 38.
20. The idea of reading Naido's voice as a squeaky wooden drawer that links her to Josie Packard was developed through personal correspondence with Timothy Morton, so credit is due to that collaborative conversation. Cheers, Tim.

WORKS CITED

Carroll, Michael. 1993. "Agent Cooper's Errand in the Wilderness: *Twin Peaks* and American Mythology." *Literature/Film Quarterly* 21.4: 287–295.

Clover, Joshua. 2009. *1989: Bob Dylan Didn't Have This to Sing About*. Berkeley: University of California Press.

Deleuze, Gilles. 1986. *Cinema 1: The Movement-Image*. Translated by Hugh Tomlinson and Barbara Habberjam. Minneapolis: University of Minnesota Press.

DiPaolo, Amanda. 2019. "The Politics and Use of Nostalgia in *Twin Peaks*." In *The Politics of* Twin Peaks, edited by Amanda DiPaolo and Jamie Gillies, 35–52. New York: Lexington Books.

Frost, Mark. 2016. *The Secret History of Twin Peaks: A Novel*. New York: Flatiron Books.

Gillies, Jamie. 2019. "Rural and Suburban Lynch: Characterizations of Hard Times in Reagan's and Trump's America." In *The Politics of* Twin Peaks, edited by Amanda DiPaolo and Jamie Gillies, 55–67. New York: Lexington Books.

Hageman, Andrew. 2014. "Dale Cooper and the Mouthfeel of *Twin Peaks*." In *Food on Film: Bringing Something New to the Table*, edited by Thomas J. Hertweck, 141–156. New York: Scarecrow Press.

Lange, Jeva. "The Scariest Thing about *Twin Peaks* is the Pacific Northwest." 18 May 2017. *The Week*. https://theweek.com/articles/699012/scariest-thing-about-twin-peaks-pacific-northwest.

Lavery, David. 1995. "Introduction: The Semiotics of Cobbler: *Twin Peaks'* Interpretive Community." In *Full of Secrets: Cultural Approaches to* Twin Peaks, edited by David Lavery, 1–21. Detroit: Wayne State University Press.

Lewis, Simon L., and Mark A. Maslin. 2015. "Defining the Anthropocene." *Nature* 519: 171–180. https://doi.org/10.1038/nature14258.

Lynch, David. 2005. *Lynch on Lynch*, edited by Chris Rodley. New York: Farrar, Strauss, Giroux.

McFarland, Melanie. 2019. "A Colorless Sky: On the Whiteness of *Twin Peaks*." In *The Women of David Lynch: A Collection of Essays*, edited by Scott Ryan and David Bushman, 33–44. Columbus, OH: Fayetteville Mafia Press.

McNeill, John Robert. 2016. *The Great Acceleration: An Environmental History of the Anthropocene Since 1945*. Cambridge, MA: Belknap/Harvard University Press.

Morton, Timothy. 2013. *Hyperobjects: Philosophy and Ecology After the End of the World*. Minneapolis: University of Minnesota Press.

Nochimson, Martha. 1995. "Desire Under the Douglas Firs: Entering the Body of Reality in *Twin Peaks*." In *Full of Secrets: Cultural Approaches to* Twin Peaks, edited by David Lavery, 144–159. Detroit: Wayne State University Press.

Shimabukuro, Karra. Spring 2016. "The Mystery of the Woods: 'Twin Peaks' and the Folkloric Forest." *Cinema Journal*. 55.3. 121–125.

Vint, Sherryl. 2016. "'The Owls Are Not What They Seem': Animals and Nature in *Twin Peaks*." In *Return to* Twin Peaks: *New Approaches to Materiality, Theory, and Genre on Television*, edited by Jeffrey Andrew Weinstock and Catherine Spooner, 71–86. New York: Palgrave Macmillan.

Weideman, Paul. "'Northwest Passage' Turns Valley into a Movie Set," *Snoqualmie Valley Record* (North Bend, WA), March 2, 1989.

———. "The Pies Behind 'Twin Peaks,'" *Snoqualmie Valley Record* (North Bend, WA), April 8, 1990.

Žižek, Slavoj. 2010. *Living in the End Times*. New York: Verso.

Dark Americana

*Identity, Frontiers and Heterotopias
in David Lynch's Dreams*

Marko Lukić

The extensive research dedicated to the study of the American frontier, its myth and mythology, as well as the different occurrences and aspects that marked this lengthy historical and cultural process, rationally stands apart from both David Lynch and his vision of what the American myth is. Although strongly anchored in the American tradition through a rich tapestry of symbolism deeply rooted in the American imagination, an actual connection in Lynch's work with the myth of the Frontier appears either nonexistent or scarcely researched. This, however, does not mean that a frontier-based discourse is not present within Lynch's opus. It is precisely within the boundaries of various mainstream historical, political, and philosophical discourses that we can spatially and philosophically locate Lynch and his creations.

In the process of debating the historical, social, or political aspects of the American frontier—and acknowledging the multifaceted artistic production that evolved as a consequence to its "myth-building" nature—an unavoidable starting analytical point is Frederick Jackson Turner's lecture "The Significance of the Frontier in American History" presented on July 12, 1893, to a meeting of the American Historical Association in Chicago. In his presentation, Turner offers a concise but meaningful reading of the symbolic nature of the frontier, which acts as both a necessary prerequisite for the basis of the American experience and formation of a national subconscious, as well as the subsequent formation of the American identity. It is through its differentiation from the European notion of a frontier as "a fortified boundary line running through dense populations" that Turner starts elaborating the specific nature of the American one, dominantly characterized by the notion of free land and resources located in a still unconquered wilderness. As he states "[t]he frontier is the line of most rapid and effective Americanization" where "[t]he wilderness masters the colonist."[1] This idea of the (initially) subdued pioneer and colonist develops into a myriad of interpretations. However, two dominant, mutually interdependent narratives emerge, the first presenting the concept of the frontier as an actual geographically definable boundary between civilization and wilderness. Then, Turner presents a separate, more abstract and symbolic understanding of the frontier as a space of adventure, opportunity, and richness that is simultaneously full of dangers, challenges, and potential death. As Turner continues, the frontier with its wilderness finds the intruding individual as a proper representative of the European scientific and cultural tradition, only to strip him in the next moment of his "garments of civilization and arrays him in the hunting shirt and the moccasin."[2] What follows is the testing provided by the austerities and hardships of the unconquered wilderness, which, if survived, will result not in the establishment of a European existential or geographical context, but instead in something new—something identifiably uniquely American.

Among the various positive and negative reactions to the frontier thesis, Richard Slotkin proposed an interesting elaboration on Turner's ideas. Slotkin, in an attempt to re-contextualize the formation of the American frontier conquering myth, articulates an idea of American identity not exclusively premised on unavoidable hardships, but instead on the violence connected to these adversities. In his seminal texts, *Regeneration Through Violence: The Mythology of the American Frontier, 1600–1860* and *Gunfighter Nation: The Myth of the Frontier in Twentieth-Century America*, Slotkin argues that the frontier space, as well as the accompanying violence, are key elements in both the process of (national) progress, and the redefining of the Turnerian European individual into a violent pioneer. These violent individuals, later mythologized as gunfighters, conformed to the necessities of the times, or more precisely to the unstoppable greed of progress, and under the later guise of the American frontier mythology waged the so-called Indian war. As described by Slotkin, this was a uniquely American experience, which functioned and was justified by opposing the "English Puritan colonists against a culture that was antithetical to their own."[3] The consequences of such war(s), as well as other similarly violent enterprises, influenced the formative process of the national identity, and further promoted what will become known as the myth of national unity. What is important to notice are the processes and (in)voluntary mechanisms used to recount, elaborate, and even justify the various violent patterns and occurrences that characterized the lengthy process of taming the frontier spaces. Slotkin goes on to elaborate that Americans turned to the printed word in order to help them deal with problems of faith, anxiety, and aspiration, causing literature to become "the primary vehicle for the communication of mythic material."[4] A similar argument can be found in Richard Ruland and Malcolm Bradbury's *From Puritanism to Postmodernism: A History of American Literature*, where they emphasize the importance of the Indian captivity narratives for both the development of literature and the creation and perpetuation of a specific angst- and fear-based relationship with everything located on the other side of the dividing line between civilization and the wilderness.[5] The often-demagogic tales of captures of innocent settlers whose only goal was to survive, and the horrors they then had to endure, reflected themselves on the creation of an idea of foreboding spaces lurking with danger. Consequently, these types of tales became the premise for the formation of a self-referential loop that allowed the forming of a "good natured," "well intentioned," or otherwise positive identity in opposition to the apparent darkness lying on the other side of the frontier.[6]

To place David Lynch and his opus within such a frontier-based theoretical context is potentially troublesome. Engulfed in his surrealist explorations of the human condition, as well as the dark side of human nature, Lynch positions himself almost completely detached from the solely survival-based existential paradigm proposed by Turner. By placing most of his narratives within a loosely defined but nevertheless contemporary setting, Lynch avoids any actual or metaphoric confrontations with nature. In his work the survival experience is then reduced to a metaphor of a battle between good and evil inside a particular character. Furthermore, although present within Lynch's narratives, violence is not articulated as a key factor necessary for survival or for achieving a specific goal. Instead, it functions as an unavoidable extension of the human character, part of a trial between good and evil, within which sometimes darkness prevails.

However, it is precisely Lynch's surrealism, heavily layered with symbolism, that allows for a more specific positioning of his narratives in relation to the Frontier mythology and the American experience in general. More specifically, much like the inner natures of his characters as well as their public lives, a particular duality appears to be dominant in his representation of actual and symbolic spaces. This spatial duality in turn is articulated through a frontier-like prism, where once again traditionally perceived civilizational values are embodied in the everyday lives of his characters, their usually unpretentious ordinary occupations and dreams. Additionally, Lynch stresses the notion of the frontier through the idea of a borderline that is physically or symbolically present within his storylines. Its purpose is to indicate not only the possible (physical and symbolic) limitations of the existence of these characters, but also the presence of something else: an unknown threat, as well as conceivable promise of knowledge, power, or other rewards.

In the attempt to define a theoretical outline for this spatial division, one construct is suitable to reconcile the various interpretative connections between Lynch's opus and the notion of the American frontier. Michel Foucault in his 1966 text *The Order of Things* articulates a theory regarding space, founded on the idea of alternative types of spaces: heterotopias, which influence language and spatiality. More precisely, heterotopias "secretly undermine language, because they make it impossible to name this and that, because they shatter or tangle common names, because they destroy 'syntax' in advance, and not only the syntax with which we construct sentences but also that less apparent syntax which causes words and things (next to and also opposite one another) to 'hold together.'"[7] Heterotopias function as such while simultaneously bringing together things that usually are not necessarily related.[8] Foucault elaborates on this in a 1967 lecture titled "Of Other Spaces," where he lists a number of different, so-called heterotopian spaces that exist parallel to ordinary sites. Foucault builds his argument on the notion that heterotopian spaces not only exist parallel to ordinary sites, but also function as a mirror, reflecting qualities that oppose those of normal spaces. These heterotopian sites "have the curious property of being in relation with all the other sites, but in such a way as to suspect, neutralize, or invert the set of relations that they happen to designate, mirror, or reflect."[9]

Consequently, what the notion of heterotopian spaces provides is a potential geographical binary, recognizing and allowing the coexistence of a known, regulated, and domesticized type of space and a reflection controlled by a different (positive or negative) set of rules and regulations. Furthermore, in his attempt to elaborate on the dynamics between these spaces, Foucault introduces the notion of heterotopias of deviation. These are spaces within which we can locate "individuals whose behavior is deviant in relation to the required mean or norm."[10] Suggested spaces, such as rest homes, psychiatric hospitals, and prisons, indicate not only the existence of an alternative and self-regulated spatial context, but also a narrowing of the interpretative possibilities of the function of these spaces. This particular type of space and the individuals within it are unable to break out or distance themselves from their specifically coded spaces, and are therefore locked within a particular narrative. It is because of these parameters that heterotopias can almost perfectly be laid over the theoretical construct of the frontier, especially over those segments that surpass the physical and measurably geographical context to extend into the symbolical and later mythical. Whether the subject of a potential analysis is an Indian captivity narrative, or a tale describing the hardships of winning the West, a spatial polarity is perpetually emphasized, character-ized by three different features—the security of the conquered/controlled domestic space, the danger and unpredictability of the space beyond the frontier, and the unavoidable changes that various characters are subject to once they decide to cross the threshold of safety. As most classic narra-tives argue, the Puritans, and later pioneers and prospectors, enjoyed the safety of their made-up civilized spaces, with perpetual danger looming within the reflection of their own spaces just across the fictitious line of the frontier. Untamed nature, wildlife, and violent natives are perennially locked within this heterotopian space, or more precisely, within this het-erotopia of deviation. It is here that we can locate Lynch's narratives as a third layer to the already existing construct of Frontier space through and heterotopias.

An almost ideal example of the superposition of a Lynchian spatial construct and a logical continuation of the frontier and heterotopian dis-course is the narrative presented in *Blue Velvet* (1986). The film begins with a straightforward sequence presenting the viewer an immaculate version of the American dream. Sanitized American images, including a white picket fence, rose garden, slow-moving fire truck with waving fireman and Dalmatian, as well as children crossing a street while being supervised by a friendly crossing guard, are presented early in the film. The viewers are immersed in a scene of calm. The presented space is peaceful, projecting a series of positive symbols connected with the idealized theoretical prom-ise of American suburbia. The scene is then brought to an abrupt stop with the image of an older man collapsing on the ground. The camera slowly pans from the unfortunate individual to a close-up of the grass, and then deeper, into the soil, where it stops on an unintelligible aggregate of bat-tling insects accompanied by foreboding background music. This quick and simple transition sets both the spatial and narrative tone for the rest of the movie.

The storyline continues by following college student Jeffrey Beau-mont, the son of the previously collapsed man, who on his way back from the hospital discovers a severed human ear in an abandoned lot. Engulfed by curiosity, Jeffrey decides to do some detective work, and things soon spiral out of control. The established polarity between light and dark-ness deepens, increasingly balanced between the safety of daylight and all associated activities, and the expanding discovery of a parallel reality of the town during night-time. As Todd McGowan elaborates in *The Impos-sible David Lynch*, Lumberton as a town functions as a double reality—during daytime it is an ideal small-town fantasy, while during night-time it becomes a nightmarish fantasy of a big city.[11] These two fantasies corre-spond to Foucault's idea of a heterotopian spatial construct. Lumberton, although functioning more as a utopian space rather than a real one within Lynch's narrative, presents itself as a benchmark of normality and realism. Concurring with McGowan's reading, this is only true during the daytime, when space is defined and articulated by an all-American idealized and potentially suburban system of values. With the approach of night-time, the spatial aspect of the town expands in proportion to the dissolution of the established system of values. While still reflecting the contours of the initially proposed space, what Lumberton transmutes into is an actual heterotopian space. As Foucault states, heterotopian spaces are "like counter-sites ... in which the real sites, all the other real sites that can be found within the culture, are simultaneously represented, contested, and inverted."[12]

Jeffrey's role within such a construct is a polyvalent one. Initially portrayed as a young man desiring affirmation and the breaking of the suburban existential pattern, he reflects a specific character trope of the post–World War II generation—a type of naïveté combined with self-assurance in one's personal capabilities.[13] This leads him to discover the connection between the severed ear and local night club singer Dorothy Vallens, as well as their connection to the criminal Frank Booth, who has forced Dorothy into sexual slavery by abducting her husband and child.[14] The discovery of a different urban reality does not startle him, and instead of backing down, Jeffrey becomes even more decisive in his attempts to save Dorothy, while at the same time unraveling the mystery surrounding Frank's criminal activities. This attitude, which causes Jeffrey to cross into the heterotopian space of the night-time city, allows him to live through a number of different experiences ranging from a sadistic sexual encounter with Dorothy, to being attacked, humiliated, and finally beaten up by Frank after a failed attempt to help her. His venture into heterotopian space, or to use Turner's idea, his venture into a space "that is too strong for the man," only prepares him for that final moment when the untamed spaces need to be finally conquered.[15] The moment arrives as a climax toward the end of the movie, when Jeffrey, chased and finally cornered in Dorothy's apartment, picks up a revolver and in a dramatic fashion shoots Frank in the head. What follows is a re-establishment of the spatial order and the re-affirmation of the film's initially-presented American Dream, as well as the affirmation of Jeffrey's identity as a now functional and satisfied member of the suburban spatial and ideological paradigm. By following the traditional Western genre trope, as well as Richard Slotkin's notion of the necessity of violence for the articulation of the American national identity, Jeffrey kills the "bad guy," thus completing the required rite of passage and becoming a man. The subverting heterotopian space is now gone, the frontier has been conquered, and the viewers are left to once again enjoy the slow-paced image of the fire truck, the waving fireman, and the white picket fence adorned with roses.

While the storyline of *Blue Velvet*, as well as the frontier/heterotopian discourse, revolves around a town/city, and the exploration and subsequent interaction of a singular character with the subverting qualities of heterotopian spaces, Lynch's *Lost Highway* (1997) articulates the concept of the Frontier as a profoundly personal and subjective experience.

A meticulous outlining of events is not a necessity for a meaningful explanation of the storyline's sequence of events. Rather, due to Lynch's non sequitur development of the storyline, the presentation of the entire narrative arc allows for the recognition of characteristic patterns. Initially set in the house of saxophonist Fred Madison, the story opens with a puzzling message on the intercom: "Dick Laurent is dead." This is followed the next morning by a VHS tape left on the doorstep and discovered by Fred's girlfriend Renee. The sense of eeriness is emphasized by the introduction of an unknown figure described in the credits as the Mystery Man. Fred first dreams of him and later meets him in person during a party that both he and Renee attend. The climax occurs with Fred watching one last tape in which he observes himself killing and dismembering Renee. Lynch immediately cuts from Fred's confusion and horror to his interrogation and incarceration by the police. What follows within Fred's cell is his transmutation into another person, Pete Dayton.

Without any evidence of wrongdoing or any plausible explanation, Pete is released into the care of his parents as the second act of the film ensues. The second storyline sees Pete, an auto mechanic, fixing, among other things, the car of a local gangster named Mr. Eddy, also known as Dick Laurent, a producer of pornographic films. Pete later meets Mr. Eddy's mistress Alice Wakefield, and the two of them start an affair shortly afterward. Through a series of events as Lynchian and convoluted as the first part of the film, Pete and Alice attempt an escape, only to end up in the desert, making love in the sand in front of a cabin.[16] Soon after, Alice disappears and Pete transmutes again into Fred. He enters the cabin where he finds the Mystery Man, who comes after him with a camera in his hand. Fred flees and goes to the Lost Highway Hotel where Mr. Eddy and Renee are having sex. Renee leaves and a few moments later Fred attacks and kidnaps Mr. Eddy, puts him in the trunk of the car, and drives him someplace in the desert. There a final confrontation between the two occurs, where Fred, aided now by the Mystery Man, cuts Mr. Eddy's throat during a struggle. Fred then witnesses the Mystery Man shooting the already dying Mr. Eddy in the head. The Mystery Man whispers to Fred a few words and disappears. Fred drives back to the house where the story began, rings the intercom, and mutters the previously heard sentence: "Dick Laurent is dead."

Although the presence of arguments regarding frontier/heterotopian spaces can be observed through different manifestations throughout the entire film (activities in daylight as opposed to night-time, urban environment as opposed to the desert, etc.), a very simple spatial dichotomy presents itself at the beginning, one that will define the polarity dominating the film. After running away from the party and the Mystery Man and returning home, Fred now stares in a pitch-black corner inside the house. He steps into it and completely disappears, only to face his own image a moment later. The presence of a mirror once again coincides with Foucault's debate about the importance of mirrors to understanding heterotopian space. As he states "[f]rom the standpoint of the mirror I discover my absence from the place where I am since I see myself over there," indicating an unavoidable uneasiness being birthed from that position of misplacedness.[17] The awareness of the possible existence of an alternative space/reality adds to anxiety and fear, mimicking initially mentioned fears relating to the concept of frontier space and what lies on the other side.

This is also the mechanism used by Lynch to propose not only the existence of danger within his other/heterotopian spaces but also the incursion of these into our own realities. As debated by Parezanović and Lukić, these alternate spaces can be defined as "dark heterotopias" structured around the ability "to subvert the traditional notions of spatial polarity, pervasively imposing itself over intimate homely places and thus indicating certain problems...."[18] This act of pervasively imposing and therefore influencing reality is visible a few moments later when Fred emerges from darkness with a determined, cruel expression on his face, followed by the scene of his watching the final tape of himself murdering Renee. This act of graphic and primordial violence relates to yet another previously established trope: the connection between violence and identity, articulated now through Fred's transformation into Pete. The appearance of Pete, however, does not only symbolize the second segment of the film, but also offers a new character and narrative arc. It is Pete that in his own way has to imitate Fred, or even Jeffrey from *Blue Velvet*, and discover, cross over into, and subsequently confront the metaphoric frontier standing between his reality and heterotopian space. After his arc is spent the viewers are once again introduced to Fred, who after an act of (assisted) violence, goes back to his house (and, supposedly, in time) only to restart the cycle again. If a tentative time frame for the events was to be sketched, Pete's appearance could be observed as the initial point of departure of the narrative loop. A much more innocent and less violence-prone character of Pete, after discovering the existence of an alternative reality, crosses over, and through the interaction with the frontier/heterotopian space changes into Fred, whose violent and disillusioned identity forces the continuation of the violent cycle, or as Richard Slotkin would define it, the process of regeneration through violence.

If an argument is to be made about the relevance of a Frontier/American-based discourse within Lynch's stories, it needs to be made, at least in part, from the perspective of the theory of space, or in this case from a Foucauldian heterotopian perspective, while simultaneously considering the different historical and cultural phenomena which characterized the process of conquering of the frontier. By acknowledging this spatial turn and its applicability to Lynch's storytelling, viewers become privy to a continuous re-creation of the previously mentioned third (purely Lynchian) spatial layer. The existence of such strata, woven out of frontier myths and heterotopian constructs, allows not only for a better understanding of the social and cultural undertones of Lynch's narratives—at least those that are not completely dislocated within a surreal context—but also the importance of the Puritan frontier experience for the entirety of the subsequent development of the American imagination.

Notes

1. Frederick Jackson Turner, "The Significance of the Frontier in American History," *nationalhumanitiescenter.org*, accessed February 6, 2020, http://nationalhumanitiescenter.org/pds /gilded/empire/text1/turner.pdf.

2. *Ibid.*

3. Richard Slotkin, *Regeneration Through Violence: The Mythology of the Western Frontier, 1600–1860* (Middletown: Wesleyan University Press, 1974), 21.

4. *Ibid.*, 19.

5. Richard Ruland and Malcolm Bradbury, *From Puritanism to Postmodernism: A History of American Literature* (New York: Penguin, 1991), 26–27.

6. *Ibid.*

7. Michel Foucault, *The Order of Things: An Archaeology of the Human Sciences* (Routledge, 2005), xix.

8. Turner, "The Significance," 2.

9. Michel Foucault, "Of Other Spaces," trans. Jay Miskowiec, *Diacritics* 16, no. 1 (1986): 24.

10. *Ibid.*

11. Todd McGowan, *The Impossible David Lynch* (New York: Columbia University Press, 2007), 92.

12. Foucault, "Of Other Spaces," 3.

13. The actual time period of the events presented in the film remains unclear, spanning somewhere between the 1950s and the late 1970s. However, the presented aesthetic strongly suggests a time frame between the post-World War II period and the 1960s.

14. The main distinction between the two female protagonists and Jeffrey's love interests—Dorothy Vallens, and Jeffrey's neighbor and daughter of a detective, Sandy Williams—is the color of their hair. While Sandy, being representative of the suburban utopian setting is a white, very blonde, and almost asexual girl, Dorothy belongs to the metaphoric underbelly of the town and is a dark-haired woman, elegantly dressed and using makeup that evokes the image of a femme fatale.

15. Turner, "The Significance," 2.

16. The characters of Alice and Renee are played by the same actress (Patricia Arquette),

with the only difference between the two being Alice's blonde hair as opposed to Renee's, which is dark.

17. Foucault, "Of Other Spaces," 24.

18. Marko Lukić and Tijana Parezanović, "Challenging the House: Domesticity and the Intrusion of Dark Heterotopias," *Komunikacija i Kultura Online* 7, no. 7 (2016): 29, http://doi.fil.bg.ac.rs/volume.php?pt =journals&issue=kkonline-2016–7-7&i=2.

Works Cited

Foucault, Michel. "Of Other Spaces." Translated by Jay Miskowiec. *Diacritics*, 16 (1) (1986): 22–27.

Foucault, Michel. *The Order of Things—An Archaeology of the Human Sciences*. New York: Routledge, 2005.

Lukić, Marko, and Tijana Parezanović. "Challenging the House—Domesticity and the Intrusion of Dark Heterotopias." *Komunikacija i kultura online*, Vol. 7, No. 7 Article 2 (2016): 22–37. http://doi.fil.bg.ac.rs/volume.php?pt=journals&issue=kkonline-2016-7-7&i=2.

Lynch, David, dir. *Blue Velvet*. 1986; High Fliers Films, 2014. DVD.

Lynch, David, dir. *Lost Highway*. 1997; Universal Pictures UK, 2012. DVD.

McGowan, Todd. *The Impossible David Lynch*. New York: Columbia University Press, 2007.

Ruland, Richard, and Malcolm Bradbury. *From Puritanism to Postmodernism—A History of American Literature*. New York: Penguin, 1991.

Slotkin, Richard. *Regeneration Through Violence: The Mythology of the American Frontier, 1600–1860*. Middletown: Wesleyan University Press, 1974.

Turner, Frederick Jackson. "The Significance of the Frontier in American History." 1893. Accessed February 6, 2020. http://nationalhumanitiescenter.org/pds/gilded/empire/text1/turner.pdf.

PART II

Indigeneity and Representation

A Discussion on the Treatment of Indigeneity in *Twin Peaks*

An Interview with Geoff Bil

Rob E. King

As his profile for the University of Delaware states, "Dr. Bil is a historian of science and European empires, with specialization in nineteenth- and twentieth-century botany, anthropology, empire, and Indigenous history."[1] His credentials could fill up another half page, but he will be most recognizable to readers of this collection as the author of "Tensions in the World of Moon: *Twin Peaks*, Indigeneity and Territoriality" for *Senses of Cinema*. Geoff's discussion contextualizes the settler colonialism elements he critiqued in his original essay. The essay is cited multiple times in this collection, and it is reasonable to say that its publication was a hallmark for a Western studies approach to Lynch's films.

RK: This collection is examining regionalism as it pertains to the North American West—that covers topics on indigeneity, road narratives following nineteenth-century westward expansionism, and Western genre elements. Where do you see potential for identifying statements on the American West in David Lynch projects?

GB: There's a lot here. Like most *Twin Peaks* scholars, I'm a big David Lynch fan, and the theme of superficial fantasy, juxtaposed with darker underlying realities, runs throughout his work. And I think this goes beyond settler colonialism, although that's certainly part of it. *Blue Velvet*, in which a horrifying subterranean shadow world is concealed behind a veneer of respectability and neighborliness, is probably the most salient example. In the opening scene, the camera literally penetrates a suburban green lawn to reveal the violence unfolding amongst the insects at the roots—which could be seen as a commentary about the land itself and the violence of occupying it. The obvious superficiality of all the happiness and wholesomeness of Lumberton—the flowers and white picket fence at the beginning, the ridiculously fake robin at the end, and the hilarious and hackneyed 1950s-era dialogue—makes this violence appear to be all the more real and terrifying. There's a similar kind of tension in *Mulholland Drive*, in which the fantasy of becoming a Hollywood star encounters the reality of what Hollywood is and what it does to people. In *Lost Highway*, the reality of the main character murdering his wife and then appearing on death row segues into a fantasy in which he imagines his reality as something completely different—though in the end, he fails to escape this reality. *Eraserhead* likewise begins with something like a fantasy of bourgeois family life and turns into a complete nightmare. Even the *Elephant Man* foregrounds the duality between Bytes and Treves, who are purportedly very different people, but who both, in their own ways, carve out a living and reputation through exploiting Joseph Merrick. We see a number of close-ups of steam, smoke and machinery representing Victorian industry and empire. This is where the sausage is made—where all the wealth comes from that bolsters the pomp and superficial display of the Victorian period. And although Bytes resides physically very close to this world of violence and conquest in the dregs of the imperial city, both Bytes and Treves are participants in this system. The theme of bourgeois hypocrisy is inescapable here, and aptly parallels the representation of settler colonial culture in *Twin Peaks*. Settler cultures are often represented—especially in film and on television—in a righteous and wholesome and civilizing light, but they come into being materially through displacing and murdering people, stealing children from parents, environmental racism, and so on.

RK: As an acknowledgment, in your article, you stated that:

> *Although Snoqualmie have never held formal title to the falls or its vicinity, it has remained a symbolically important site for meditating, bereaving lost loved ones, making important decisions, or obtaining spiritual sustenance for their children. The absence of governmental recognition in the form of tribal property rights from 1953 to 1999, in fact, arguably made the falling waters and their mists even more important as a locus of cultural identity.*[2]

It was announced on November 1, 2019, in The Seattle Times *that the Snoqualmie Tribe was able to buy the Salish Lodge and adjacent land.*[3] *Is there anything particularly interesting to you about region in the films of Lynch and* Twin Peaks *and how they might edge against real issues of colonization? What is important for fans to keep in mind from your perspective?*

GB: I do remember the 2019 purchase. I also remember that it was preceded, quite interestingly, by the Muckleshoot tribe purchasing the lodge and hoping to expand it. On the one hand, this put the property rightfully in Indigenous hands, but it wasn't in Snoqualmie hands, so it's nice to see that there's been some restitution there.

In general, for fans of *Twin Peaks*, or of any media representation of settler colonialism, it's tremendously important to remember that Indigenous peoples are still here, and that the struggles faced by Indigenous peoples are essentially continuous over the longue durée of settler colonialism. That might seem self-evident, but it's not what dominant media representations tend to show, nor has it been common in many settler colonial education systems—whether in Canada, the U.S. or elsewhere. It's still very commonplace to speak about Native peoples as if they do not exist, and to speak about settler colonialism as something that happened in the distant past. Even academics frequently write about what they call the "colonial era" as if it's something that happened a hundred years ago.

The reality is that these tensions and displacements never stopped. The last residential school in Canada didn't close until 1996, for instance. And there are ongoing struggles surrounding the Dakota Access Pipeline, as well as the proposed Trans Mountain Oil Pipeline expansion, of which the Canadian government took direct ownership in 2018, and which runs right through unceded Indigenous territories. So, when *Twin Peaks* applies a version of the Indian graveyard horror trope to present colonialism as something that happened in the distant, mist-enshrouded past, it actually participates in the discourse surrounding processes that are still taking place.

RK: *Yeah, in my next question—I think it kind of touches on that, a little bit—the continual colonization. And that is where you were discussing some of the theosophy points that show up in* Twin Peaks. *And there, you know, Mark Frost was into esoteric spirituality a little bit. So, some of that bleeds in, but how does that affect Hawk's function or his portrayal of the native mystic? I know you talk about that in the article—but maybe just to elaborate a little bit on here.*

GB: In preparation for our discussion, I actually went back and revisited Brad Duke's *Reflections: An Oral History of* Twin Peaks—namely, the portion in which Michael Horse relates New Age spiritualism to Indigenous belief systems, particularly in the Pacific Northwest.

Of course, it's not my place to say whether his take in that interview is correct or not. The article cites work by Philip Deloria and Wendy Rose, who call out these New Age movements as examples of cultural appropriation.[4] But I'm also very open to the possibility—more so now, perhaps, than when I wrote the article—that there are other kinds of stories happening alongside these appropriations from Indigenous cultures and peoples.

Another book I reference is by the historian Joy Dixon, who examines theosophy in the context of the British empire in India—which is a separate but related colonial context. On the one hand, theosophy definitely played on stereotypes that in some ways reinforced the rule of "rationalistic" Britain over purportedly "spiritual" and less cognitively developed societies. At the same time, it also explicitly opposed white supremacy by conceding a great deal of authority and legitimacy to the belief systems of Indigenous and colonized peoples.[5] I think you can have both happening at the same time: It doesn't necessarily have to be one or the other.

RK: So, beyond some of the tensions that you note in your article—and then there is obviously more to mine there—but what do you appreciate about Frost and Lynch's inclusion of indigeneity in the series? Do you think that does something for viewers, just the way they kind of approach it or....

GB: I suppose it depends on the viewers, many of whom I'm sure view *Twin Peaks* from a very conventionally colonialist perspective. But in preparation for our conversation, I took the chance to look over some of my old notes and found an essay draft that included a discussion of *The Cowboy and the Frenchman* [dir. David Lynch, 1988]. Have you seen it by any chance?

RK: Yes, I have. I watched it a couple of times the past couple of years, and it gets a brief mention in the book. I was surprised it didn't come up a little bit more. So, I'm curious to hear your take on that.

GB: Well, it's only a short film, but it's a hilarious one. It has Jack Nance and Harry Dean Stanton, and Michael Horse playing a Native American character named Broken Feather. Alongside a kind of slapstick caricature of a Frenchman [played by Frederic Golchan], Horse's character is very, very funny, even more so than he was in *Twin Peaks*. The article references a scene in which Hawk transitions between what Barbra Meek calls "Hollywood Injun English" and sounding very modern and conventional.[6] The transition is even more pronounced in *The Cowboy and the Frenchman*, in which Broken Feather opens by informing the cowboys that that he tracked the Frenchman and considered him to be a "peyote nightmare" from the "Great Spirit," but closes the film by speaking in perfectly fluent, conversational English.

So, in addition to the standard settler colonial tropes in *Twin Peaks*, I think there's something else happening there as well. And at the risk of engaging in purely counterfactual speculation, I do wonder, if they'd continued with the series, whether Hawk would have gotten a more interesting backstory? Other than having a girlfriend with a Ph.D. from Brandeis, would we learn more about him? Would he have played a more active role in the main events of the series? I can't help but wonder if some of these details would have been fleshed out more effectively if the third season had happened when it should have, back in the early 90s.

RK: Have you had the chance to read Mark Frost's The Secret History of Twin Peaks?

GB: I started reading it, and from what I could see, it kind of takes the esoteric elements of *Twin Peaks* and just kind of runs away with it. It's all over the place. From what I can recall, the original *Twin Peaks: Access Guide to the Town* also has a lot of that stuff in there.[7] It's something I have to sit down and spend some time with some day. When I first read it, my initial impressions were—my goodness, on a certain level, this is so offensive. But in light of how I'm looking at some of this material now, I would want to go back and read the entire thing in context alongside watching the series again before I say anything definitive about it.

RK: Absolutely. The reason I brought it up is—there is a section in there where Michael Horse—well, Hawk—gets to tell the story of Big Ed and Norma from his point of view. And he talks about his background in Vietnam with Big Ed, and he cusses more in his dialogue. His voice is a little bit like—he's allowed to be a little bit more Michael Horse than Hawk. And I think that was kind of a gift from Mark Frost to Michael Horse. So, I'll just follow up—have you found yourself looking back at the series with any new questions or following the article's publication? Have you thought of any topics that you wish you had included or just explored differently?

GB: Yeah, I've thought a lot about this. There are ways in which I might approach the material a bit differently. When I'm not writing about *Twin Peaks*—which is, for better or worse, most of the time—my specialization is actually in the history of colonial science, and more particularly with the kinds of relationships between Indigenous and European and American people that come into being around scientific collecting, especially botany and anthropology—collecting plants, Indigenous artifacts, and so on. And part of what this work entails is exploring how impossibly complicated these kinds of situations are for Native people.

On the one hand, if you accommodate Western interests in any way—if you have anything to do with colonial structures or colonial institutions—on some level, you risk legitimizing those structures and institutions. On the other hand, there are instances in which you have to take that risk, literally, for survival. It's how you feed yourself and your family. Given that settler colonialism is premised on the extinction or assimilation of Indigenous peoples, simply surviving—or even thriving—as an Indigenous person is itself a form of resistance, even if that involves working with colonial institutions. And obviously there is a long history of Indigenous people doing just that—surviving as a form of resistance—such that it has its own portmanteau term: survivance.[8] You might be a surveyor or a scientist; you might be a guide; you might be a teacher or a business owner; you might play some role in government; you might be trading with colonizers; or you might be working in film and television.

I just finished a fantastic book by Margaret Bruchac [*Savage Kin: Indigenous Informants and American Anthropologists*] that examines situations in which Native people assist anthropologists and archaeologists in collecting, and in some cases wind up becoming anthropologists themselves, or even carving out lucrative acting careers. She gives the example of a woman named Beulah Tahamont (who is Abenaki) and her daughter Bertha, who did precisely this in the early twentieth century. In some respects, they were giving cinematic representations of Indigenous people that settler audiences wanted or expected to see. At the same time, their success also provided real resources to Native communities in California, including through their activism surrounding things like anti–Indigenous prejudice in the rental housing market, and representation of Indigenous peoples on the silver screen.[9]

This framework can be extended in various ways. Coll Thrush, whom I also cite in the article, writes similarly about how cities like Vancouver, Seattle and London are on the one hand colonizing entities—premised on exploitation and so on—but have also emerged as meaningful places for Indigenous peoples and other marginalized groups.[10] We could even ask what it means to work at a university, right? Working at an American or Canadian university means you're working in an institution that was built on occupied land. Many U.S. campuses were also built using slave labor and with funds—if you work at a land grant university like I do—derived from stolen Indigenous lands in the western U.S.[11] So, if you work at these places as a Black scholar or an Indigenous scholar, or if, like me, you come from a white settler background but want to try to use your position to aid the work of decolonization in some way, that still requires living within these institutions and in some ways contributing to them, whether you like it or not.

That's useful context, I think, for understanding Michael Horse's comments with respect to Hawk being a positive representation of Native people.[12] If that means working with a system—or within a narrative—that plays into certain colonial expectations, then so be it. You have to take victories where you can get them. Another thing that comes out in the oral history and elsewhere was that the actual filming of *Twin Peaks* often played out with a great deal of humor and laughter. There were a lot of inside jokes that didn't necessarily translate to viewers. One anecdote that I can remember is when Hawk bends down to look at a piece of grass, when they were tracking Jacques Renault to his cabin, and he immediately knows just where to go—this, of course, playing into the stereotyping of Native Americans having superhuman tracking abilities. Everyone on set, including the director, and including Horse, who just improvised this on the spot, knew how ridiculous it was, and they were all very much in on the joke.[13] I was nineteen or twenty years old when I first viewed this material, and was completely oblivious to a lot of this humor. But looking back at it now, part of me wonders how many viewers, particularly viewers from a Native American background, might have been in on the joke too. That's pure speculation on my part, but that's something I'd be interested in knowing further via oral history.

So, if I were writing this article today, I would maintain my polemical criticisms of these narrative structures—of good and bad Indians, righteous frontiersmen, and so on. But I would also be more open to the likelihood that, within these structures to which all of us, both inside and outside *Twin Peaks*, are forced to relate, there are probably many different kinds of stories happening simultaneously. There are different audiences that are going to read this stuff differently. And I think that if we're going to try and pay attention to the specificity and materiality of Pacific Northwest colonialism and Snoqualmie struggles alongside Indigenous representation in *Twin Peaks*, which I try to do in the article, it also helps to pay attention to the specificity of these other kinds of stories happening within the series. I think they're important, and that they serve a very useful function in undermining the narratives we want to criticize.

Notes

1. University of Delaware, Arts & Sciences, Department of History, "Geoffrey Bil," accessed February 27, 2021, https://www.history.udel.edu/people/faculty/gbil?uid=gbil&Name=Geoffrey%20Bil.

2. Geoff Bil, "Tensions in the World of Moon: *Twin Peaks*, Indigeneity and Territoriality," *Senses of Cinema* 79 (2016).

3. Paige Cornwell, "Snoqualmie Tribe buys Salish Lodge and adjacent land for $125 million, halting nearby development," *The Seattle Times*, November 1, 2019, accessed February 27, 2021, https://www.seattletimes.com/seattle-news/eastside/snoqualmie-tribe-buys-salish-lodge-and-adjacent-land-for-125-million/.

4. Philip J. Deloria, *Playing Indian* (New Haven: Yale University Press, 1998), 169–78; Wendy Rose, "The Great Pretenders: Further Reflections on White Shamanism," in Susan Lobo and Steve Talbot, eds., *Native American Voices: A Reader*, 2nd ed. (Upper Saddle River, New Jersey: Prentice Hall, 2001), 330–43.

5. Joy Dixon, *Divine Feminine: Theosophy and Feminism in England* (Baltimore: Johns Hopkins University Press, 2001).

6. Barbra A. Meek, "And the Injun Goes 'How'!: Representations of American Indian English in White Public Space," *Language in Society* 35:1 (2006), 94–102.

7. Richard Saul Wurman, David Lynch, and Mark Frost, *Welcome to Twin Peaks: Access Guide to the Town* (London: Penguin, 1991).

8. Gerald Vizenor, *Native Liberty: Natural Reason and Cultural Survivance* (Lincoln: University of Nebraska Press, 2009), 1–10, 24, 100–1.

9. Margaret M. Bruchac, *Savage Kin: Indigenous Informants and American Anthropologists* (Tucson: University of Arizona Press, 2018), 84–113.

10. Coll Thrush, *Indigenous London: Native Travelers at the Heart of Empire* (New Haven: Yale University Press, 2016); Thrush, *Native Seattle: Histories from the Crossing-Over Place* (Seattle: University of Washington Press, 2007).

11. Robert Lee and Tristan Ahtone, "Land-grab universities," *High Country News*, March 30, 2020, accessed March 31, 2021, https://www.hcn.org/issues/52.4/indigenous-affairs-education-land-grab-universities.

12. Brad Dukes, *Reflections: An Oral History of* Twin Peaks (Nashville: short/Tall press, 2014), 104.

13. Dukes, *Reflections*, 104.

"It has something to do with your heritage"

Indigenous Arts in Twin Peaks

David Titterington

Preface

Indigenous North American art objects exist alongside their manufactured doppelgängers in the backgrounds of Mark Frost and David
Lynch's *Twin Peaks*. In this essay I review the complicated history of Native
art in Euro-American establishments like hotels, and I explore one of the
most overlooked actors in the show: a gigantic Heiltsuk formline being
that lives in Ben Horne's office at The Great Northern. This vibrant entity
shows up during key moments in all three seasons yet is never acknowledged by characters within the show nor within *Twin Peaks* scholarship. I
conclude that Frost and Lynch loaded all three seasons of *Twin Peaks* with
"Indian" imagery on purpose, partaking in their settler heritage, but also
holding up a mirror to the inland empire and helping us to unsettle settler
colonialism.

Introduction

Much of *Twin Peaks* (1990–2017) takes place inside a fictional hotel,
The Great Northern, perched atop a giant waterfall in the Pacific Northwest. This breathtaking location is real and is one of the tallest and most
powerful waterfalls in the USA—Snoqualmie Falls—a sacred site filled
with secrets. Physically comparable to Niagara Falls, some call it "the
Garden of Eden," because it is where, in the Snoqualmie myth-histories,
the first humans emerged.[1] The mythic falls and the television show have

now become inextricably linked, the site now "sacred" for a second set of reasons.

We quickly discover that The Great Northern doubles as both a gateway to Canadian drugs and teenage prostitution and as a Native American art museum. Glass cases line the walls near the front desk and conference rooms, displaying an impressive collection of Native American baskets. More art objects—pottery, dolls, masks—are displayed on ledges, walls, and mantles. Most arresting are the Northwest Coast tribal formline crest designs painted on the cedar walls and printed on the café menus and security guard uniforms. They look authentic—because that's what tourists want, right? That's what we expect to find when visiting ancient American sites: something "authentic," something "Indian"—"Native Otherness."[2] Special Agent Dale Cooper (Kyle MacLachlan), our protagonist, *lives* inside this Indian art hotel for the entire first two seasons.

Many of the artworks we see in the hotel are in fact real Native artifacts. They are not copies or mere props. They were collected by Robert "Bob" Riebe (1937–2009), the previous owner of the Kiana Lodge in Poulsbo, Washington, where the pilot was filmed. Riebe's art collection now belongs with the Suquamish Tribe, who purchased the Kiana Lodge from him in 2004.

It's not uncommon for tourist sites in the Pacific Northwest to have "Indian dens" or "Indian corners"—cluttered bric-a-brac displays of Native art objects. This settler American tradition dates back more than 150 years.[3] In this sense, The Great Northern is authentic to its time and place.

Turning one's home or business into a tiny Native art museum served many functions. It helped people present themselves as sophisticated citizens—traveled, educated, knowledgeable—and, as Marshall McLuhan would put it, it's part of a well-known colonial pattern of cultural conquest where the previous environment becomes a work of art in the new invisible environment.[4] We can see this pattern exaggerated in the park-enfolding Crystal Palace of the 1851 London Exhibition and its "festival of empire," or we can see it take shape in Disneyland's "It's A Small World" ride with its hyperreal, simulated imperialism and so-called Disneyism that helps Americans distance the evil of conquest and genocide. This pattern reaches back to the beginning of empire: the Romans loved to surround and domesticate symbols and artworks of the Indigenous.[5] But of course, the Egyptian statues and Nilescapes that decorated dining rooms in Pompeii tell us more about the Romans than they do about the Egyptians. Likewise, the totem poles, formline paintings, and trade baskets of *Twin Peaks* speak most about Lynch and Frost, their production, and their non–Native characters' "imaginary Indians."[6] Pictures of the Other are often a kind of self-portrait. What can we learn about Ben Horne by looking at his art collection? What can we learn about Dale Cooper by looking at the miniature totem pole and tiny Chief Joseph figurine he keeps next to his bed?[7]

Non-Natives collecting Native art may be textbook "imperialist nostalgia," Renato Rosaldo's term, where agents of colonialism "yearn for" and "celebrate" the cultures they have destroyed.[8] Rosaldo also calls this a kind of "mystification," and it's one reason why the United States names its states, cities, streets, cars, corporations, military helicopters, and sports teams after Indigenous cultures.[9] Idealized fantasies gloss over violence and brutality. It may be why David Lynch leans so heavily on Native imagery in *Twin Peaks*.

Glass cases and the eye-dazzling zigzag patterns of Suquamish baskets survive well into Season 3, when all-American dreamer Dale Cooper disappears into the basket zigzag of the Black Lodge, and twenty-five years later re-appears inside a giant glass box. Glass boxes resonate and echo within the show and the larger context of the American West. They take the form of televisions—another method of collecting and displaying Native imagery—but also high school trophy cases, aquaria, and green houses. These rhetorical spaces frame, surround, and museumize images from our past, and we need to be careful around them. Sometimes the seemingly innocuous behavior of art collectors—of displaying things in glass boxes—aligns with genocidal prerogatives. Take for example Luiseño artist James Luna's 1987 *Artifact Piece,* where he installs himself in an exhibition case in the San Diego Museum of Man, much to the surprise of visitors. See also Rebecca Belmore's 1988 Olympics-disturbing performance art *Artifact #671B*, and Guillermo Gómez-Peña and Coco Fusco's 1992 world-traveling performances dubbed *The Couple in the Cage*, marking the Columbus quincentennial.

There is an attempt to make Native peoples and the things that represent them "decorations" for non–Native spaces, partially because encountering these artworks gives the tourist a potent whiff of a different time, a time unbounded and untouched by industrial machinery and modern capitalist insanity.[10] In some cases, collecting and appreciating Native art became a symbolic protest against modern industrialized life.[11] These works were "handmade," and became perfect receptacles for the American unconscious: our dreams of the past. Their creators were perceived as closer to the source—prelapsarian children of nature, both wild and angelic—and the fine craftsmanship and durable, natural materials were considered therapeutic.[12] They could even boost a boy's masculinity.[13] Native art was understood by some settlers as a key to establishing contact with both our "primitive past" and our elusive subconscious, both of which were believed to be more "authentic" than our conventional, waking, industrialized personae.[14] For *Twin Peaks* fans, the show itself may fulfill this dual role.

Especially at the turn of the twentieth century, settlers used baskets, blankets, and masks to get a taste of pasts both real and imaginary, and they paid good money for these art objects. Fanatics vied with one another to fill their Indian corners with elaborate, expensive displays. Collectors valued baskets in particular—some of Louisa Keyser's baskets sold for tens of thousands of dollars *each*.[15] Otis Mason of the Smithsonian described this frenzy for Native baskets as "a disease-like craze," *Canastramania*.[16]

"I haven't found any Indians"

Native imagery is ever-present in *Twin Peaks* even as Native Americans are near absent. The totem poles, baskets, rugs, and formline paintings at The Great Northern produce what Natalie K. Baloy calls "holographic Indigeneity," a Native presence that is hyper-visible from some angles and invisible from others.[17] This is typical of Northwest Coast hotels and public places like parks, and is part of that ongoing strategy of settler colonialism: remove Native peoples and replace them with their art.

Some scholars and archeologists point out that Northwest Coast artworks collected by non–Natives were not mere commodities but acted as "double agents," able to occupy and "possess" collectors, "converting the imperial legacy of collection into the quite different project of recollection."[18] Nevertheless, the so-called "scramble for Northwest Coast artifacts" turned violent. Tourists and settlers would invade and alter the landscapes *and peoples* in search of something authentically "Indian" (and therefore, authentically American).[19] In 1889 John Muir described the behavior of tourists in Alaska: "There was a grand rush on shore to buy curiosities and see totem poles. The shops were jammed and mobbed, high prices being paid for shabby stuff manufactured expressly for the tourist trade."[20]

Some art was made for tourists, but stories abound of collectors paying desperate Natives to go against their tribal laws and sell ceremonial objects and cultural patrimony not meant for outsiders. The Zuni reportedly *killed* anyone caught selling their wooden Ahayu'da sacred War Twins.[21] Some works, especially ones considered living beings, were simply not for sale, but collectors often didn't care. In fact, for the ones that were not for sale, they paid double! And because the art market was very lucrative, many impoverished communities quickly made a small fortune from satisfying the white market's wild appetite.

Sometimes it was cheaper to buy art made at Indian boarding schools-turned-sweatshops. Native children at these schools were "colonized through art," in that they were forced to make designs that did not align with their own tribal traditions but were chosen by their white art teachers to sell to the white market.[22] Encouraging art-making in these boarding schools killed two birds with one stone: it turned Native peoples into productive citizens and it nurtured and protected the United States national soul—due to settler guilt, assimilation shifted to preservation.[23] What this all means is that Native American artworks, such as the ones we see at The Great Northern, are both powerful agents of survivance (Gerald Vizenor's term)—agents that protect and carry cultures and identities forward—but are also tools used by settlers to both hasten and assuage the guilt of conquest and genocide.

These Native art objects play another, even more basic, role in the United States and in *Twin Peaks*. In spaces such as hotels, Indigenous and Indigenous-looking objects interact with their settings to construct ideas of "civilized" and "primitive," "foreign" and "familiar," "self" and "other." Recently, social scientists and scholars of material culture have pointed out how the construction of "self" and "otherness" is anchored specifically in Indigenous art objects and even tourist souvenirs.[24] This is partially due to the fact that displaying artworks as artifacts reinforces stereotypes used to support Eurocentric views of the evolution of humanity. Settlers love anything that helps them situate races, cultures, and environments in a hierarchical order, a "chain of being."[25] By not including *contemporary* Northwest Coast art in the television show, Lynch and the fictional Ben Horne promote only one kind of Native presence: one that doesn't make history, but is history. It entertains and even encourages the problematic worldview that sees "authentic" Indigeneity as forever from the past, made up of "images of the vanquished," or simply ghosts.[26]

Daniel Gunderson applies this lens of Native erasure and "ghosting" to *Twin Peaks*, where he argues real Natives are replaced with simulations. Gunderson trains his eyes on BOB (Frank Silva) as a "spectral native," and adds a new dimension to our understanding of how images of Native art in *Twin Peaks* reflect the greater extent to which Americans "may be truly haunted by something which refuses to stay buried: the undeniable horrors that enabled the foundation and expansion of our nation."[27]

Playing Indian

In the pilot episode, Lynch/Frost consistently juxtapose American Indian imagery with images of trauma. A large, Tlingit-style totem pole (carved by non–Native Duane Pasco) appears behind Pete Martel (Jack Nance) the moment he discovers the body of Laura Palmer (Sheryl Lee). Later, formline designs and Native baskets wreathe Leland Palmer (Ray Wise) at The Great Northern when he is told by Sheriff Truman (Michael Ontkean) that Laura is dead. This is the moment when we get that transcendent, blood-curdling scream from Sarah Palmer (Grace Zabriskie). Shortly thereafter we are introduced to Ben Horne's son, Johnny (Robert Bauer), who is clearly distressed, wearing a fake Plains Indian headdress, and banging his head against a doll house that resembles The Great Northern.

The next episode that Lynch wrote and directed (Season 1, Episode 3) also deploys Native imagery. It opens with a long shot of the Horne family eating dinner in a large room at The Great Northern. For an entire minute, the camera does not move or cut away, and we get a good look at the *moving painting* Lynch has made for us. Ben Horne (Richard Beymer) sits closest to the camera, while the rest of his family huddles at the other end of the table. Nobody speaks. Johnny is the most animated, wearing his fake Indian headdress, sitting Indian style in his chair, and speaking incoherently beneath a soundscape of crickets, clinking silverware, and eating sounds. No one else does much of anything for a full minute.

A gigantic formline tribal crest design, painted on the wall, frames the shot and looks directly into the faces of both Ben and the viewer. This polymorphic being or "person" frames many Ben Horne scenes, such as his mental breakdown while watching movies about his childhood (Season 2, Episode 11) and his famous green bicycle story (Season 3, Part 12), where, shortly after he learns that his grandson is a murderer, he regresses to his childhood again. In front of the huge sea monster's open mouth—perhaps speaking to the viewer?—we see a world globe, reminiscent of the Tibetan paintings of Mara eating the six realms of being.

The double-eyed spirit-being painted behind Ben Horne's desk is an enlarged copy of one that appears on a Heiltsuk cedar bentwood burial chest in the collection of the Canadian Museum of History in Gatineau, Quebec.[28] It looks like the Haida sea spirit Konankada, who is essentially Death, Master of Souls, and whose image is found all along the Northwest Coast, from Washington to Alaska.[29] But it seems unlikely that this matters to the characters, for none ever acknowledge it.[30]

If we read Lynch's mise-en-scène as a painting—as he probably intended—then it's basically a feathered Indian headdress superimposed on a settler American family as they eat dinner surrounded by formline artwork. That is to say, it's a picture of white people "playing Indian."[31] The image also suggests a haunting by a still-living, now-dissociated way of being that the characters cannot see, a presence in the room that is there to observe them.

In any other film or television show, we could overlook these art-works as mere props and stereotypes, what some historians call "white people's Indian art."[32] But in Lynch's projects, objects are sentient beings. Anthony Ballas describes the universe in *Twin Peaks* as made of "vibrant matter" (after Jane Bennett's book by that name).[33] Ryan Coogan describes it best. "[I]n Lynch's world, objects act as humans do, humans are often object-like, and there is no distinct hierarchy between the anthropocentric and the inert."[34] Ballas says this is one reason Lynch's work is so disturbing: it echoes the posthuman "object-turn" in philosophical discourse.[35]

Lynch offers his viewers access to an unsettling, posthuman world where seemingly inanimate objects such as logs, telephone poles, jewelry, ceiling fans, pictures, statues, coins, and pies all have power over human people. *Twin Peaks* is also filled with shapeshifters. An arm turns into a man and then into a tree. A person becomes a doorknob. Lynchian objects have their own wants and impulses that change the world, and are not directed or controlled by humans. In this way, perhaps *Twin Peaks* unsettles (as in *decolonizes*) because it *decenters* human agency and the anthropocentric universe associated with settler colonialism and capitalism, focusing instead on "thing-power," "objectal agency," and the lives and stories of the often-overlooked "other-than-human persons"—persons, or better yet, *relatives*.[36]

The Log Lady is ostensibly married to her log, and even if this seems like a surrealist image from Lynch, an entire genre of Indigenous American oral stories concerns intimate relations between humans and other-than-human entities like sticks and rocks.[37] In *Getting Dirty: The Eco-Eroticism of Women in Indigenous Oral Literatures*, Anishinaabe scholar Melissa Nelson writes that "the metaphysics of eco-erotics teaches us that we are related to everything through a visceral kinship and that our cosmo-genealogical connections to all life demand that we treat our relatives with great reverence and appreciation."[38] She says that decolonizing begins with "an honest inventory of our pansexual natures and visceral connections to the more-than-human world." This is why the Log Lady is completely at home within an Indigenous worldview and may even nudge us into unsettlement. Nelson states that "Within many Indigenous worldviews, it is common—dare I say, 'natural'—for young women to fall in love with these other beings: to marry them, make love, and live together as lovers and married couples."[39] Nelson recounts a particularly fascinating story called "Stick Husband" about a Coast Yuki woman who marries a stick.

Lynch's world of living objects aligns, albeit superficially, with Indigenous worldviews—totemic and animist-ontologies, multi-species kinship, nonhuman persons, and family claims to real local spirits and their portraits.

The Crest

Which brings us back to the domesticated spirit-being living with Ben Horne that no one ever talks about (or recognizes as an agency in its own right). Similar clan designs are found on totem poles, canoes, Tlingit screens and plank houses, Heiltsuk big houses, Chilkat blankets, Kwakwa̱-ka'wakw transformation masks, and, interestingly, Tsimshian soulcatchers. Without a doubt, these clan designs are some of the most sophisticated and powerful drawings in the world. Visually akin to the mind-boggling tessellations of M.C. Escher, forms join like puzzle pieces, and the longer one looks, the more puzzle pieces appear.[40] *Twin Peaks* itself has been likened to an M.C. Escher drawing, complete, intricate, and "distorted" just like a formline crest.[41]

These drawings are also similar to tattoos and magic sigils that can signal identity and influence the future. Nobody knows where they came from because they have always been here. Artists will copy the ancestors' designs, or rather the designs copy themselves through human bodies.

The *formline* of the tribal crest design behind Ben Horne's desk is the continuous black outline that swells and constricts as it manifests the main animal, or in this case, spirit. Haida artist Bill Reid refers to this inimitable linework as "restrained tension."[42] He argues that all of the elements in the design must *remain in tension,* "for if one were to release the tension, the design would collapse."[43] Art historian and philosopher Alfred Gell calls symmetrical, complicated tribal design work a "technology of enchantment" because it disturbs the viewer's normal cognitive functioning. Art ensnares, and Gell argues that dazzling patterns become "psychological weapons" meant to destabilize the spectator, "to weaken his grip on himself."[44] When considering the gestalt effects these drawings have on human perception, Gell half-jokingly points to ethology and the eyespots on butterfly wings meant to frighten predatory birds.[45]

Thinner and more colorful secondary and tertiary formlines fill up the negative spaces of the primary design with more entities, creating an evenly distributed, balanced composition. One can also see within the design examples of "split representation," a kind of mirroring or doubling of an image to expose two sides of a single being at once. These drawings can therefore be mentally "wrapped" around a three-dimensional surface before carving.[46] This illustrates a multi-perspectival space and time that predates cubism by hundreds of years. We perceive faces inside faces, minds inside minds, stories inside stories, and higher dimensional space mapped onto lower dimensional space. It seems worth noting that some Northwest Coast tribes like the Tlingit believe in reincarnation.[47]

This large Heiltsuk formline person, both radically out of place and at home in a different way at The Great Northern, shrinks everything and everyone around it. I count twenty-two eyes in the painting, two of them with clear pupils. It is more present in this way, even when unnoticed, than the other characters. What is it doing in Ben Horne's office? Anthropologist Sergei Kan writes that, for the Tlingit, the crest design is "the most important symbol for the matrilineal group, as well as its most jealously guarded possession" (note the story of the 1996 repatriation of a Tlingit Killer Whale sculpin clan hat valued at over $150,000).[48] In the past, the gifting or earning of these designs sometimes involved human sacrifice.[49]

Formline crests serve as a kind of seal, shield, guardian, and record of a clan's history—a tag from "myth time."[50] Heads and faces are the most common motif in Northwest Coast Native art in general, and we see many of them painted throughout The Great Northern. According to Tlingit anthropologist Frederica de Laguna, the faces repeated inside the primary creature's head signify "indwelling souls," and indwelling *places* that correspond with external souls and external places.[51] Tangentially, insides and outsides are conflated in *Twin Peaks* in general, The Great Northern in particular. Production designer Richard Hoover noted how "a massive use of wood gives an outside feeling to the interiors."[52]

Each formline crest has a spirit-being and a place "behind it," linking a particular group to a particular terrain.[53] As Kiowa author N. Scott Momaday would put it, formline crests *take place*.[54] Generally, Native American religions, attitudes, and artworks all *take place* and are "fine-tuned to harmonize with the lands on which the people live."[55] Many Native communities argue that their people cannot be alienated from their land without committing genocide. This argument underpins many sacred sites cases, including that of Snoqualmie Falls.[56]

The images painted on the walls of The Great Northern also come from "myth time" and embody the intimate relationship between clan members and the other-than-human beings depicted. They "fuse" identities, places, and histories.[57] Moreover, crests are the medium through which a clan's regional "value" is expressed.[58] Like Deputy Hawk's map, they are very old but always current. They can even influence a person's future. Reportedly there is a Tlingit practice of rubbing a child's mouth with a stone depicting the clan crest to influence the child's destiny.[59]

These sacred artworks are domesticized by their constant proximity to computers, chairs, and other items in the hotel. That which was once imagined as alien now becomes part of the establishment itself. Accordingly, the hotel desks, tables, and souvenir kitsch are imbued with an other-worldliness.

Fetish Objects

After a full minute, Ben's brother Jerry (David Patrick Kelly) interrupts the aforementioned dinner, bursting onto the scene with sandwiches. The soundscape shifts to jazz and we are swept up in a Lynchian display of absurdist, italicized consumption—"a typical Lynchian juxtaposition."[60] The men are ecstatic in part because the brie sandwiches remind them of "Ginny and Jenny's down by the river." The food triggers erotic memories. As with Proust's madeleine, or like the smell of engine oil later in the show, sensual engagement with objects unlocks memories of "lost time." This is not dissimilar to the power of Native art objects in non–Native homes, hotels, and tourist sites. The strange objects function as a fetish.[61]

Most Indigenous artworks lose their original function when they enter hotels and museums, but acquire new ones, new forms of magic. What we see happening in The Great Northern is a revealing expression of United States heritage. Settler cultures tend to take and display the sacred symbols of the cultures they defeat, not only as a way to flex, but also, it appears, as a way to cope. Imperialist nostalgia helps to assuage settler guilt. From one perspective, to suddenly celebrate the imagery and artworks from the culture you have just nearly destroyed is perverse. And yet, as Jean Baudrillard astutely notes, we invest in objects what we find impossible to invest in human beings.[62] Baudrillard, known for his theories of simulacra and simulations, suggests that collectors are incomplete people who dream up an alternate reality through their collections in order to retreat and regress.[63] There is also an almost sexual pleasure collectors experience when acquiring things and arranging, handling, even fondling them.[64] It is a brand of paraphilia or objectophilia. Collecting (and hoarding) probably correlates with the genital stage in developmental psychology, where "all kinds of tensions and frustrated energies [are] grounded and calmed."[65]

Season 1, Episode 3 of Twin Peaks juxtaposes the fetishistic consumption of Native art with the fetishistic consumption of food. In fact, the consumption of sandwiches specifically runs all the way to the penultimate "joke" in Season 3: an absurd overabundance of sandwiches.[66]

Lynch/Frost then connect the consumption of food and Native imagery to the consumption of women. After Jerry interrupts the quiet dinner, we learn of Ben's sex casino on the side, and the homosocial relationship he has with his brother (they presumably share virgin prostitutes)—and notice (for the first time?) Old Glory waving proudly behind their boat.

A Message from the Log

The title of this essay comes from something Margaret Lanterman (Catherine E. Coulson), better known as The Log Lady, says to Deputy Hawk (Michael Horse) in the first episode of Season 3. Actually, the Log tells Hawk through The Log Lady that "Something is missing and you have to find it. It has to do with Special Agent Dale Cooper. The way you will find it has something to do with your heritage. This is a message from the log." We discover that what is missing is part of Laura Palmer's diary, and that "something to do with your heritage" does indeed have to do with the Nez Perce, Hawk's tribe, but not as we might expect. Laura's missing story turns out to be hidden inside a bathroom stall door made by "Nez Perce Manufacturing." This is probably not a real Native company (see Wikipedia's incomplete list of company names derived from Indigenous peoples). Part of Deputy Hawk's "heritage," therefore, according to the Log, is either having his tribe's name and image appropriated by a toilet stall manufacturer, or his tribe's survival by adapting to produce undignified goods settlers need.

Also part of Deputy Hawk's heritage—and that of many of the viewers—is the psychopomp that leads him to the bathroom door: a Buffalo Nickel, also known as an Indian Head Nickel, designed by none other than *End of the Trail* sculptor James Earl Fraser. This tiny coin speaks volumes about settler colonialism. It does not commemorate a specific person for their accomplishments or contributions (as does all other currency bearing someone's image), but instead presents a generic Plains Indian head. Frazer himself said, "my purpose was not to make a portrait but a type."[67] The Indian is every bit as nameless as the buffalo on its reverse. Likewise, because we know next to nothing of Hawk's actual Native heritage, his primary function in the series is arguably that of a generic Native American "tasked with ameliorating settler guilt."[68]

Conclusion

Twin Peaks reveals that settler colonial households and "private" spaces, like those depicted in The Great Northern, are important actors and even microcosmic empires. These sites make arguments. They brim with information, and we should be alert to them and what they signal. At the same time, moved into background ubiquity, the mute Indigenous symbols form a hyperobject, an atmosphere in which the dramatic narrative flares.[69] In a figure/ground reversal, the characters and their nightmares become a work of art in a new invisible environment. Nothing is as it seems. Colonization turns people into objects, whereas decolonization turns objects into people. *Twin Peaks*, then, is a Möbius strip on which both movements flow.

When we cross the themes in *Twin Peaks* with the themes and histories of Northwest Coast art, the two superimposed stories generate a third, moiré-like pattern; a new image that is neither merely Lynchian nor Native American. If we step way back and examine it from multiple angles, we can find a flickering, shadowy portrait of the American psyche.

The Native art in *Twin Peaks* connects us with our subconscious mind, our settler heritage, and our Indigenous past, present, and future. When we foreground the Indigenous characters in the show, we get a broader view of both *Twin Peaks* and of what is currently known as the United States. We get a better view of our heritage. We may not like what we see—that shadowy, shifting moiré pattern in the glass box—but as Carl Jung said, "One does not become enlightened by imagining figures of light, but by making the darkness conscious."[70]

Acknowledgments

This essay benefited considerably from conversations with teachers, colleagues, and students at Haskell Indian Nations University and at the University of Kansas. Special thanks to Gina Adams; Norman Akers; Raven Chacon; Carrie Cornelius; Alicia Cox; Christopher Forth; Nicholas Galanin; Devlin Gandy; Tanya Hartman; Rob King; Michael King; Kylie Kookesh; Majesta Roach; M.J. Ruff; Eli Stogsdill; Evan Thomas; Michael Verney; Daniel Wildcat; Diamond Williams; the staff at the Kiana Lodge; my parents; and my supportive and patient husband, Jack Miles. I am also grateful to Michael Garfield of the Santa Fe Institute for his insights, criticisms, and editing of this essay. All errors and shortcomings are, of course, my own.

NOTES

1. Kenneth D. Tollefson and Martin L. Abbott, "From Fish Weir to Waterfall," *American Indian Quarterly* 17, no. 2 (1993), 209–225.

2. Paige Raibmon, *Authentic Indians: Episodes of Encounter from the Late-Nineteenth-Century Northwest Coast* (Duke University Press, 2005); Renisa Mawani, "Imperial Legacies (Post)Colonial Identities: Law, Space, and the Making of Stanley Park, 1859–2001," *Law/Text/Culture* 7 (2003): 98–141; Mawani, "From Colonialism to Multiculturalism?: Totem Poles, Tourism, and National Identity in Vancouver's Stanley Park," *ARIEL: A Review of International English Literature* 655, no. 35 (2006): 31–57. Totem poles and baskets have come to symbolize "authentic" Native art that is desired and consumed by tourists and visitors. This perceived authenticity, as Mawani puts it, is premised on an

inauthenticity: on a singular, homogenized, imagined and "fixed" Indigenous identity that does not capture the complicated and diverse histories and experiences of real indigenous communities in Pacific Northwest. This is how certain representation can also eclipse and erase cultures.

3. Elizabeth Hutchinson, *The Indian Craze: Primitivism, Modernism, and Transculturation in American Art, 1890–1915* (London: Duke University Press, 2009); Molly Lee, "Appropriating the Primitive: Turn-of-the-Century Collection and Display of Native Alaskan Art," *Arctic Anthropology* 28, no. 1 (1991): 6–15; Lee, "Tourism and Taste Cultures: Collecting Native Art in Alaska at the Turn of the Twentieth Century," *Unpacking Culture: Art and Commodity in Colonial and Postcolonial Worlds*, ed. Ruth B. Phillips and Christopher B. Steiner, 1st ed. (University of California Press, 1999), 267–281.

4. Marshall McLuhan, "The Emperor's Old Clothes," In *The Man-Made Object*, ed. G. Kepes (New York: George Brazillier, Inc. 1966), reprinted in *Marshall McLuhan Unbound* (20), eds. E. McLuhan and W.T. Gordon (Corte Madera, California: Gingko Press, 2005), 9.

5. Stephanie Malia Hom, "Simulated Imperialism," *Traditional Dwellings and Settlements Review*, 25, no. 1 (2013): 25–44; William Irwin Thompson, *The American Replacement of Nature* (Doubleday, 1991); Caitlín Eilís Barrett, *Domesticating Empire: Egyptian Landscapes in Pompeian Gardens* (Oxford University Press, 2019).

6. Daniel Francis, *The Imaginary Indian: The Image of the Indian in Canadian Culture* (Vancouver, BC: Arsenal Pulp Press, 1992).

7. For detail shots of Cooper's room and The Great Northern Hotel, visit Steven Miller's "Vacant Peaks" at *Twin Peaks Blog*, https://www.twinpeaksblog.com/category/vacant-peaks/.

8. Renato Rosaldo, "Imperialist Nostalgia," *Representations* no. 26 (1989): 107–22.

9. *Ibid.*, 109.

10. T. Jackson Lears, *No Place of Grace: Antimodernism and the Transformation of American Culture, 1880–1920* (New York: Pantheon, 1981).

11. Lee, "Appropriating the Primitive," 12.

12. Philip J. Deloria, *Playing Indian* (Yale University Press, 1998), 106–108.

13. Hutchinson, *The Indian Craze*, 31.

14. Jackson Rushing, "Ritual and Myth: Native American Culture and Abstract Expressionism," in *The Spiritual in Art: Abstract Painting 1890–1985*, ed. Tuchman and Maurice (New York: Abbeville Press, 1986); Wanda M. Corn, *The Great American Thing: Modern Art and National Identity, 1915–1935* (Berkeley: University of California Press, 1999).

15. Marvin Cohodas, *Basket Weavers for the California Curio Trade: Elizabeth and Louise Hickox* (The University of Arizona Press, 1997); Phillips, Ruth B., and Christopher B. Steiner, eds., *Unpacking Culture: Art and Commodity in Colonial and Postcolonial Worlds*, 1st edition (University of California Press, 1999).

16. Otis Tufton Mason, "Aboriginal American Basketry: Studies in a Textile Art without Machinery," *Annual Report of the Smithsonian Institution for the Year Ending June 30, 1902, Report of the U.S. National Museum*, Part II (Washington, DC: Government Printing Office, 1904), 187–188.

17. Natalie J.K. Baloy, "Spectacles and Spectres: Settler Colonial Spaces in Vancouver," *Settler Colonial Studies* 6, no. 3 (2016): 209–234.

18. Isaiah Lorado Wilner, "Transformation Masks: Recollecting the Indigenous Origins of Global Consciousness," in *Indigenous Visions: Rediscovering the World of Franz Boas*, ed. Isaiah Lorado Wilner and Ned Blackhawk (New Haven: Yale University Press, 2018), 3–41. University of Chicago's Isaiah Lorado Wilner argues that these Northwest Coast artworks have an agency of their own and act as "mnemonic devices that archive the global propagation of knowledge." Wilner argues that transformation masks specifically became a "survival strategy by the Kwakwa̲ka'wakw, a network of peoples, "who utilized the anthropologist Franz Boas as a host body to enter and alter the world that came to colonize them."

19. Douglas Cole, *Captured Heritage: The Scramble for Northwest Coast Artifacts* (Vancouver and Toronto: Douglas and McIntyre, 1985).

20. Robert Campbell, *In Darkest Alaska: Travel and Empire Along the Inside Passage*

(Philadelphia: University of Pennsylvania Press, 2007), 166; Aldona Jonaitis, "Northwest Coast Totem Poles," *Unpacking Culture: Art and Commodity in Colonial and Postcolonial Worlds*, ed. Ruth B. Phillips and Christopher B. Steiner, 1st edition (University of California Press, 199): 104.

21. Chip Colwell, *Plundered Skulls and Stolen Spirits: Inside the Fight to Reclaim Native America's Culture.* (University of Chicago Press, 2017).

22. Lentis, Marinella Lentis, *Colonized through Art: American Indian Schools and Art Education, 1889–1915* (Lincoln: University of Nebraska Press, 2017).

23. John Ott, "Reform in Redface: The Taos Society of Artists Plays Indian," *American Art* 23, no. 80–107 (2009). On the one hand, settler support for Native art announced a positive shift in attitudes towards Native peoples: preservationist rather than assimilationist, "and more inclined towards "noble" rather than "savage" stereotypes." Caroline Jean Fernald, "The Visualization of the American Southwest: Ethnography, Tourism, and American Indian Souvenir Arts," PhD diss. (University of Oklahoma, 2017), 7. On the other hand, their display perpetuated romantic and homogenizing conceptions of Native Americans as simple, carefree, and ultimately incapable of joining modern life. Fernald argues that natives also engaged in auto-ethnography and self-preservation through this treacherous time, when populations in the U.S. dropped to around 250,000, "for the sake of future generations," by replicating their culture, sharing protected knowledge with anthropologists, modeling for artists and photographers, and producing traditional arts for sale to tourists.

24. Rojek, Chris Rojek and John Urry, *Touring Cultures: Transformations of Travel and Theory* (New York, Routledge: 1997).

25. David Hume, *Tourism Art and Souvenirs: The Material Culture of Tourism* (New York: Routledge, 2014), 73.

26. Ann McMullen, "Reinventing George Heye: Nationalizing the Museum of the American Indian and Its Collections," in *Contesting Knowledge: Museums and Indigenous Perspectives*, ed. Susan Sleeper-Smith (Lincoln: University of Nebraska Press, 2009), 69.

27. Daniel Gunderson, "That Which Refuses to Stay Buried: *Twin Peaks* and the Spectral Native of American Discourse," MA thesis (Humboldt State University, 2015), 32–33.

28. These are extremely powerful cedar bentwood boxes that act like safes, but also like animal hide bundles, and even tombs or reliquaries for Northwest Coast dignitaries. Sometimes these burial chests are inserted into totem poles.

29. Hope B. Werness, *The Continuum Encyclopedia of Native Art: Worldview, Symbolism, and Culture in Africa, Oceana, and Native North America* (New York: Continuum, 200), 167–168.

30. Nicholas Galanin, *Let Them Enter Dancing and Showing Their Faces/Yéil Ya-Tseen: Nell Has Yaxdaxoon* (Minor Matters Book, , 2018), 61–62. The Hornes, as far as we know, are not Native. Technically, the crest on their wall is not either. This specific Heiltsuk symbol was copied onto a set by some L.A. stagehand hired by art director Cara Brower. The originals were painted by Pasco, and even though he is a well-known, respected artist, his work still signals a persistent problem. I asked Nicolas Galanin, Tlingit artist and carver, what he thought of Pasco's artwork we see in the pilot. Although Galanin remarked that Pasco seems like a nice guy, Galanin lamented that Pasco's work "still takes up space." I am reminded of Galanin's 2014 installation and performance called *White Carver*, which I think is worth looking at because its one of the best descriptions of what is going on with the appropriation of Northwest Coast art: We take what we want and leave the body behind. In the performance, a white man in an apron is sitting on a stool, whittling an object. Portraits of past White Carvers hang on the walls, acknowledgment of the legacy to which he is connected. The wooden, ceremonial "fetish" object White Carver is copying is by Galanin. It is a fleshlight or "pocket pussy," made out of yellow cedar (an extremely spiritual substance to many Northwest Coast people). The raw wood "doubles down on fetish," Galanin says. "The masturbation tool has a singular function–to satisfy desire without intimacy with a partner. The fetishization of the pocket pussy as a small part removed from the physical, mental, and emotional wholes of a person stands in for the small part of the Pacific Northwest indigenous culture that is fetishized and separated by non-indigenous consumer culture."

31. Philip J. Deloria, *Playing Indian*. Deloria, professor of history and son of famed teacher Vine Deloria, Jr. (*God Is Red*), explores why the settler often needs to feel Indigenous, even if only for fun. "Playing Indian" is a powerful U.S. pastime, beginning with the Boston Tea Party and continuing all the way into the people walking down my street in Kansas City right now, hollering drunkenly outside my window in KC Chiefs gear. The Chiefs had just won the 2020 Super Bowl, and the parade was today. Scholars and historians often point to "Indian play" and native appropriation as a kind of colonizer coping mechanism—a way to alleviate the pressure and horror of living on stolen land.

32. Hutchinson, *The Indian Craze*; Robert F. Berkhofer, *The White Man's Indian: Images of the American Indian, from Columbus to the Present* (Vintage Books, 1979). Fergus Bordewich, *Killing the White Man's Indian: Reinventing Native Americans at the End of the Twentieth Century* (New York: Archer Books, 1997).

33. Anthony Ballas, "'My Log Has A Message For You,' or Vibrant Matter and Twin Peaks: On Thing Power and Subjectivity," *Critical Essays on* Twin Peaks: The Return, ed. Antonio Sanna (New York: Palgrave Macmillan, 2019), 135.

34. Ryan Coogan, "'Here's to the Pie That Saved Your Life, Dougie':The Weird Realism of *Twin Peaks*," *ibid.*, 135.

35. Ballas, "Here's to the Pie," 121; Jeffrey Andrew Weinstock, "Wondrous and Strange: The Matter of *Twin Peaks*," in *Return to* Twin Peaks: New Approaches to Materiality, Theory, and Genre on Television (New York: Palgrave Macmillan, 2016), 29–31.

36. Ballas, *ibid.*; Philippe Descola, *Beyond Nature and Culture*, trans. Janet Lloyd (Chicago: University of Chicago Press, 2013); Graham Harvey, *Animism: Respecting the Living World* (London: Hurst & Co., 2005); David Posthumous, *All My Relatives: Exploring Lakota Ontology, Belief, and Ritual* (Lincoln: University of Nebraska Press, 2018); Nurit Bird-David, "Persons or Relatives? Animistic Scales of Practice and Imagination," in *Rethinking Relations and Animism: Personhood and Materiality* (New York: Routledge, 2018); Vine Deloria, Jr., *God Is Red: A Native View of Religion* (Colorado: Fulcrum Publishing, 2003).

37. Nelson, Melissa K. 2017. "Getting Dirty: The Eco-Eroticism of Women in Indigenous Oral Literatures," in Joanne Barker, *Critically Sovereign: Indigenous Gender, Sexuality, and Feminist Studies* (Duke University Press, 2017), 237.

38. *Ibid.*, 235.

39. *Ibid.*, 237.

40. Alfred Gell, 'The Technology of Enchantment," in *Anthropology, Art and Aesthetics*, ed. Jeremy Coote and Anthony Shelton (Oxford University Press, 1992). The visual properties of these designs can cause anyone who tries to look at them as a whole to experience peculiar, non-ordinary optical sensations. The "opposed volutes," lead the eye off in opposite directions. "Figure-ground" confusions force the brain to reconcile visual paradoxes. As it is with most good visual artworks, certain colors and shapes have "glamouring effects" on the human mind.

41. William J. Devlin and Shai Biderman, *The Philosophy of David Lynch* (University Press of Kentucky, 2011), 17.

42. William Reid and Robert Bringhurst, *Solitary Raven: The Essential Writings of Bill Reid* (Vancouver: Douglas & McIntyre, 2009), 17.

43. *Ibid.*

44. Gell, "The Technology of Enchantment," 45.

45. *Ibid.* Gell half-seriously points to ethology to explain the human "disposition" to respond to particular perceptual stimuli in predetermined ways. He jokes that when an ethnologist sees complex symmetry in tribal artworks like this, they "without a doubt, mutter 'eye-spots!' and immediately start pulling out photographs of butterflies' wings likewise marked with bold, symmetrical circles, and designed to have much the same effect on predatory birds…"

46. Janet Catherine Berlo and Ruth Phillips, *Native North American Art* (Oxford University Press, 2015), 216.

47. George Thornton Emmons and Frederica de Laguna, *The Tlingit Indians / George Thornton Emmons; edited with additions by Frederica de Laguna and a biography by*

Jean Low (Seattle: University of Washington Press, 1991), 32, 287–288. More and more faces appear the longer you look at the tribal crests in *Twin Peaks* due to the plethora of "ovoids"—a shape that looks like a bean but contains multiple forms. Haida artist Lyle Wilson shows the "evolution of the ovoid shape" as beginning with the prominent eye-spots on the wings of big skates, *Raja binoculata*, from the Latin for "two eyes." These rings blend with the more squared eyeholes of the human skull, and then finally are super-imposed onto the eyespot shapes on killer whales (see Wilson's *Origins/Coalition* painting from 2011). Ovoids also conform to the pentagon shape of the communal plank house fronts, which suggests that they can refer to entire houses; Judith Ostrowitz, *Privileging the Past: Reconstructing History in Northwest Coast Art* (Seattle: University of Washington Press, 1999), 76. There are "inner" and "outer" ovoids, like there are inner and outer rooms in a house, and since the same "design units" are used for different animal body parts, these drawings encourage "visual puns"; Berlo and Phillips, *Native North American Art*, 216–217. Sometimes U-forms can be eyes or fins, and Tsimshian formline artist Terry Starr argues that tails can sometimes qualify as wolf cubs. Northwest Coast artists still, today, exploit the polysemous capacity of the complicated designs to the full, using it to, as Berlo and Phillips put it, "play on fundamental philosophical perceptions of structural dualities, the deceptiveness of appearances, mythic processes of transformation, and the paradoxical coexistence of two truths as a single juncture in time and space."

48. Sergei Kan, *Symbolic Immortality: The Tlingit Potlach of the Nineteenth Century* (Seattle: University of Washington Press, 2016), 72; Rosita Worl, "Tlingit At.oow: Tangible and Intangible Property," PhD diss. (Harvard University, 1998). Sometimes these crests are described as "tangible and intangible property" or at.oow, in that they qualify as "cultural patrimony," or communally owned objects (like bones), that in the U.S. fall under the repatriation laws of NAGPRA.

49. Zachary Jones, "Clan At.óowu in Distant Lands: A Survey of Tlingit Art in European and Russian Museums," *Box of Knowledge* 1, no. 1 (1998): 1–35, Sealaska Heritage Institute Coccational Papers; Worl, "Tlingit At.oow."

50. Marjorie Myers Halpin, "The Tsimshian Crest System: A Study Based on Museum Specimens and the Marius Barbeau and William Beynon Field Notes," PhD thesis (University of British Columbia), 17–18.

51. Frederica de Laguna, "Under Mount Saint Elias: The History and Culture of the Yakutat Tlingit: Part Two," *Smithsonian Contributions to Anthropology* (1972): 761.

52. Weinstock, "Wondrous," 30.

53. Thomas Thornton, *Being and Place among the Tlingit* (Seattle: University of Washington Press, 2008). Thomas Thornton calls these formline paintings "settings," spatio-temporal "genres," and "chronotopes" (after Mikhail Bakhtin). Thornton even compares them to European landscapes paintings, "because they [both] explicitly appropriate and idealize places and therefore shape the perception and experience of those landscapes."

54. N. Scott Momaday, *The Names: A Memoir* (New York: Harper and Row, 1964), 142.

55. Deloria, *God Is Red*, 69.

56. The Red Nation, *The Red Deal* (Brooklyn, NY: Common Notions, 2021); Andrea Smith, *Conquest: Sexual Violence and American Indian Genocide* (Duke University Press, 2005), 122. Geoff Bil, "Tensions in the World of Moon: *Twin Peaks*, Indigeneity and Territoriality," *Senses of Cinema* 79 (2016).

57. Thornton, *Being and Place*, 32.

58. Kalervo Oberg, *The Social Economy of the Tlingit Indians. American Ethnological Society* (Seattle and London: University of Washington Press, 1973), 125; Kan, *Symbolic Immortality*, 353.

59. Kan, *Symbolic Immortality*, 73.

60. Jeff Johnson, *Pervert in the Pulpit: Morality in the Works of David Lynch* (Jefferson, NC: McFarland, 2004), 153.

61. Ruth B. Phillips and Christopher B. Steiner, eds. *Unpacking Culture: Art and Commodity in Colonial and Postcolonial Worlds*. 1st ed. (University of California Press, 1999). David Hume argues that souvenirs are endowed with the same supernatural powers of the fetish (term first used in 1757, by French philosopher Charles De Brosses, and applied to

the analysis of primitive religions associated with the African continent). They are a "substitution for that which is not available."

62. Jean Baudrillard, *The System of Objects* (London: Verso, 2005), 96.

63. *Ibid.*, 95.

64. McMullen, "Reinventing George Heye," 67; Werner Muensterberger, *Collecting: An Unruly Passion: Psychological Perspectives* (Princeton, New Jersey: Princeton University Press, 1994), 234.

65. Baudrillard, *The System of Objects*, 96.

66. Martin Fradely and John A. Riley, "Dirty Bearded Men in a Room!" in *The Politics of* Twin Peaks, ed. Amanda DiPaolo and Jamie Gillies (Lexington Books, 2019), 69–92. Donuts may also substitute for sandwiches in *Twin Peaks*, and their round shape and decorated surfaces rhyme with baskets. There are at least two dozen Native American baskets in the pilot, and neat rows of at least six dozen donuts in the Sheriff's station.

67. David Bowers, *A Guide Book of Buffalo and Jefferson Nickels* (Atlanta, Ga.: Whitman Publishing, 2007), 38–39.

68. Geoff Bil, "Tensions in the World of Moon: *Twin Peaks*, Indigeneity and Territoriality," *Senses of Cinema* 79 (2016). Furthermore, the image of a Plains Indian head representing all Indians facilitates more Indigenous erasure, and the ubiquitous synecdoche links Native peoples with food and consumption. It appears on packaging for chips, beef jerky, orange juice, cornmeal, cereal, honey, and butter, and on convenience stores and gas stations, including the Indian Head Gas Station that Agent Cooper and Sheriff Truman visit in Season 1 Episode 5.

69. Timothy Morton, *Hyperobjects: Philosophy and Ecology After the End of the World* (University of Minnesota Press, 2013).

70. Carl Gustav Jung and R.F.C. Hull, *Alchemical Studies* (Routledge & Kegan Paul, 1967), 255–256.

Works Cited

Ballas, Anthony. 2019. "'My Log Has A Message For You,' or Vibrant Matter and *Twin Peaks*: On Thing Power and Subjectivity." *Critical Essays on* Twin Peaks: The Return, edited by Antonio Sanna. Palgrave Macmillan: 119–134.

Baloy, Natalie J.K. 2016. "Spectacles and Spectres: Settler Colonial Spaces in Vancouver." *Settler Colonial Studies*, 6, no. 3: 209–234.

Barrett, Caitlín Eilís. 2019. *Domesticating Empire: Egyptian Landscapes in Pompeian Gardens.* Oxford University Press.

Baudrillard, Jean. 2005. *The System of Objects.* London: Verso.

Berkhofer, Robert F. 1979. *The White Man's Indian: Images of the American Indian, from Columbus to the Present.* Vintage Books.

Berlo, Janet Catherine, and Ruth Phillips. 2015. *Native North American Art.* Oxford University Press.

Bil, Geoff. 2016. "Tensions in the World of Moon: *Twin Peaks*, Indigeneity and Territoriality." *Senses of Cinema*, no. 79 (2016): Web [n.p.]. [Online Access]

Bird-David, Nurit. 2018. "Persons or relatives? Animistic scales of practice and imagination." In Miguel Astor-Aguilera and Graham Harvey, *Rethinking Relations and Animism: Personhood and Materiality.* London: Routledge.

Bordewich, Fergus. 1996. *Killing the White Man's Indian: Reinventing Native Americans at the End of Twentieth Century.* New York: Archer Books.

Bowers, David. 2007. *A Guide Book of Buffalo and Jefferson Nickels.* Atlanta: Whitman Publishing.

Campbell, Robert. 2007. *In Darkest Alaska: Travel and Empire Along the Inside Passage.* Philadelphia: University of Pennsylvania Press.

Cohodas, Marvin. 1997. *Basket Weavers for the California Curio Trade: Elizabeth and Louise Hickox.* The University of Arizona Press.

Cole, Douglas. 1985. *Captured Heritage: The Scramble for Northwest Coast Artifacts*. Vancouver and Toronto: Douglas and McIntyre.

Colwell, Chip. 2017. *Plundered Skulls and Stolen Spirits: Inside the Fight to Reclaim Native America's Culture*. University of Chicago Press.

Coogan, Ryan. 2019. "'Here's to the Pie That Saved Your Life, Dougie':The Weird Realism of *Twin Peaks*." *Critical Essays on* Twin Peaks: The Return. Edited by Antonio Sanna, pp. 135–148. Palgrave Macmillan.

Corn, Wanda M. 1999 *The Great American Thing: Modern Art and National Identity, 1915–1935*. Berkeley: University of California Press.

De Laguna, Frederica. 1972. "Under Mount Saint Elias: The History and Culture of the Yakutat Tlingit: Part Two." *Smithsonian Contributions to Anthropology*. 1–1395.

Deloria, Philip J. 1998. *Playing Indian*. Yale University Press.

Deloria, Vine. 2003. *God Is Red: A Native View of Religion*. Golden, CO: Fulcrum Publishing.

Descola, Philippe. 2013. *Beyond Nature and Culture*. Janet Lloyd (trans.). Chicago: University of Chicago Press.

Devlin, William J., and Biderman, Shai. 2011. *The Philosophy of David Lynch*. The Philosophy of Popular Culture. University Press of Kentucky.

Emmons, George Thornton, and Frederica de Laguna. 1991. *The Tlingit Indians*. Seattle; New York: University of Washington Press; American Museum of Natural History.

Fernald, Caroline Jean. 2017. "The Visualization of the American Southwest: Ethnography, Tourism, and American Indian Souvenir Arts." Dissertation submitted to the Graduate Faculty, University of Oklahoma. Online.

Fradely, Martin, and John A. Riley. 2019. "Dirty Bearded Men in a Room!" In Amanda DiPaolo and Jamie Gillies (eds.), *The Politics of* Twin Peaks. Lanham, MD: Lexington Books, 2019, 69–92.

Francis, Daniel. 1992. *The Imaginary Indian: The Image of the Indian in Canadian Culture*. Vancouver, BC: Arsenal Pulp Press.

Galanin, Nicholas. 2018. *Nicholas Galanin: Let Them Enter Dancing and Showing Their Faces/Yéil Ya-Tseen: Nell Has Yaxdaxoon*. Seattle: Minor Matters Books, LLC.

Gell, Alfred. 1992. "The Technology of Enchantment." In Jeremy Coote and Anthony Shelton (eds.), *Anthropology, Art and Aesthetics*. Oxford: Oxford University Press.

Gunderson, Daniel. 2015. "That Which Refuses To Stay Buried: *Twin Peaks* and the Spectral Native of American Discourse." Thesis for Master of Arts in English Literature, Humboldt State University.

Halpin, Marjorie Myers. 1973. "The Tsimshian Crest System: A Study Based on Museum Specimens and the Marius Barbeau and William Beynon Field Notes," Thesis (Ph.D.), University of British Columbia.

Harvey, Graham. 2005. *Animism: Respecting the Living World*. London: Hurst & Co.

Hom, Stephanie Malia. 2013. "Simulated Imperialism." *Traditional Dwellings and Settlements Review* 25, no. 1 (2013): 25–44. Online.

Hume, David. 2014. *Tourism Art and Souvenirs: The Material Culture of Tourism*. New York: Routledge.

Hutchinson, Elizabeth. 2009. *The Indian Craze: Primitivism, Modernism, and Transculturation in American Art, 1890–1915*. Durham, NC: Duke University Press.

Johnson, Jeff. 2004. *Pervert in the Pulpit: Morality in the Works of David Lynch*. Jefferson, NC: McFarland.

Jonaitis, Aldona. 1999. "Northwest Coast Totem Poles." In Ruth B. Phillips and Christopher B. Steiner (eds.), *Unpacking Culture: Art and Commodity in Colonial and Postcolonial Worlds*, 1st ed. Berkeley: University of California Press. 104–121.

Jones, Zachary. 2012. "Clan At.óowu in Distant Lands: A Survey of Tlingit Art in European and Russian Museums," *Box of Knowledge* 1, no. 1: 1–35. Sealaska Heritage Institute Coccational Papers.

Jung, Carl Gustav, and R.F.C. Hull. 1967. *Alchemical Studies*. New York: Routledge & Kegan Paul.

Kan, Sergei. 2016. *Symbolic Immortality: The Tlingit Potlach of the Nineteenth Century*. Seattle: University of Washington Press.

Lears, T. Jackson. 1981. *No Place of Grace: Antimodernism and the Transformation of American Culture, 1880–1920*. New York: Pantheon.

Lee, Molly. 1991. "Appropriating the Primitive: Turn-of-the-Century Collection and Display of Native Alaskan Art." *Arctic Anthropology* 28, no. 1: 6–15.

Lee, Molly. 1999. "Tourism and Taste Cultures: Collecting Native Art in Alaska at the Turn of the Twentieth Century." In Ruth B. Phillips and Christopher B. Steiner (eds.), *Unpacking Culture: Art and Commodity in Colonial and Postcolonial Worlds*, 1st ed. Berkeley: University of California Press, 267–281.

Lentis, Marinella. 2017. *Colonized through Art: American Indian Schools and Art Education, 1889–1915*. Lincoln: University of Nebraska Press.

Mason, Otis Tufton. 1904. "Aboriginal American Basketry: Studies in a Textile Art Without Machinery." *Annual Report of the Smithsonian Institution for the Year Ending June 30, 1902, Report of the US National Museum*, Part II. Washington: Government Printing Office. 171–548.

Mawani, Renisa. 2003."Imperial Legacies (Post)Colonial Identities: Law, Space, and the Making of Stanley Park, 1859–2001." *Law/Text/Culture* 7: 98–141.

Mawani, Renisa. 2006."From Colonialism to Multiculturalism?: Totem Poles, Tourism, and National Identity in Vancouver's Stanley Park." *ARIEL: A Review of International English Literature*, 655(Special Issue on Law, Literature and Postcoloniality) 35 (1–2): 31–57.

McLuhan, Marshall. 2005. "The Emperor's Old Clothes." In G. Kepes (ed.), *The Man-Made Object* (90–95). New York: George Brazillier, Inc. Reprinted in E. McLuhan and W.T. Gordon (eds.), *Marshall McLuhan Unbound* (20). Corte Madera, CA: Gingko Press.

McMullen, Ann. 2009. "Reinventing George Heye: Nationalizing the Museum of the American Indian and Its Collections." In Susan Sleeper-Smith (ed.), *Contesting Knowledge: Museums and Indigenous Perspectives*. Lincoln: University of Nebraska Press.

Momaday, N. Scott. 1964. *The Names: A Memoir*. New York: Harper and Row.

Morton, Timothy. 2013. *Hyperobjects: Philosophy and Ecology After the End of the World*. Minneapolis: University of Minnesota Press.

Muensterberger, Werner. 1994. *Collecting: An Unruly Passion: Psychological Perspectives*. Princeton, NJ: Princeton University Press, 1994.

Nelson, Melissa K. 2017. "Getting Dirty: The Eco-Eroticism of Women in Indigenous Oral Literatures." In Joanne Barker, *Critically Sovereign: Indigenous Gender, Sexuality, and Feminist Studies*. Durham, NC: Duke University Press.

Oberg, Kalervo. 1973. *The Social Economy of the Tlingit Indians*. American Ethnological Society. Monograph 55. Seattle: University of Washington Press.

Ostrowitz, Judith. 1999. *Privileging the Past: Reconstructing History in Northwest Coast Art*. Seattle: University of Washington Press.

Ott, John. 2009. "Reform in Redface: The Taos Society of Artists Plays Indian." *American Art* 23. Chicago: University of Chicago Press. 80–107.

Phillips, Ruth B., and Christopher B. Steiner, editors. 1999. *Unpacking Culture: Art and Commodity in Colonial and Postcolonial Worlds*. Berkeley: University of California Press.

Posthumus, David. 2018. *All My Relatives: Exploring Lakota Ontology, Belief, and Ritual*. Lincoln: University of Nebraska Press.

Raibmon, Paige. 2005. *Authentic Indians: Episodes of Encounter from the Late-Nineteenth-Century Northwest Coast*. Durham, NC: Duke University Press.

Reid, William, and Robert Bringhurst. 2009. *Solitary Raven: The Essential Writings of Bill Reid*. Vancouver: Douglas & McIntyre.

Rojek, Chris, and Urry, John. 1997. *Touring Cultures: Transformations of Travel and Theory*. New York: Routledge.

Rosaldo, Renato. 1989. "Imperialist Nostalgia." *Representations*, no. 26: 107–22.

Rushing, Jackson. 1986. "Ritual and Myth: Native American Culture and Abstract Expressionism." In Maurice Tuchman (ed.), *The Spiritual in Art: Abstract Painting 1890–1985*. New York: Abbeville Press.

Smith, Andrea. 2015. *Conquest: Sexual Violence and American Indian Genocide*. Durham, NC: Duke University Press.

"The Red Nation." 2021. The Red Deal. *Common Notions.*

Thompson, William Irwin. 1991. *The American Replacement of Nature.* New York: Doubleday.

Thornton, Thomas. 2008. *Being and Place Among the Tlingit.* Seattle: University of Washington Press.

Tollefson, Kenneth D., and Martin L. 1993. "From Fish Weir to Waterfall." *American Indian Quarterly* 17, no. 2: 209–25.

Vizenor, Gerald R. 2008. *Survivance: Narratives of Native Presence.* Lincoln: University of Nebraska Press.

Weinstock, Jeffrey Andrew. 2016. "Wondrous and Strange: The Matter of *Twin Peaks.*" In Jeffrey Andrew Weinstock and Catherine Spooner (eds.), *Return to* Twin Peaks: *New Approaches to Materiality, Theory, and Genre on Television.* New York: Palgrave Macmillan.

Werness, Hope B. 2000. *The Continuum Encyclopedia of Native Art: Worldview, Symbolism, and Culture in Africa, Oceana, and Native North America.* New York: Continuum.

Wilner, Isaiah Lorado. 2018. "Transformation Masks: Recollecting the Indigenous Origins of Global Consciousness." In Wilner Isaiah Lorado and Blackhawk Ned (eds.), *Indigenous Visions: Rediscovering the World of Franz Boas.* 3–41. New Haven, CT: Yale University Press.

Worl, Rosita. 1998. "Tlingit At.oow: Tangible and Intangible Property." Doctoral dissertation, Harvard University.

"Very old, but always current"

Indigenous Geographies in Twin Peaks

Garrett Wayne Wright

In *Twin Peaks* Season 3, Part 11, Deputy Tommy "Hawk" Hill (Michael Horse) presents a hide-skin map to Sheriff Frank Truman (Robert Forster). "This map is very old," Hawk explains, "but it is always current. It's a *living thing*." The old map contains several symbols with different meanings: twin, snowy peaks represent White Tail and Blue Pine mountains, the latter being Hawk's and Truman's destination and a sacred site for local Indigenous peoples; a fire symbol represents what Hawk describes as "more like modern-day electricity"; and black corn represents the opposite of fertility—death.[1] Hawk's explanation of the map is brief and is ultimately interrupted by phone calls from Margaret Lanterman (Catherine E. Coulson) and Lucy Brennan (Kimmy Robertson). Still, the map and its symbolism contain powerful representations of Indigenous art, history, and cartography.

Hawk's map is an example of ledger art, an art style that gets its name from nineteenth-century Indigenous artists who used scrap paper as their canvases on reservations. Using pages from old Bibles, government documents, and even love letters, these artists would depict important moments from their respective peoples' histories. Long before ledgers were used for these paintings, artists refined their style in paintings on bison hides. *The Three Villages Robe*, for example, was one such painting made by a Quapaw artist and gifted to French officials in Louisiana in the 1740s to celebrate and cement the alliance between the Quapaws and the French.[2] Further north on the Great Plains of what is now North and South Dakota, artists from the Očhéthi Šakówiŋ (Great Sioux Nation) and the Blackfoot Nation recorded notable events and people on documents known as winter counts—hide paintings that operated as a calendar of events over the course of many years.[3]

Importantly, the map in Season 3 of *Twin Peaks* was made by Michael Horse, the actor who plays Deputy Hawk. Horse, who is of Yaqui, Mescalero, and Zuni ancestry, has described the moment he first encountered ledger art as nothing short of eye-opening. "I realized," he said in a 2008 interview, "this was *my* history, from *my* point of view." As he attests, sources created by Indigenous people almost always force people to re-think familiar histories. Moreover, Horse views his own ledger art as being part of a long tradition of Native art, saying that "a lot of modern Indigenous art gets it start from this form of aboriginal art." To Horse and many others, such art forms serve as a potent way to maintain cultural traditions and keep Indigenous histories alive.[4]

That is not to say that this particular representation of Native art and histories is all positive. Indeed, plenty of ink has been spilled on analysis— and criticism—of the role of Native people and archetypes in *Twin Peaks* and Lynch's *oeuvre* more generally. Michael Carroll, for example, has argued that the show recreates the old dualistic archetypes commonly cast upon Indigenous characters: the "evil Indian" (BOB, portrayed by Frank Silva) and the "noble savage" (Hawk). Comparing characters in *Twin Peaks* to characters from other artifacts of the American literary canon, such as James Fenimore Cooper's *The Last of the Mohicans*, Carroll analyzes the show within the context of Joseph Campbell's idea of the monomyth.[5] More recently, historian Geoff Bil applied settler colonial theory to Carroll's analysis of Indigenous archetypes in *Twin Peaks* to argue that the show's first two seasons buy into and perpetuate harmful representations of Native people. Bil shows how Lynch and Frost appropriated aspects of Native cultures that were not themselves native to the area in which *Twin Peaks* exists, which is the ancestral homeland of the Snoqualmies. Instead, as Bil shows, Hawk symbolizes an amalgam of Native Americans—an extremely diverse category—whose main task in the show is to "ameleiorat[e] settler guilt."[6] Taken together, Carroll and Bil encourage viewers to critically examine the roles of Native characters—and, inversely, the absence of such characters—in Lynch's works and in popular culture more generally.

This essay locates the ways in which Indigenous geographies broadly conceived can be found in *Twin Peaks*. Both Carroll and Bil wrote their essays before Season 3 aired in 2017 (Bil's essay was part of a collection written on the eve of the season's premiere). This essay uses Hawk's ledger map as an entry point to discuss how Indigenous epistemologies regarding space and place made their way into the show.

The authenticity and respect with which the show's creators treat Indigenous histories and characters deserves commendation. In focusing on Indigenous geographies, however, *Twin Peaks*, like much of American popular media, has a complicated relationship with Indigeneity. That is, the show (especially in Season 3) includes a representation of authentic Indigenous epistemologies, notably place-making through art and maps, but it does so by drawing upon traditions among American Indians from the Great Plains rather than the Pacific Northwest, where the show is set. In identifying the show's geographically dislocated representations of Indigenous traditions, this essay situates it within a long history of Hollywood portrayals of American Indians.

Hawk's ledger map is a good starting point for a discussion of Indigenous epistemologies—in this case, conceptions of space and place-making—as represented in *Twin Peaks*. It exists within a long tradition of Indigenous cartography, which predated European colonialism in North America and resulted in artifacts that provide visions of the continent that are unfamiliar to non–Native people.

Map-making is an act of place-making, the process by which a people or a community understand the space in which they live and situate themselves. It is also an expression of power. During the colonial era, the North American continent was up for grabs by many groups. At the time of the American Revolutionary War, hundreds of sovereign Indigenous and European polities claimed and contested homelands across the continent. In this time period, as well as others, the ways in which Europeans represented space on a map often said more about their own ambitions than the reality on the ground.[7]

Speaking to European maps of colonial territories during the seventeenth and eighteenth centuries, many historians have argued that European maps were "intensely political documents," ascribing European control over vast swaths of territory that was predominantly controlled by varying groups of American Indians.[8] In representing space as something defined by European power, these imperial cartographers literally and figuratively erased the presence, power, and histories of Indigenous peoples who had lived there for centuries before Europeans knew that North America existed.[9] To state it differently, in 1803 when the United States bought Louisiana from France for only a few thousand dollars, French women and men lived in the territory. Tens of thousands—if not more than 100,000—Indigenous peoples, however, did as well, and they would not have seen the transfer of their homeland from one imperial power to another in a European parlor as a legitimate claim to the region.

Sheriff Frank Truman's presence in the scene with Hawk's map drives home the contrast between Western cartography and American Indian conceptions of space. The scene in Season 3 begins with Truman frustratedly finding his destination based on Major Garland Briggs's (Don S. Davis) coded message on Google Maps. Having found the location via coordinates, Truman realized that it is nevertheless inaccessible: though Google Maps displays the spot precisely, it is covered by a mass of trees and, as Sheriff Truman remarks, there is "no road—it's gone." Enter Deputy Hawk, with his "very old, but always current" map, which confirms information given to them by Major Briggs. Namely, the date listed in Major Briggs's message corresponds with Hawk's reading of the stars on the map. Where western cartography and technology failed, Hawk's "living" map provided the local knowledge necessary to find Jackrabbit's Palace, where they eventually traveled and found Naido (Nae Yuuki) before Deputy Andy Brennan (Harry Goaz) was summoned to meet with the Fireman (Carel Struycken). All of this was possible because of Hawk's map, which represented space differently, and in this case more usefully, than Truman's online search.

This contrast holds true throughout history. When focus shifts to maps and other artifacts made by Indigenous peoples, space looks very different. Rather than the vast bird's-eye-view of most European maps, Native-origin maps tend to be more relational, reflecting a different way of viewing the land itself. Whereas European maps represent land as territory to be claimed by Europeans, or what one scholar called "anticipatory geography," Indigenous maps tend to reflect Native people's connections to the land itself—to particular places, resources, and even to their sense of identity.[10] Anthropologist Tim Ingold has argued that to Indigenous peoples and mapmakers, "land is not a lifeless substrate but rather a lively presence or a ground from which things, including people, develop and grow."[11] Similarly, in his groundbreaking work *Wisdom Sits in Places*, anthropologist Keith Basso put forward the idea that "what people make of their places is closely connected to what they make of themselves as members of society and inhabitants of the earth," and that, for Western Apaches, the past "lies embedded in features of the earth … which together endow their lands with multiple forms of significance that reach into their lives and shape the way they think."[12]

In other words, if European maps present space as territory that they anticipate will soon be claimed and inhabited by settler colonists, then most Indigenous maps represent space that is already inhabited, situating themselves within the land on the ground rather than separated from it through a bird's eye view. Moreover, Indian maps operate as what one scholar called "an illustration of the Native American's oral landscape," thereby encompassing generations of knowledge in one document, or in Hawk's words something that is "always current."[13]

This sense of place, identity, and connection to one's homeland is embodied in Hawk's ledger map. As previously mentioned, the map contains numerous symbols that reflect Hawk's people's understanding of their ancestral homeland. Although Hawk only reveals the meaning of a few symbols on the map, such maps almost always included locations of the map-maker's towns, which may be represented by the tipi-like structures on Hawk's map, or other markers that represented how a people view themselves within a particular space.[14] As a map that has presumably been passed down for generations, it also offers a perspective on Hawk's people's history as preserved through oral tradition.

The map, Hawk says, is "very old." It seems probable that it originated in the early nineteenth century, when a Nez Perce chief named Twisted Hair mapped the Clearwater River basin on bison hide for Meriwether Lewis and William Clark on their westward expedition. According to the fictionalized version of Clark's journals found in *The Secret History of Twin Peaks*, Twisted Hair created the map and gave Lewis the "artifact" that we now know as the Owl Ring, which Twisted Hair had been given by Lodge entities he describes as "white people" who lived "near those [water] falls," the location that would later become the town of Twin Peaks.[15] How Hawk ended up with the map, if it is indeed the same map, is unclear, but its inclusion in *The Secret History of Twin Peaks* corroborates Hawk's claim about its age.

In actual history, Twisted Hair *did* make a map for Lewis and Clark. Indeed, his map was the first Native map used by the pair, but many more followed, including one made by an Arikara man named Too Né in 1804. A hereditary chief of the Arikaras, Too Né welcomed Meriwether Lewis and William Clark to his town on the Upper Missouri River, from which he guided them to Mandan and Hidatsa villages farther west. At some point along the way, Too Né created a map for his new American friends that situated Lewis and Clark among the geographic and demographic landscape of the world of the Arikaras, spanning the entire Missouri River basin and stretching as far south as Spanish New Mexico. The map was vital for the U.S. travelers and eventually made its way back to Washington, D.C., where Thomas Jefferson added it to his private collections. Like Twisted Hair's map (i.e., Hawk's map in the canon of *Twin Peaks*), Too Né's map allowed Lewis and Clark to successfully travel westward to the Pacific Ocean.[16]

In this way Hawk's ledger map lies within a long tradition of non–Native explorers using Native knowledge and cartography to understand and navigate territory that at first seemed to be uncharted.[17] Throughout American history European and American travelers relied upon Indigenous knowledge of and guidance within the American landscape. In the case of *Twin Peaks*, we see this same process play out, albeit in a supernatural way through the portals between our world and the territory of Lodge entities such as BOB, MIKE (Al Strobel), and the Fireman.

This role for Hawk extends back into Seasons 1 and 2, when he first acted as the authority of all things local and strange for Special Agent Cooper (Kyle MacLachlan) and his comrades at the Twin Peaks Sheriff's Department. Hawk's centrality to supernatural entities and journeys becomes heightened toward the end of Season 2 when Cooper tries to locate the Black Lodge in his effort to stop Windom Earle (Kenneth Welsh). Hawk is vital to this effort, as his people's legend of the Black Lodge provides guidance to Cooper and Sheriff Harry S. Truman (Michael Ontkean) as they try to interpret the meanings of various petroglyphs on the walls of the Owl Cave.

The Native American guide or spiritual counselor is a common trope, one that has been justifiably critiqued as stereotypical.[18] Yet, an examination of Indigenous cartography in expeditions such as the Lewis and Clark shows that Native knowledge has been central to non–Native journeys for centuries. Moreover, the representations of space on Hawk's map and within the Owl Cave gel with the real history of Indigenous place-making through cartography.

In including Hawk's ledger map, *Twin Peaks* thus presents an authentic representation of Indigenous art and place-making. Not only was the map created by a Native artist, Michael Horse himself, it also reflects the general epistemologies and cosmologies of many Indigenous peoples, especially those from the Great Plains. Yet the character of Hawk identifies as Nez Perce, and the ledger map is much more firmly in the tradition of Plains Indians, a fact that that Horse, himself a member of nations from the Southwest, has readily admitted.[19] Indigenous nations from the Pacific Northwest had discernably different artistic traditions than, say, the Pawnees on the Central Plains or people within the Očhéthi Šakówiŋ who would have created ledger art that resembles Hawk's map.[20] Thus, even in an authentic representation of one way that Indigenous people thought about space, the show implicitly erases the ways of knowing and conceiving of the world within the communities who lived and continue to live in the Pacific Northwest.

There is a long history of conflating Plains Indian culture with Native American culture, thereby flattening what it meant and continues to mean to be Indigenous. For decades, if not centuries, the typical image of an American Indian in popular media and art has tended to resemble a Comanche warrior, a man on horseback with his face painted and his head adorned with a feather headdress.[21] It is important to recognize that "American Indian" is a diverse category made up of many different people who speak a multitude of languages, have distinct religious beliefs, and operate within various forms of social organization. That the ledger map in Season 3 of *Twin Peaks* was created by an Indigenous artist is a huge step forward from Bil's criticisms of Seasons 1 and 2. Perhaps if viewers are lucky enough to see more of the show in their lifetimes, its representation of Indigeneity will expand to include ideas, practices, art, and actors from the Indigenous Northwest, as well.[22]

NOTES

1. For a more detailed analysis of the symbols on Hawk's ledger map (as well as a high-resolution image of the map), see Gisela Fleischer, "'It's a Living Thing'—Analyzing Hawk's Map," *25YearsLater*, August 7, 2017, https://25yearslatersite.com/2017/08/07/its-a-living-thing-analyzing-hawks-map/.

2. Kathleen DuVal, *The Native Ground: Indians and Colonists in the Heart of the Continent* (Philadelphia: University of Pennsylvania Press, 2006), 83; Morris Arnold, *The Rumble of a Distant Drum: The Quapaws and Old World Newcomers, 1673–1804* (Fayetteville: University of Arkansas Press, 2007), 65–69.

3. Colin G. Calloway, *One Vast Winter Count: The Native American West before Lewis and Clark* (Lincoln: University of Nebraska Press, 2003), 11–13; Blanca Tovías, "The Right to Possess Memory: Winter Counts of the Blackfoot, 1830–1937," *Ethnohistory* 61, no. 1 (2014): 99–122.

4. Michael Horse, "Ledger Art," pts. 1 and 2, *YouTube*, 2008, accessed on May 24, 2020, https://www.youtube.com/watch?v=Z0dHIkTTj2U. https://www.youtube.com/watch?v=kV6MA6BCEZk&t=245s; Rob E. King, "Interview: Michael Horse on The Return, the 'Living Map,' Ledger Art, and More!" *25YearsLater*, 2018, accessed on May 26, 2020, https://25years latersite.com/2018/06/19/interview-michael-horse-on-the-return-the-living-map-ledger-art-and-more/.

5. Michael Carroll, "Agent Cooper's Errand in the Wilderness: *Twin Peaks* and American Mythology," *Film/Literature Studies* 21, no. 4 (1993): 290–292.

6. Geoff Bil, "Tensions in the World of Moon: *Twin Peaks*, Indigeneity and Territoriality," *Senses of Cinema* 79 (2016), accessed May 25, 2020, http://sensesofcinema.com/2016/twin-peaks/twin-peaks-indigeneity-territoriality/.

7. Juliana Barr, "Geographies of Power: Mapping Indian Borders in the 'Borderlands' of the Southwest," *William and Mary Quarterly* 68, no. 1 (2011): 7, 9; Juliana Barr and Edward Countryman, "Maps and Spaces, Paths to Connect, and Lines to Divide," in *Contested Spaces of Early America*, eds. Juliana Barr and Edward Countryman (Philadelphia: University of Pennsylvania Press, 2014), 4.

8. *Ibid.*

9. Barr, "Geographies," 7.

10. J. Brian Harley, "Rereading the Maps of the Columbian Encounter," *Annals of the Association of American Geographers* 82, no. 3 (1992): 532; Calloway, *One Vast Winter Count*, 11–12; Brian Francis Egan, "From Dispossession to Decolonization: Towards a Critical Indigenous Geography of Hul'qumi'num Territory," PhD diss. (Carleton University, 2009), 55–56; Barr, "Geographies," 7.

11. Tim Ingold, *The Perception of the Environment: Essays in Livelihood, Dwelling, and Skill* (New York: Routledge, 2000); Egan, "From Dispossession," 56.

12. Keith Basso, *Wisdom Sits in Places: Landscape and Language among the Western Apache* (Albuquerque: University of New Mexico Press, 1996), 7, 34.

13. Mark Warhus, *Another America: Native American Maps and the History of Our Land* (New York: St. Martin's Press, 1997), 3–4.

14. Fleischer, "It's a Living Thing."

15. Mark Frost, *The Secret History of Twin Peaks* (New York: Macmillan, 2016), 11; Ali Sciarabba, "The Secret History of Twin Peaks: The Lewis & Clark Expedition and the Nez Perce," *25YearsLater* (2017), accessed May 26, 2020, https://25yearslatersite.com/2017/11/05/the-secret-history-of-twin-peaks-the-lewis-clark-expedition-and-the-nez-perce-secrets-and-mysteries-part-2/.

16. James P. Ronda, "'A Chart in His Way': Indian Cartography and the Lewis and Clark Expedition," *Great Plains Quarterly* 4, no. 1 (1984)): 43–44, 46; Christopher Steinke, "'Here is my country': Too Né's Map of Lewis and Clark in the Great Plains," *William and Mary Quarterly* 71, no. 4 (2014): 589–610.

17. See Alan Taylor, *American Colonies: The Settling of North America* (New York: Penguin Books, 2001) for an overview of this in various regions and time periods of colonial American history. As Taylor notes, "Indians became indispensable to the European contenders for North American empire. On their contested frontiers, each empire desperately needed Indians as trading partners, guides, religious converts, and military allies ... [and] Indian relations were central to the development of every colonial region" (49). See also Barr and Countryman, *Contested Spaces in Early America*, 16, 23–24, 125; G. Malcolm Lewis, ed., *Cartographic Encounters: Perspectives on Native American Map Making and Map Use* (Chicago: University of Chicago Press, 1998); Robert Paulett, *An Empire of Small Places: Mapping the Southeastern Anglo-Indian Trade, 1732–1795* (Athens: University of Georgia Press, 2012).

18. Bil, "Tensions."

19. Horse, "2 Ledgers"; King, "Interview."

20. Bill Holm, *Northwest Coast Indian Art: An Analysis of Form* (Seattle: University of Washington Press, 2015).

21. Ward Churchill, "Fantasies of a Master Race: Categories of Stereotyping of American Indians in Film," in *Fantasies of the Master Race: Literature, Cinema and the Colonization of American Indians*, ed. M. Annette Jaimes (Monroe, ME: Common Courage Press, 1992), 232–239; John Mihelich, "Smoke or Signals? American Popular Culture and the Challenge to Hegemonic Images of American Indians in Native American Film," *Wicazo Sa Review* 16, no. 2 (2001): 129–137; Ken Nolley, "The Representation of Conquest: John Ford and the Hollywood Indian," in *Hollywood's Indian: The Portrayal of the Native American in Film*, 2nd edition, eds. Peter C. Rollins and John E. O'Connor (Lexington: University Press of Kentucky, 2003), 78–80. See also William H. Goetzmann, *The West of the Imagination* (Norman: University of Oklahoma Press, 2009).

22. Bil, "Tensions."

Works Cited

Arnold, Morris. 2007. *The Rumble of a Distant Drum: The Quapaws and Old World Newcomers, 1673–1804.* Fayetteville: University of Arkansas Press.

Barr, Juliana. 2011. "Geographies of Power: Mapping Indian Borders in the 'Borderlands' of the Southwest." *William and Mary Quarterly* 68 (1): 5–46.

Barr, Juliana, and Edward Countryman. 2014. "Maps and Spaces, Paths to Connect, and Lines to Divide." In *Contested Spaces of Early America*, edited by Juliana Barr and Edward Countryman, 1–28. Philadelphia: University of Pennsylvania Press.

Basso, Keith. 1996. *Wisdom Sits in Places: Landscape and Language among the Western Apache.* Albuquerque: University of New Mexico Press.

Bil, Geoff. 2016. "Tensions in the World of Moon: *Twin Peaks*, Indigeneity and Territoriality." *Senses of Cinema*, issue 79. http://sensesofcinema.com/2016/twin-peaks/twin-peaks-indigeneity-territoriality/.

Blakeslee, Donald J. 2010. *Holy Ground, Healing Water: Cultural Landscapes at Waconda Lake, Kansas.* College Station: Texas A&M University Press.

Calloway, Colin G. 2003. *One Vast Winter Count: The Native American West before Lewis and Clark.* Lincoln: University of Nebraska Press. 11, 13.

Carroll, Michael. 1993. "Agent Cooper's Errand in the Wilderness: *Twin Peaks* and American Mythology." *Film/Literature Studies* 21 (4): 287–296. ProQuest.

Churchill, Ward. 1992. "Fantasies of a Master Race: Categories of Stereotyping of American Indians in Film." In *Fantasies of the Master Race: Literature, Cinema and the Colonization of American Indians*, edited by M. Annette Jaimes. Monroe, ME: Common Courage Press. 231–241.

Dorsey, George A. (1906) 1997. *The Pawnee Mythology*. Reprint, Lincoln: University of Nebraska Press. Citations refer to the reprinted edition.

DuVal, Kathleen. 2006. *The Native Ground: Indians and Colonists in the Heart of the Continent*. Philadelphia: University of Pennsylvania Press.

Egan, Brian Francis. 2009. "From Dispossession to Decolonization: Towards a Critical Indigenous Geography of Hul'qumi'num Territory." PhD Dissertation, Carleton University. ProQuest.

Fleischer, Gisela. 2017. "'It's a living thing'—Analyzing Hawk's Map." *25 Years Later*. https://25yearslatersite.com/2017/08/07/its-a-living-thing-analyzing-hawks-map/.

Frost, Mark. 2016. *The Secret History of Twin Peaks*. New York: Macmillan.

Harley, J. Brian. 1992. "Rereading the Maps of the Columbian Encounter." *Annals of the Association of American Geographers* 82 (3): 522–536.

Holm, Bill. 2015. *Northwest Coast Indian Art: An Analysis of Form*. Seattle: University of Washington Press.

Horse, Michael. 2008. "Ledger Art." 2 parts. YouTube. https://www.youtube.com/watch?v=Z0dHIkTTj2U; https://www.youtube.com/watch?v=kV6MA6BCEZk&t=245s.

Ingold, Tim. 2000. *The Perception of the Environment: Essays in Livelihood, Dwelling, and Skill*. New York: Routledge.

King, Rob E. 2018. "Interview: Michael Horse on The Return, the 'Living Map,' Ledger Art, and More!" *25 Years Later*. https://25yearslatersite.com/2018/06/19/interview-michael-horse-on-the-return-the-living-map-ledger-art-and-more/.

Mihelich, John. 2001. "Smoke or Signals? American Popular Culture and the Challenge to Hegemonic Images of American Indians in Native American Film." *Wicazo Sa Review* 16 (2): 129–137.

Nolley, Ken. 2003. "The Representation of Conquest: John Ford and the Hollywood Indian." In Peter C. Rollins and John E. O'Connor (eds.), *Hollywood's Indian: The Portrayal of the Native American in Film*, 2nd ed. Lexington: University Press of Kentucky. 73–90.

Riding In, James Thomas. 1991. "Keepers of Tirawahut's Covenant: The Development and Destruction of Pawnee Culture." PhD Dissertation, University of California Los Angeles.

Ronda, James P. 1984. "'A Chart in His Way': Indian Cartography and the Lewis and Clark Expedition." *Great Plains Quarterly* 4 (1): 43–53.

Sciarabba, Ali. 2017. "The Secret History of Twin Peaks: The Lewis & Clark Expedition and the Nez Perce." *25 Years Later*. https://25yearslatersite.com/2017/11/05/the-secret-history-of-twin-peaks-the-lewis-clark-expedition-and-the-nez-perce-secrets-and-mysteries-part-2/.

Steinke, Christopher. 2014. "'Here is my country': Too Né's Map of Lewis and Clark in the Great Plains." *William and Mary Quarterly* 71 (4): 589–610.

Tovías, Blanca. 2014. "The Right to Possess Memory: Winter Counts of the Blackfoot, 1830–1937." *Ethnohistory* 61 (1): 99–122.

Warhus, Mark. 1997. *Another America: Native American Maps and the History of Our Land*. New York: St. Martin's Press.

Weltfish, Gene. 1965. *The Lost Universe: Pawnee Life and Culture*. Lincoln: University of Nebraska Press.

Wright, Garrett. 2019. "Paawaarihuusu: Travel and the Central Great Plains." PhD Dissertation, University of North Carolina at Chapel Hill.

"I am the FBI"

American Identity in Twin Peaks

MOLLY O'GORMAN

In *The Psychology of the Western*, William Indick argues that the foundation of the American mythos is the frontier myth.[1] The frontier was presented as a boundary between the civilized and the barbarous—the barbarous or "savage" frequently referred to Native Americans—while white conquest was presented as the spreading of civilization. Indick notes, however, that understanding barbarity as the archetypal feature of the Native American on film is simplistic, although their depiction as such is a useful foil to demonstrate white superiority. He argues that the real prize to be conquered is the West itself, which is consistently fetishized as a wild entity to be tamed and owned.[2] The depictions of both the wildness of the Native American as well as the white desire to conquer them, establish the Native American as synecdochising the American landscape. This link has solidified the second stereotype of the Native American on film, the noble savage, a more primitive person than the white civilized American who is closer to the natural and spiritual world.

Both sides of the indigenous stereotype are seen in *Twin Peaks* through Hawk and BOB, whose depiction draws on the "Evil Indian" trope from Western film. White American identity is constructed in opposition to this, as Cooper and the FBI's repeated venturing into other worlds can be read as a form of imperial imposition of settler law. Indigenous Americans are either excluded from this concept of America or absorbed into it, with characters like Hawk only able to take their place in the white community by actively replicating racially oppressive behaviors. By reading *Twin Peaks* through the lens of postcolonial cinematic criticism, this essay proposes that the show upholds colonial ideology, not only in its depiction of indigenous types but also in its treatment of the supernatural as a frontier in a manner descended from Western cinema, and its imposition of settler American law beyond borders both natural and supernatural.

The Displacement of White Evil

> HARRY: I've seen some strange things, but this is way off the map—I'm having a hard time believing.
> COOPER: Harry, is it easier to believe that a man would rape and murder his own daughter? Any more comforting?
> HARRY: No.
> GARLAND: An evil that great in this beautiful world … finally … does it matter what the cause?
> COOPER: Yes, because it's our job to stop it.
> GARLAND: Yeah.
> ALBERT: Maybe that's all BOB is. The evil that men do. Maybe it doesn't matter what we call it [*Twin Peaks*, Season 2, Episode 16, "Arbitrary Law"].

This moment between the law enforcement articulates a central tension to *Twin Peaks*; is it Leland or BOB who kills Laura Palmer? Albert's claim that BOB is "[t]he evil that men do" is an oft quoted explanation for Leland's demonic possession, but his latter claim that "it doesn't matter what we call it" deserves questioning. The abstract conceptualization of evil through BOB has been criticized by many writers, including Michael Carroll, who points out BOB's long greasy hair, threatening grimace, and forest dwelling all link to the Western image of the threatening Native American.[3] This can be added to BOB's position in *Twin Peaks'* pseudo-indigenous mythology, as well as his silence which is broken only by screams or laughter, both indicative of a barbarous Otherness. Geoff Bil goes further in pointing out that the rape and murder of a young white woman is not only the central premise of *Twin Peaks*, it is the central premise of many Westerns and other founding stories of the American mythos, forming part of the framework that has caused indigenous people to be viewed in the same barbarous terms in which BOB is contrived.[4] With this in mind, Cooper's framing of Harry's question in terms of ease is troubling. Are we displacing white violence onto a native-coded demon in order to comfort ourselves?

The centrality of "ease" in this conversation should ring alarm bells, having replaced the more conventional principle of "truth" in solving a crime. Furthermore, the extended canon of *Twin Peaks* suggests that what is easy to believe is not the truth. In *The Secret History of Twin Peaks*, Frost (as Lawrence Jacoby) writes of Leland's incestuous rape and murder of Laura:

> Nightmares like this don't take root in native or aboriginal homes. *Ever.* In affluent, urban American families it's, increasingly, a specialty of the house. Strange, isn't it? All those "gifts" we think of as advantages, the ones we're

socially programmed to strive for, the "dream" no one questions because it looks so seductive on television or in the pages of glossy magazines. But my own prejudices and predispositions got in the way. I'd never seen an anomaly like Laura's family up close before. I plain missed it. I'm still convinced I don't know the real story.[5]

The suggestion that incest is a specifically suburban American crime is not so clear cut here as Jacoby's initial declaration suggests. Although he is admittedly a dubious psychologist, his missing of Laura's abuse despite his belief that incest is a "speciality" of the suburban home implies a more complicated relationship between crime and American-ness than he originally suggests. The alliterative highlighting of "prejudices and predispositions" suggests that there was something in Jacoby's mindset blocking his understanding, and his use of the term "anomaly" despite the previous use of "specialty" demonstrates that whatever he might say, he cannot fully conceive of the affluent American home as the seat of evil. We might also note that "affluent" and "aboriginal" are not opposites, yet Jacoby sets them up as such; noticing that BOB is denim-clad, a material associated with laborers, demonstrates that it is not only through race, but also through class, that BOB is set up as the anti-suburban. The prejudices found in Jacoby's writing are not confined to his narrative but thus present through the show's ostensibly neutral angle. Jacoby's claim that he still doesn't know "the real story" is undermined by his acknowledgment of his own prejudices, and the audience that knows "the real story" as BOB are invited to look at BOB in light of Jacoby's predisposition to trust the affluent American family. Here, Jacoby's yen to find an alternative explanation for Leland's actions recalls Cooper's suggestion that BOB is a "more comforting" explanation.

The suggestion that incest has a suburban demographic, however, also raises several problems. It essentializes indigenous Americans into noble savages, a race of humans uncorrupted by civilization, by positing fundamental differences between races. However, if we understand from this essentialization that BOB represents the evil committed by Leland, the question of why the creators chose a native-coded figure to express what is a suburban crime is pressing. If crimes of incest originate with the settler rather than the native person, BOB's image is not chosen to represent the nature of the crime but rather a generic barbarity that draws on decades of filmic and literary representation. The displacement of human barbarity onto an abstract native entity ties into pseudoscientific theories of unilineal human development which suggest that the civilized mind of the Western man has mastered his animal instincts in a way that "primitive" people could not. These theories were used to justify colonial mastery, and we can see that discourse of mastery in microcosmic detail in the dramatic irony that the creators employ. The audience's knowledge that Leland/BOB is the killer leaves them willing to believe that Leland is able to control BOB and reclaim his morals. This maps onto a larger discourse about the need for civilization which is inextricable with the American mythos. It is worth recognizing, of course, that Frost's persona is that of Lawrence Jacoby in *The Secret History of Twin Peaks* and that the declaration that Leland's crime is one typical of his milieu is not authorial. However, Jacoby's role as a psychoanalyst should give the audience, as analysts themselves, pause. Our job, much like Jacoby's, is to interpret what has happened to Laura, and Jacoby's failure to get to the bottom of Leland's abuse because of his predisposition to trust him should make us question the usefulness of displacing the evil outside the home, away from the white man.

The question of incest as a crime typical to white suburbia begs the question: against whom is this crime committed? Judith Butler, drawing on Claude Lévi-Strauss's analysis of the incest taboo, has posited the incest taboo as emerging from the treatment of women as objects of exchange, a behavior which has been fundamental to the existence of patriarchy.[6] It can thus be argued that Laura's rape and murder were not merely committed against her, but against the nuclear family and its larger patriarchal counterpart, white, middle-class America. It is this which allows the murder of Laura Palmer to take on so much significance in comparison to the less privileged Teresa Banks, and which makes sense of Cooper's claim that

> I've only been in Twin Peaks a short time but in that time I have seen decency, honour and dignity.... Laura Palmer's death has affected each and every man, woman and child because life has meaning here, every life. That's a way of living I thought had vanished from the Earth, but it hasn't, Albert—it's right here in Twin Peaks [*Twin Peaks*, Season 1, Episode 3, "Rest in Pain"].

The implication of this vanishing moral utopia is that it is vanishing from Twin Peaks, too. Although the town generally mourns Laura, the value that the town places on life has been ruptured by Leland's actions. Cooper's claim that "life" is the value system of Twin Peaks is simplistic, however. The soap opera parody allows us to see Twin Peaks as made up of a series of interconnected families (Martells, Hornes, Palmers, Haywards etc.), suggesting that Cooper's nostalgia is not merely for morality but for the post-war American ideal of a society made up of co-operative nuclear family units. The crime of incestuous rape and murder is chosen to shock, but it also represents the extreme opposite of the value system represented by Twin Peaks. Incest destroys the nuclear family like no other crime. Cooper's claim so early to be motivated by the values of the town suggests an ideological motivation to his investigation that goes beyond the simple desire to solve. His attempt to save Laura can in this light be seen as an attempt to restore the American fantasy after the destruction of BOB. The fact that his failure plunges Cooper/Richard and Laura/Carrie into an alternate world, seemingly inhabited by spirits in the form of the Tremonds, only highlights the dichotomy between white America and the supernatural Other, which the show roots in indigenous mythology.

The native coding of the evil Other is made more palpable by the obvious whiteness of Twin Peaks. The only notable exceptions to this are Hawk and Josie, whose plots are tied up in their ethnicities. The worlds of indigenous mythology and the Hong Kong mafia are allowed to intrude on Twin Peaks through the obvious difference inherent in these characters' bodies, but the rest of the town remains white. Where ethnicity does not serve a plot-relevant purpose, white is thus reverted to as the neutral, clearly homogenizing America. This is not without reason. The aesthetic of *Twin Peaks* is based on 1950s American suburbia in the post-war boom, deconstructing it to show the darkness at the heart of the suburban idyll. Such themes are typical of Lynch's work. *Blue Velvet* (1986) presents a similar critique of suburbia, whilst *Mulholland Drive* (2001) substitutes the gloss of suburbia with the glamour of Hollywood, similarly dressed in a post-war aesthetic. Such depictions are necessarily majority white, because it is the post-war ideology of the middle-class nuclear family in which Lynch is largely interested, and this is an ideology from which people of color have generally been excluded.

However, despite dismantling this ideology to show the darkness underneath it, its whiteness is never interrogated and thus arguably the most obvious hidden evil remains hidden. Melanie McFarland compares the treatment of women of color like Jade and Naido to Lynch's woodworked objects, their nudity taking precedence over personalities and thus demonstrating that a fetishized brown skin tone marks an entirely superficial engagement with them.[7] We might contrast this to the treatment of Laura Palmer. Although her depiction is often criticized for aestheticizing violence against women, the focus on Laura as subject in *Twin Peaks: Fire Walk with Me* is a recentering which highlights the effect of small-town violence and corruption rather than simply presenting its luridness. McFarland is right to recognize that non-white characters are never afforded that radical recentering. When applied to the show's indigenous characters and plot lines, this estheticizing and sidelining of people of color presents a troubling vision of America, which is only deepened when considering the native coding of the supernatural Other, a move which in itself lends the show a superficially eerie aesthetic at the expense of the indigenous image.

Parodying the Western

The Cowboy and the Frenchman (1988) shows that Lynch was thinking about national stereotypes around the same time that *Twin Peaks* was taking shape. The show was pitched to ABC in the same year.[8] Lynch was asked to provide a short for *The French as Seen By...*, and whilst his slapstick depiction of French stereotypes is amusing, what is telling is the equal space given to American stereotypes. Harry Dean Stanton and Jack Nance play stereotypically unworldly cowboys, whose intelligence does not match their ability to reach for their holsters. A comparison between Hawk in *Twin Peaks* and Michael Horse's appearance as Broken Feather, the Native American following the Frenchman, however, can give insight into the relationship between settler and Native American identities in Lynch's work.

National stereotypes are played for comedy in this short: the removal of baguettes, souvenirs of the Eiffel Tower, a plate of cheese and a plate of snails among other objects from Pierre's bag forms an increasingly long and ludicrous catalogue of stereotypes. The impossibility that these would all fit into Pierre's bag implies unreality to the exaggeration. Although not so explicitly dismantled, the placement of American stereotypes beside this French one allow us to revel in their similar ridiculousness. The gun-toting violence and ignorance of the white American cowboys match up with the half-naked Native American stalking the Frenchman like prey. These are not stereotypes meant to be taken seriously.

Broken Feather first appears naked from the waist up, seemingly hunting Pierre. Just as the sight of Pierre coming down the mountain was accompanied by the typically French accordion, the first appearance of Broken Feather is scored with percussion, a sound associated with Native Americans on film.[9] His second appearance is similarly scored, and similarly juxtaposed, though this time with Slim's rendition of the cowboy classic *Git Along Little Dogies*, and the percussion appears and disappears as Broken Feather does. When he speaks, his syntax is generically broken. These stereotypes are not without their subversions. The intermittent timpani is played for comic effect, and his poor English is increasingly juxtaposed to his professionalized language ("livestock," "personnel") and intelligent regard for business, undermining such a depiction. Furthermore, Broken Feather's resentment, initially depicted as an irrational anger, is shown to be because one of the cowboys owes him money. This can be read as a microcosmic rationalizing for the much larger antagonism of Hollywood's Native Americans and undermines the single-faceted idea of violence without reason. Generally, then, the stereotype of the Native American is parodied just as the stereotypes of the titular cowboy and Frenchman are.

Despite Lynch's rejection of the indigenous stereotype, however, Broken Feather is not given equal weight to the rest of the characters. He is absent from the short's title. He has very few lines by comparison to characters from other ethnic groups, and he is visually sidelined, often placed on the edge of the group, away from the main action. Furthermore, although admittedly hyperbolic, examples of French and non-indigenous American culture feature heavily in the second half of the film, but Broken Feather's culture does not intrude at all. The only musical association we get with him is basic percussion. Yang Kaiyuan writes that percussion is frequently used to depict Native Americans on film but often only reductively draws on an indigenous percussive musical culture, reducing the musical complexity to a dissonant percussion to contrast with the more developed consonant Western romantic tradition.[10] Although this reductive stereotype is mocked in the short, indigenous culture is not showcased further, unlike the musical performances of the white cast members. Furthermore, although at first sight the playful mockery of the indigenous stereotype seems to match the treatment of the white stereotypes, the two cannot be equal. White stereotypes have long existed but do not form the basis of an entire genre of film. On top of this the continued systematic oppression of indigenous Americans is arguably furthered by their dehumanized portrayal in the mass media, something which does not apply to the stereotypes of the cowboy or the Frenchman. Making light comedy from all three stereotypes side by side, particularly when the Native American character is so consistently relegated to the periphery, does not take into account the importance of cinematic representation for marginalized groups nor the gravity of their misrepresentation.

Despite these problems the satirizing of such stereotypes demonstrates Lynch's rejection of the concept of Native American barbarism. With this in mind we can analyze how Native Americans are depicted in *Twin Peaks*. The most prominent indigenous character in *Twin Peaks* is Hawk, played by Michael Horse, who also played Broken Feather in *The Cowboy and the Frenchman*. Horse's presence in both works provides a point of intertextuality, bringing the two characters into dialogue with one another. Carroll, who sees BOB as the stereotype of the "evil Indian," writes that he "is counterpoised by his diametric opposite, the 'noble savage,' albeit in rather subdued form, in Deputy Hawk, friend of the white man who yet preserves some of his Indian ways and is possessed of mystic knowledge."[11] Hawk's role as lawman opposes him to the lawless Broken Feather; his uniform symbolizes his conformity with the settler. His speech is typically intelligent and insightful, with none of Broken Feather's syntactical slips, and he has no musical theme. Whilst the characterization of Broken Feather is played for comedy—a comedy that acknowledges its ridiculousness—Hawk's never is, suggesting that this is a characterization that Lynch takes more seriously. Carroll's claim, however, that Hawk is not a movement away from the world of stereotypes but simply a move to a different stereotype, carries weight. He notes that Hawk's character resembles the "noble savage" character type that developed in later Western films. Writing about the depiction of Native Americans on film, Harry M. Benshoff and Sean Griffin write that they are frequently portrayed as childlike, unthreatening people with a purer connection to the natural world than the white man.[12] The former of these traits is not applicable to Hawk, but his cultural connection to nature and the spiritual world is vital to the show's plot. Benshoff and Griffin explain that whilst these seem like positive traits, the depiction of a more natural human being who is guided by instinct removes human intellect and agency from indigenous characters, instead animalizing them. Such animalizing is the flip side to the barbaric animalistic depiction satirized in *The Cowboy and the Frenchman.*

The "noble savage" character type is sometimes referred to as the "spiritual guide" because it typically reinforces white centrality to the narrative, and *Twin Peaks* is no exception. Hawk fills the role of the "good native American" who aids white people against villains who are coded as indigenous. Admittedly, despite the show's mythos declaring itself to be native American, it draws instead on theosophy, a nineteenth-century occult movement which draws heavily on eastern religion and particularly Tibet. Despite this, Native American imagery is much more obvious within *Twin Peaks*. But even though the show claims to center indigenous myth systems, Hawk does not take a leading role in penetrating the Lodge. Instead, his knowledge is used to guide Cooper on his quest, reinforcing Cooper's centrality even in a world to which he is a clear outsider. Furthermore, the masquerading of a theosophic tradition as Native American provides the same effacement of indigenous culture that we see in the musical exclusion of Broken Feather from *The Cowboy and the Frenchman*, except on a far grander scale. *Twin Peaks* traded on its eerie premise of the demons of indigenous mythology, yet this can be read as a form of mythological redface; the adoption of indigenous mythology is superficial, using familiar imagery to draw on a filmic tradition of the indigenous Other whilst not conceptually engaging with it.

Issues of race are rarely confronted so head on in *Twin Peaks* as they are in *The Cowboy and the Frenchman*. Two key moments where prejudice against indigenous people are confronted come in conversation with Lucy, a primarily comic character, thus tonally matching the treatment of race in the short. In the second series, Lucy's sister, Gwen, says to Hawk: "God, after all we've done to you, how you must hate us white people." Hawk merely replies: "Some of my best friends are white people" (*Twin Peaks,*

Season 2, Episode 15, "Drive with a Dead Girl"). Hawk's response is a twist on the white person's common defense of racism, but this engagement is as superficial as that of *The Cowboy and the Frenchman*. Gwen's lack of intelligence throughout her brief appearance is played for laughs, and she initially treats Hawk as something of a stereotype, calling him "Eagle Eye." This name is more stereotypically Native American than Hawk, being hyperbolically majestic and double barreled, and the dramatic irony of the situation means that this blunder is played for comedy. This reduction of Hawk to a character type is similar to that of Broken Feather and suggests a simplicity and incomprehension on Gwen's part. The fact that she is the only character to voice the question of racism is therefore problematic. Hawk's dismissal of Gwen's assumption is a dismissal of the adversarial relationship between indigenous and settler populations seen in *The Cowboy and the Frenchman*. The dismissal of stereotypes as silly is something thus seen in both texts, rather than a recognition either of their gravity or of continued systemic oppression. The other engagement with indigenous oppression comes indirectly through Lucy's misuse of the term "Indian," which occurs in a scene where she suggests that chocolate might be an indigenous remedy for gas (*Twin Peaks*, Season 3, Part 3, "Call for Help"). Lucy recurs in both these moments, signifying the comic tone of both. Her perception of Hawk is not figured as a symptom of oppression but as a moment of farce, extending white perception of Native Americans to hyperbolic conclusions just as in *The Cowboy and the Frenchman*. Although this mocks stereotypes that prevail in majority-white film, it undermines their gravity and also refuses to acknowledge the stereotypes that continue to play into indigenous characters in *Twin Peaks*.

Law Enforcement as Colonization

The abundance of natural imagery in *Twin Peaks* reflects a colonial mindset through its depiction of the wildness of the American landscape. The iconic waterfall shot of Snoqualmie Falls from the opening credits, for example, connotes the painting style of the Hudson River school not only in its wild beauty but in the brown tones of the rocks and in its portrayed isolation, despite in fact being beside the Great Northern. The color palette and action depicted recall works such as Frederic Edwin Church's *Niagara Falls from the American Side* (1867) and John Frederick Kensett's *Niagara Falls* (1855), Church and Kensett both being key artists of the Hudson River school.

Such connotations do not exist in an ideological vacuum. John K. Howat argues that the fascination with the untamed landscape seen in such paintings is something that distinguishes American art from that of Western Europe in this period largely because of the settler mindset that understands the land as something to be tamed.[13] Sally J. Morgan has written about the adaptation of the Hudson river school of painting into the Western film, where American landscapes are frequently depicted as untouched and untamed, with lingering landscape shots to draw out the comparison. *Twin Peaks'* depiction of Snoqualmie Falls draws on both traditions to suggest the same untamed power, as does its depictions of Ghostwood Forest.[14] The show cuts to a shot of Snoqualmie Falls at moments of unbridled terror such as directly following Maddy's death, and to Ghostwood Forest directly after Leland's suicide (*Twin Peaks*, Season 2, Episode 14, "Lonely Souls" and Season 2, Episode 16, "Arbitrary Law"). Thus, the cinematographic link between the indigenous-coded BOB and the landscape implies a colonial aspect to Cooper's role as law enforcement, implying the need to rehabilitate a wild landscape. Given the indigenous connotations as well as the provenance of such images in a colonial understanding of America, law enforcement in *Twin Peaks* is implicitly intertwined with ideas of white settling.

The show's iconic waterfall is Snoqualmie Falls, a site which is sacred to the Snoqualmie Tribe. Glastonbury Grove provides the link to the Lodge, which Hawk describes in terms of Nez Perce folklore. The spirits in the trees, the ghosts of Ghostwood Forest, are visually associated with the indigenous totems of the Great Northern through Josie's absorption into the hotel wood as well as the otherworldly noise emanating from it in Season 3. Physical embodiments of the supernatural other are thus unmistakably coded as indigenous. But this indigeneity is superficial. Frost has acknowledged that the Black and White Lodge, among other aspects of *Twin Peaks* lore, derive from theosophy rather than the indigenous origins claimed in the show.[15] Despite only being superficial, however, the choice of Native American landscapes and imagery is important because of the colonial narrative it implies in the law enforcement. Bar Hawk and Albert, all of the law enforcement is white. Hawk fits into the stereotype of spiritual guide, backing up the law rather than questioning its philosophy.

This philosophy is one of the frontier. The frontier is central to *Twin Peaks*. Borders between worlds are defining spaces, such as Glastonbury Grove or Jack Rabbit's Palace, and the climaxes of the second and third series center on Cooper, the pioneer figure, venturing into another, wilder world. More neutral terms such as "explorer" do not fit Cooper. His motivation for moving between worlds is to redress wrongs committed in the United States, rehabilitating the world(s) of the lawless into American law. Cooper's morality seems initially unambiguous; kidnapping, rape and murder, the crimes against which he positions himself, are not morally negotiable. However, we might view these moments of frontier transgression in the light of a previous attempt by Cooper to universalize American principles of justice, crossing the border to Canada during his sting on One-Eyed Jack's. When questioned by the Canadian police about border crossing, the deaths that took place on the sting and the drug transaction, Cooper replies: "I admit to the border crossing. You already know the extent of my involvement with the killings. I hope you know me better than to suspect I'd have any part of a drug transaction" (*Twin Peaks*, Season 2, Episode 17, "Dispute Between Brothers"). Despite underplaying the severity of his actions, what is interesting is Cooper's unwillingness to excuse his interjurisdictional trespass. Earlier, he justifies it by claiming its relevance to the Laura Palmer case, not acknowledging his violation of Canadian law. Cooper is willing to impose his law beyond his jurisdiction in the interest of his concept of justice, foreshadowing his journey to the Lodge. This attitude links directly to the conquering pioneer. Although Cooper does not want to materially possess other worlds, his desire to bring an American order can be read as an attempt at civilization, an attempt which is undeniably colonial.

Cooper's personal sense of pioneering justice is inextricable from the legal system presented in the show. Upon his declaration after waking in Season 3 that "I am the FBI," the emotional peak of the show's theme tune cues up, highlighting the significance of the statement (*Twin Peaks*, Season 3, Part 16, "No Knock, No Doorbell"). Much like the opening shots of the robin, mill, waterfall, and town sign have become synonymous with *Twin Peaks* in the public imagination—and indeed neatly summarize the aesthetic of the town—the theme music suggests that this moment summarizes the essence of *Twin Peaks*. The colonial justice that Cooper attempts to enforce beyond his remit is institutionally American. Sue Lafky writes that "the evil portrayed is an individual evil that is outside of social and political structures." She argues that this is a refusal to acknowledge society's complicity in the crimes against Laura.[16] However, when viewed in racial terms, this is more pernicious. This external placement of evil is a demonization of the racial Other and an ideological universalization of American law.

Conclusion: "The evil in the woods"

The imposition of this justice onto a pseudo-indigenous enemy thus parallels patterns of colonial justice that, in the form of the Western, create much of the identity of America on film. They also parallel real colonial ideologies, which continue to play out today against indigenous people in

America. The centrality of the FBI to Cooper's quest positions the white settler as essential to the concept of America, which is set up in opposition the native-coded Other. The creation of a moral binary through the White and Black Lodge which requires the Black Lodge to be controlled by American law enforcement does not merely position white settlers as cinematic "good guys" over indigenous "bad guys," but specifically relies on the colonial imposition of settler law. Although the frontier that Cooper pioneers is a supernatural one, *Twin Peaks'* Western heritage, both in cinematography and in native-coding, racializes it. Although *Twin Peaks* critiques middle class white American identity through its depiction of the horrors lurking underneath suburbia, the refusal to recognize the non-white victims of white America, nor indeed its systemic roots in the legal system, lead to a work which, despite its critique, fundamentally upholds the values of white America. In *Twin Peaks,* White American identity is thus built on the violent exclusion of the indigenous, which can only be remedied by their forced inclusion on colonial terms.

NOTES

1. William Indick, *The Psychology of the Western: How the American Psyche Plays Out on Screen* (Jefferson, NC: McFarland, 2008), 2.

2. *Ibid.*, 16.

3. Michael Carroll, "Agent Cooper's Errand in the Wilderness: 'Twin Peaks' and American Mythology," *Literature/Film Quarterly* 21, no. 4 (1993): 291.

4. Geoff Bil, "Tensions in the World of Moon: *Twin Peaks,* Indigeneity and Territoriality," *"I'll See You in 25 Years": The Return of Twin Peaks and Television Aesthetics* 79 (2016), *Senses of Cinema,* https://www.sensesofcinema.com/2016/twin-peaks/twin-peaks-indigeneity-territoriality/.

5. Mark Frost, *The Secret History of Twin Peaks* (New York: Flatiron Books, 2016), 307.

6. Judith Butler, *Gender Trouble: Feminism and the Subversion of Identity* (New York: Routledge, 1990), 52–53.

7. Melanie McFarland, "A Colorless Sky: On the Whiteness of *Twin Peaks*," in *The Women of David Lynch: A Collection of Essays* (Columbus, OH: Fayetteville Mafia Press, 2019), 38.

8. David Canfield, "Between Two Worlds," *Slate* (May 3, 2017), accessed June 30, 2020, https://slate.com/culture/2017/05/twin-peaks-creators-david-lynch-and-mark-frosts-strange-sublime-collaboration-a-history.html.

9. Yang Kaiyuan, "Savages and Romantics: How Hollywood Soundtracks Construct Native Americans," *folio* (January 12, 2015), https://foliojournal.wordpress.com/2015/01/21/savages-and-romantics-how-hollywood-soundtracks-construct-native-americans-by-yang-kaiyuan/.

10. *Ibid.*

11. Carroll, "Agent Cooper," 291.

12. Harry M. Benshoff and Sean Griffin, *America on Film: Representing Race, Class, Gender, and Sexuality at the Movies,* 2nd ed. (Malden, MA: Wiley-Blackwell, 2009), 98.

13. John K. Howat, ed. *American Paradise: The World of the Hudson River School* (Metropolitan Museum Publications, 1987), xvii.

14. Sally J. Morgan, "The Ghost in the Luggage—Wallace and Braveheart: Post-Colonial 'Pioneer' Identities," *European Journal of Cultural Studies* 2, no. 3 (1999): 385–386.

15. Kevin Jackson, "Higher Peaks in View: The Man Who Wrote Twin Peaks Has Plans to Get Weirder. Mark Frost Talked to Kevin Jackson about Sherlock and Warlocks," *The Independent*, August 22, 1992, https://www.independent.co.uk/arts-entertainment/higher-peaks-in-view-the-man-who-wrote-twin-peaks-has-plans-to-get-weirder-mark-frost-talked-to-1541807.html.

16. Sue Lafky, "Gender, Power, and Culture in the Televisual World of *Twin Peaks*: A Feminist Critique," *Journal of Film and Video* 51, no. 3/4 (1999): 5–19.

Works Cited

Benshoff, Harry M. and Sean Griffin. 2009. *America on Film: Representing Race, Class, Gender, and Sexuality at the Movies.* Malden, MA: Wiley-Blackwell.

Bil, Geoff. 2016. "Tensions in the World of Moon: *Twin Peaks*, Indigeneity and Territoriality." *Senses of Cinema*, no. 79 (July). http://sensesofcinema.com/2016/twin-peaks/twin-peaks-indigeneity-territoriality/.

Butler, Judith. 1990. *Gender Trouble: Feminism and the Subversion of Identity.* New York: Routledge.

Canfield, David. "Between Two Worlds," *Slate* (May 3, 2017), https://slate.com/culture/2017/05/twin-peaks-creators-david-lynch-and-mark-frosts-strange-sublime-collaboration-a-history.html.

Carroll, Michael. "Agent Cooper's Errand in the Wilderness: *Twin Peaks* and American Mythology." *Literature/Film Quarterly* 21, no. 4 (1993): 291.

Frost, Mark. 2016. *The Secret History of Twin Peaks: A Novel.* New York: Flatiron Books.

Howat, John K., ed. 1987. *American Paradise: The World of the Hudson River School.* New York: Metropolitan Museum Publications.

Indick, William. 2008. *The Psychology of the Western: How the American Psyche Plays Out on Screen.* Jefferson, NC: McFarland.

Jackson, Kevin. "Higher Peaks in View: The Man Who Wrote Twin Peaks Has Plans to Get Weirder. Mark Frost Talked to Kevin Jackson about Sherlock and Warlocks." *The Independent.* (August 22, 1992). https://www.independent.co.uk/arts-entertainment/higher-peaks-in-view-the-man-who-wrote-twin-peaks-has-plans-to-get-weirder-mark-frost-talked-to-1541807.html.

Kaiyuan, Yang. "Savages and Romantics: How Hollywood Soundtracks Construct Native Americans." (January 12, 2015). https://foliojournal.wordpress.com/2015/01/21/savages-and-romantics-how-hollywood-soundtracks-construct-native-americans-by-yang-kaiyuan/.

Lafky, Sue. "Gender, Power, and Culture in the Televisual World of *Twin Peaks*: A Feminist Critique." *Journal of Film and Video* 51, no. 3/4 (1999): 5–19.

McFarland, Melanie. 2019. "A Colorless Sky: On the Whiteness of *Twin Peaks*," In Scott Ryan and David Bushman (eds.), *The Women of David Lynch: A Collection of Essays.* Columbus, OH: Fayetteville Mafia Press.

Morgan, Sally J. "The Ghost in the Luggage—Wallace and Braveheart: Post-Colonial 'Pioneer' Identities." *European Journal of Cultural Studies* 2, no. 3 (1999): 385–386.

PART III

Road Narrative and Genre

Thoughts on the American Southwest in Film and Television

An Interview with Monica Montelongo Flores

ROB E. KING

Monica Montelongo Flores teaches multiethnic American literature at California State University, Stanislaus. She has given multiple presentations on western elements in *Twin Peaks* and the films of David Lynch and includes the subject in her essay "Cowboy Accommodations: Plotting the Hotel in Western Film and Television," which appears in *A Fistful of Icons: Essays on Frontier Fixtures of the American Western*, edited by Sue Matheson for McFarland. In the following discussion, she shares her background in research and teaching the regionality of the Southwest and its portrayals in film and media. The interview reveals how David Lynch's films can appeal to multiethnic audiences and researchers, further illustrating the value of this volume in collecting current regional approaches to Lynch's films.

RK: I want to ask you about how you've engaged with David Lynch's filmography or with Twin Peaks *in your research and publications.*

MF: Very early in grad school I was interested in gender and I wanted to talk about gender—women in particular. A lot of the reasons I wanted to talk about gender was because I was a Lynch fan and very interested in the representation and intersections of gender, sexuality, you know, these discussions where it seems very clear that Lynch is trying to represent a type or types of female psyches. Then what happened was—I started thinking a lot more about the intersections of gender and race. That led me down a slightly different path during my MA program, but when I entered my doctoral program in West Texas, I became very

127

fascinated with the history, culture, landscape, theories, and mythologies of the American West and how all of that has played a role in my understanding of the world. And one of the ways that the West has played a role in my way of looking at the arts and the artists is through Lynch's work.

So, when I had the opportunity to start forming my dissertation chapters, I immediately knew I was going to have a chapter on something Lynch had done. I could not shake *Twin Peaks* for the life of me. I just felt like I needed to write something on it and then the more and more I started thinking about *Twin Peaks*, it seemed really clear all of the tropes are Western tropes, right? We have Washington—the American West; we have the northern border that replaces the southern border we typically see in Westerns, and all of that came flooding into my research. And so I gave conference presentations specifically on representations of the Great Northern, and I worked on a project that discussed mixed race identity, indigeneity, and settler colonialism and how it all works in *Twin Peaks*, and through that I could talk about this idea of dislocating the border. Lynch gives us this border that is somehow dislocated from the West—and at the same time still very much connected to it.

Lately, I've been really interested in *Wild at Heart*—I think because it has such a happy ending. It doesn't feel Lynchian because of that happy ending, and I have been interested in Lynch's romances and how Sailor and Lula's romance works differently than everyone else's in his work. From there, I started thinking about the portrayal of Texas, Texas, as this weird space that represents the American West, but also the American South. So, it kind of makes sense that all of this trauma and terror would occur in Texas in *Wild at Heart*. That's really what sparked my recent research interests in the film and where my interests are continuing to go. I think moving forward, I'll probably be working on that project, on *Wild at Heart*, for a while to see if I can find it a good home eventually.

RK: This isn't a Lynch-specific question—and maybe you already touched on some of this—but tell me more about some of your interests in the American Southwest and how you engage with film studies and the literature of the region.

MF: That's a good question. Like I said, you know, I am interested in the region, in the Southwest or the American West, because I guess as an inhabitant—of living my whole life in Texas and now in California—the interest comes from my own positionality as a Mexican American woman living in a region that is very much organized and manicured through colonial ideology. So, you know, I think my interest really comes from those internal struggles, trying to understand how all of that has had an impact on my own life, my own education and what I've been taught about the region throughout my life.

I've taught courses on the region in a couple of different ways. I've taught courses that focus specifically on the Western, a genre that mythologizes the American West, but I've also taught courses that surround the literature and creative productions that deal with the American West. And oftentimes we get really differing perspectives when we start to think about it outside of the genre-specific Western film, for example. So, my American West course probably looks different than a lot of others. I include art by Delilah Montoya and Natalie Diaz's poetry. I've included work by Willy Vlautin and of course Américo Paredes's *George Washington Gomez*. So, I mean, my American West courses do kind of become a— not a celebration of the West at all—but more so like a kind of unveiling of what the American West really looks like to people who haven't had the opportunity to talk about it in that way.

I will also say that I'm currently redecorating my office to be Southwest-themed, so, that doesn't deal with my work, but it does—in many ways, the fact that I want to surround myself with the Southwest says a lot about what the region means to me, the energy that it gives me. I have cactus bookends and all sorts of things in my office and wherever I work, because I do feel a certain kind of energy from all of that iconography. And I guess that's kind of where my head space is most of the time, either in the Southwest or in Texas, despite being in California currently.

RK: Yeah, maybe I'm taking a note from Mark Frost on this, but I recently decorated my office with an atomic café, Acid West theme in terms of Joshua Wheeler's book of essays. So, I have UFOs, a cow being abducted, and atomic bombs figurines. Have you read any of the Mark Frost's Twin Peaks *novels?*

MF: I actually have not. The last thing I read was The Secret Diary of Laura Palmer. *I actually haven't had the chance to read this new—what is it?* Secret History*? I haven't had a chance.*

RK: I'll contextualize it, and then we can form a different question. So, it's a dossier found in a murder victim's archive, an epistolary novel. And then you discover as you read the book whose archive that is. And it leads you— it hints at things maybe behind the third season, also known as The Return.

So, The Secret History *is like the secret history of America, but he is focusing on the Pacific Northwest. And so it gets into UFOs—Roswell is in there—and Jack Parsons, who created the Jet Propulsion Laboratory in California and was a big occultist. He worked with L. Ron Hubbard. They knew each other well, and there's a big story there. So, the idea is that as you wind through it, you are getting a history of the American West that no one wants to talk about—you know, Project Bluebook and how it connects to* Twin Peaks, *of course. How I thought we might engage with it is—what is the story of the West that as a native of the region you hope is told some- day through a medium like this? Is there a secret history that needs to be told whether we speak about literature or film? And is there anything out there today that satisfies your hopes for those kind of narratives?*

MF: That's a really good question. When I think that—gosh, there's so much when it comes to the American West more broadly. This is actu- ally something that I think of a lot. The secret history is, for me—who is doing all the labor in the West? Who are the people that are really keep- ing this whole thing running, right? And by that, I don't mean at all peo- ple in power; I mean people who literally wake up at 4:00 in the morning, are out the door at 5:00 and don't come home until after the sunset. They're tired and exhausted, and no one respects them or values them. And a lot of those histories are from undocumented workers or even documented workers. In California, the undocumented farm workers put food on everyone's tables, the entire nation, the entire world. And they do not pro- vide them with an ounce of dignity, and they don't value their labor or their lives that, you know—in terms of historically what we talk about. We don't get to—we hear about those in power, but we don't hear about those that are really making everything run. And so, for me, those stories are really important. And then, of course, when I think about reasons—I'm from the Rio Grande Valley (RGV), and I have seen little to no represen- tation, which is strange because we are a pretty significant population in Texas. We are not sparsely populated, you know, and I say "we," but I don't live there anymore, though I still consider myself a resident of the Rio Grande Valley. But there's something about that region being invisible nationally. We are invisible nationally. And a large part of the reason we are invisible nationally is because it's a bunch of Mexicans. We are a bunch of Mexicans—some of us born here, some of us not; some documented, some not. And, you know, the fact that we are so invisible nationally shows just exactly where our national values are.

So, that's always been one of the secret histories that I feel needs to be kind of uncovered and given a chance to be celebrated in some ways, and the literature and film of those areas now—let me just say—the literature of the RGV does not get as much attention as it deserves. There are a lot of artists and writers that come out of there, but we don't see them quite as often, as, you know—I would say people from maybe bigger cities—Aus- tin, San Antonio, etc. But some of the things that give me hope for these kinds of narratives to get out are writing communities, academic commu- nities, and artists' communities talking more and more about each other's work. That brings hope. But really, you don't get that kind of recognition, or you don't get that kind of representation until you have something that is really mainstream, like a mainstream television show or really mainstream film unfortunately.

You know, as of right now, I can't think of a mainstream film or television show that deals with the RGV. We definitely lack representation. So, that would be something I'd be interested in seeing. Then, of course, there are a lot that represent the U.S.-Mexico border. I guess it was—I can't remember—seven, eight years ago—they had that show, *The Bridge*, which is about the El Paso-Juarez border. But, you know, the problem with that show and shows that try to represent the border is that it's always violent. And the people there are always degenerates. They're always violent, to the point where it's not a livable area, in that show—there's nothing livable about that place. That show made you feel sorry for El Paso and people who live in El Paso and Juarez. And it didn't provide any kind of representation of the various people and cultures that live there and how they live daily. And so that's kind of the other thing—when you ask for representation of the RGV—well, what's the show going to be? Is it going to be a bunch of, you know, Border Patrol agents? Is that what we're going to be seeing when we get finally get representation? Like, what exactly is it? And so, trusting someone with your story is important, right? And I don't know if we— again, speaking as if I live in the RGV, and I don't any more—I don't know if we really have anyone in mainstream television or film that we could trust.

RK: Right, I see that. I ask you that because you get to teach about the Southwest. You are hearing what students are writing and reading about—their personal stories. When I wrote my article for New American Notes Online, *for the special issue on* Twin Peaks: The Return, *I started to hint at it, and I didn't quite know where to go—in this book, whether we were going to talk Jack Parsons from* The Secret History, *if we were to look at the idea of the nuclear explosion that we see in Part 8 of that third season as representing a broader story about the region—so, there was the Trinity Test explosion, and in* Twin Peaks *that opens kind of a Pandora's box, perhaps an origin for evil—the evil that men do, perhaps. Well, the other side of that story includes the down-winders, those people on the land. You begin to research it and try to understand that narrative. Well, very quickly, you're tied back to the land, I think.*

MF: Yes, completely. I think trauma is central in Lynch's work and so it makes sense that the impacts of that evil are essential to his narratives about the American West.

RK: So, I was looking at these ideas. If we're talking Jack Parsons's occultism and California and the sex magic rituals out in the New Mexico desert, as Frost's book suggests—I began to say, well, what about the region and the people? We have a BOB in the Pacific Northwest representing something old out in the woods, but there is an opportunity here. There is, you know—the show comes back to Odessa, Texas—West Texas. Now, we're in New Mexico. And I have this wonderful volume here, Brujerias: Stories of Witchcraft and the Supernatural in the American Southwest and Beyond. *And it's a book of oral histories from people about stories they heard from their grandparents or parents, stories that they wanted to preserve. And I think there is a fascinating opportunity, especially in your studies and what you hear, you know—there is something there, and it's about spirituality on The Plains, and it doesn't have to be evil on The Plains. You could certainly have fun with that, I think.*

So, I was just curious. I'm going to ask one more question. In your essay "Cowboy Accommodations: Plotting the Hotel in Western Film and Television," you write that "Co-creators David Lynch and Mark Frost relocate the typified Western location and landscape to the Northwestern US-Canada border, reuse the conventionalized tropes of the sheriff and Indian tracker, and merge urban and rural settings in the series." While this essay is a few years old now, can you elaborate on that—how you see The Great Northern in this post-modern western setting and perhaps how you see it now that Season 3 has aired?

MF: That article was my favorite to write. You know, it was essentially a film history survey of all of these films, including television series, how the hotel and accommodations associated with travel are used. The one thing that I point out in the chapter that I thought was really important about the Great Northern is it does merge urban and rural settings. Also, something that I talked about is that it merges the natural and the supernatural because we have the abundance of wood everywhere, right? Everything reminds us of our setting—that majestic Northwest with its grand trees—and really spooky spaces out in the woods. We have all this beautiful wood and, you know, all of these references to the nature that's surrounding the Great Northern inside. It is meant to look very much like a lodge—maybe even hinting at the masonic, something we see in the black and white flooring of the red room—reminding us of the natural world, but supernatural things occur there. And to me, it really was in Season 3— so, we see it in little moments with the electricity, the noise, the spooky sounds of electrical energy that Lynch loves to use. That all informs our suspicion that the Great Northern is this really important space, right? That, to me, confirms it. And all of the energy, all of the energy that the Great Northern had in seasons one and two, in some ways are missing from that space. I feel like in season three the Great Northern has been zapped of energy. It was empty in some way—maybe more like it's sleeping, and the presence of those sounds, the energy of electricity, it tells me that more is to come, like something's bubbling up underneath that. And that's something I'm going to keep an eye out for moving forward.

The one thing I'm saying is, I think, in terms of the post-modern—what is the commentary the Great Northern is making about the American West? And what are our expectations, our expectations when we go to a place like the Great Northern? Season 1 and Season 2, that was 1990 to '92, right? Our expectations thirty years ago were that we were going to be pampered to some degree because the Great Northern is a resort that is definitely not the motels we see Ben and Catherine having an affair in or that Laura and Ronette use, right? The Great Northern represents a class. It represents the supernatural. And the one thing I would say moving forward is we need to look at how Season 3 continues to represent an abundance of travel iconography used throughout the series. The idea of being mobile and travel itself is very colonial, right? Travel itself, the idea of traveling and going somewhere, location and tourism, things like that—it's all colonialism; it comes from a colonial approach and ideologies.

I have noticed that in season three, that kind of travel iconography continues to comes up. We have gas stations and more use of the road, right? So, I think something I would add when looking back on that part of the article, is that I now see the energy—colonial energies—from the Great Northern, all the energy the Great Northern represented earlier in the series, has kind of exploded in season three and it is spread out differently over that season. The Great Northern may be sleeping, but everything—everywhere—else is awake. That's where my mind was during my first viewing of it. That's where my mind is when I think about that particular space, which is my absolute favorite space in the whole series. I was a big fan of *The Shining*, and so creepy hotels have always been an interest for me. I was always drawn to those sites.

RK: Just clarifying, you talked about travel having a colonial aspect, in the sense of conquest? Like expansionism, or in terms of class?

MF: Well, you know, travel—put it this way. When you think about the way Western towns are set—and let's think about them historically, but also think about them in terms of mythology, right—like film mythology, how films have portrayed them. There is some truth in those portrayals, where a Western town really isn't a "place"—at least in colonial thinking—until it has a hotel. The hotel allows people to come to town. It allows for lodging, and it attracts folks to it for whatever—business, what have you—some sort of visitation. And so, the settling of the American West and the erasure of the people and place it was before colonial contact is completely wrapped up in the kind of accommodations that were established. There are some great scholars on hotels and motels and travel, and they really helped me understand that all of this kind of travel iconography, tourism, all of it was evidence of colonialism, and what it suggested was—okay, now we have a hotel, now we have a place to live, at least temporarily, now this land has become a place—our place. Before that, it wasn't, it was considered to be just space, right? It was this space that the nation was forming into something. And the deception there is that it always was a place, right? So, yeah, the Great Northern is a giant symbol of that idea, that the West has become a place through colonialism. And then, you know, you are reminded again that it was always a place by all of the indigenous art and artifacts throughout the hotel.

RK: Right, well, thank you so much for doing this. Your perspective on region in film and literature studies adds to this collection's acknowledgment of place and how scholars use Lynch's imagery to discuss it. That's valuable, and I appreciate it.

Once Upon a Time in Rancho Rosa

Reading Twin Peaks *Season 3 as a Neo-Western*

Franck Boulègue *and* Marisa C. Hayes

Introduction: Going Rogue in the Wild, Wild West

During the span of time that elapsed between Seasons 2 and 3 of *Twin Peaks*, a process of "untaming" appears to have taken place in the series. Arguably, this can be attributed to BOB and Joudy's influence, resulting in increased violence that is reminiscent of the lawlessness found in representations of the American Old West. One need only recall the myriad ways in which Mr. C sows mayhem and destruction in his wake to conjure the image of a Western outlaw, sparking fear as he moves from town to town. It appears indeed to be "a dark, dark age," as the character Janey-E asserts in Las Vegas (Season 3, Part 6), one in which "digging yourself out of the shit" with one of Doctor Jacoby's specially-designed shovels becomes a psycho-spiritual gold rush for characters such as Nadine. This essay proposes to analyze Season 3 of *Twin Peaks* through the prism of Western films, specifically their iconic geography, character types, and motifs in order to explore how co-creators Mark Frost and David Lynch have transposed and appropriated them, often using the Western to frame their deep-rooted interests in spirituality and mythology. While the Western no longer dominates screens today, its images and narrative tropes were essential cultural currency throughout much of the twentieth century—including Frost and Lynch's formative years—via radio, television, novels, painting and film. For the uninitiated, the third season of *Twin Peaks* may seem an unlikely candidate for the Western genre, yet Frost and Lynch's eighteen-part "limited event series" is exemplary of the *neo-Western*, that is revisiting the Western with "fresh eyes, offering different viewpoints and giving it a contemporary update."[1]

As Stephen Aron notes in *The American West*, "Beginning with the

1903 movie *The Great Train Robbery*, Westerns dominated American cinema for a good part of the twentieth century."[2] The intertextuality that permeates Frost and Lynch's third season of *Twin Peaks* facilitates this transposition of the Western within a contemporary context.[3] Various tropes of the genre become a vehicle for the spiritual preoccupations of the show's creators, while generationally, both Frost and Lynch witnessed the golden era of Western cinema, leaving its mark on their respective writing and visual practices. During the 1950s, the era in which Lynch and Frost grew up, the Western genre was revered and represented a vital force in popular culture.[4] The ascendency of the Western was already notable by the 1920s, when half of the film productions at major Hollywood studios, including Universal, were Westerns. This popularity endured and flourished during the post-war period with successful titles such as *Red River* (1948), *High Noon* (1952), *Shane* (1953), and *The Searchers* (1956). Westerns also proliferated on television, a fact that resonates with *Twin Peaks* and its connections to the genre. "By 1958–59, 8 of the Top 10 [television] shows were westerns; a year later there were 48 Westerns on television, including 30 in prime time."[5] The codes of the Western reflect the dual nature of the *Twin Peaks* television series that is both rooted in the present and a vintage mythology of the 1950s.

While many of the stories and landscapes featured in the Western genre are inspired by historical events, they are hybrid constructions that merge fictionalized towns with physical landscapes, and historical figures with legendary accounts. As a result, they weave documented facts and screen mythology into distinct representations of an imaginary West. In *Focus on the Western*, Jack Nachbar asserts that "The 'real' West is only the physical environment of Western movies; at their heart Westerns present the 'idea' of the West, history not as it in fact occurred but how it is imagined to have occurred."[6] The genre's depiction of an imaginary West invites a literary analysis of character types, narrative themes, and structure. Additionally, the mythic geography of the American West stimulates a strong response in relation to place, from the arid depictions of the South to the densely forested woodlands of the North, where upon first encounter in the pilot episode, Cooper exclaims, "Man, smell those trees! Smell those Douglas Firs!"

Ooh, Las Vegas: Truth Is a Pathless Land

The vast majority of *Twin Peaks* Season 3 is set west of the Mississippi River, the subject of the song, "Mississippi," performed by the Cactus Blossoms in Part 3. Moreover, most of the season's locations from South

Dakota to Texas are strongly associated with the mythos of the American West, as depicted in Western films and serials of the twentieth century. Featured prominently throughout the season, the fictional town of Buckhorn is set in the Black Hills of South Dakota near the real town of Deadwood, celebrated for the presence of gunslingers Wild Bill Hickok and Calamity Jane, among others.[7] The South Dakota Black Hills were an important center for gold prospecting and many outlaws found their way to this area, leaving a trail of death and destruction in their wake. Other settings that are significant in both classic Westerns and the third season of *Twin Peaks* include present-day Texas, Nevada, and Washington.[8] These states are associated with historical events that have become mythologized within the Western canon, including Lewis and Clark's expedition to the Pacific Northwest. The celebrated explorers' "Corps of Discovery" plays a key role in Frost's book, *The Secret History of Twin Peaks*, which like the Western seamlessly interweaves historical fact and fiction.[9]

Why this setting? Traditionally, identifying the East (where the sun rises) is the first step in navigating the four cardinal directions. While Season 3 does feature locations in the Eastern United States (New York and Philadelphia) and abroad (Buenos Aires and Paris), the majority of the plot is scattered across various state lines in the vast American West. This lack of orientation represents a striking departure from the focus on the town of Twin Peaks in the first two seasons of the series and establishes an important framework for Cooper's quest to return to the Washington locale and his fully integrated self. In addition to providing this crucial plot function, the American West provides an equally salient context for exploring the forces of good and evil. This recurring theme in Frost and Lynch's work is exemplified in the confrontation with BOB at the Twin Peaks Sheriff's Station in Part 17, a showdown akin to the archetypal denouement that has come to define the Western genre in which a "conflict of good and bad is a duel between two men."[10] Geography plays an important role in these carefully choreographed confrontations because their anticipation depends upon at least two characters from divergent locations who finally collide at the same destination.

In Westerns, this showdown is systemically preceded by travel that provides sweeping images of the local geography, doubling as both narrative advancement and metaphor for the character's inner nature. Mr. C, Cooper's evil doppelgänger, is often on the move, featured in harsh landscapes. When he does visit domestic dwellings, such as Buella's cabin and a rural farmhouse where Hutch and Chantal have murdered the owners, they are rustic, isolated places where base violence is often a way of life. Further traces of these landscapes in the form of dirt and grease on Mr. C's skin create sensorial ties to the elemental nature of these locations. The deserted setting of the Rancho Rosa housing development in Nevada also signifies Cooper's loss of identity and purpose when he embodies Dougie. Rancho Rosa, as Frost confirms, can be understood as a contemporary ghost town, a subject explored at greater length in Rob King's essay "The Horse is the White of the Eye: Pioneering and the American Southwest in *Twin Peaks*."[11]

Intertextual references of a spiritual nature are also of key importance in relation to the geographic expansion of Season 3. The West represents the direction of justice and truth in numerous Eastern spiritual traditions, of which Lynch is a follower through his dedicated Transcendental Meditation practice (including its related Vedic scriptures), and in which Frost has consistently demonstrated a strong interest.[12] For example, Frost's forthcoming book will be focused on the life of Indian philosopher and religious guru, J. Krishnamurti, whose 1929 assertion that "Truth is a pathless land," represents the core of his teachings.[13] The circumvented journey from Las Vegas to Texas that Cooper undertakes in order to fully awaken and find Laura Palmer resonates with Krishnamurti's claim. The barren landscapes featured in Nevada and Texas along the way, as well as the thick forests of the Northwest, can be symbolically understood as the Unconscious in contrast to the urban development of the domesticated East (the Ego),[14] providing a fitting backdrop for Cooper's topsy-turvy quest.

Not unlike the enlightenment described in Vedic and Buddhist traditions, the American West, inhabited by denizens ranging from pioneers to hippies, has been represented as a place of individual liberation and opportunity. If both spiritual enlightenment and ideals of freedom are westward bound, the geography of the American West is perfectly positioned, both physically and symbolically, to stage Cooper's confrontation with evil and his attempts to set the world (and time) to rights again.[15] In this regard, it is natural to ask why the West, associated with spiritual idealism, is also a stage for negative and destructive events, including the action that unfolds in Part 8.

The Trinity Test explosion is depicted as the origin of evil in *Twin Peaks*[16] The duality central to Vedic spirituality proposes that good cannot exist without evil, that one would not recognize the light without knowing darkness. Lynch returns regularly to this notion of balance in his work, reflected most explicitly in the character development depicted during Season 3.[17] In Jungian terms, it may even be argued that Cooper, Mr. C, and Dougie are all various facets of the same individual who has become fractured and must return to a unified, or balanced, self.[18] As a wise Belle in the film *I Killed Wild Bill Hickok* remarks, "There is a time for fighting, a time for peace."[19] The Western has always relied on both do-gooders and outlaws to maintain this delicate balance, or as Lynch says "there's always been the very, very good, and the very, very bad swimming in the same sea. And it's just a question of balance."[20]

Character Types and Iconic Establishment: The Good, the Bad and the Dougie

Riffing on Sergio Leone's celebrated Western, *The Good, the Bad and the Ugly* (1966), Showtime released an official t-shirt that appropriates the film's iconic triptych of characters to reference the trio of doppelgängers portrayed by Kyle McLachlan throughout Season 3.[21] Cooper, Mr. C, and Dougie correspond to an important social order established in most Westerns. The notion of good defeating evil is deeply rooted in the Western as an extension of Christian morality, or what Nachbar refers to as the need for a Christ-like figure capable of surviving the harsh environment of the American desert: "American heroes have a long tradition of serving as the Redeemer.... If the land was to be settled, it had to be tamed and purified.... The lawlessness of the frontier required a strong sense of divine justice."[22]

When in full possession of himself, Cooper embodies this role, not only applying his authority as an FBI agent but also by using less orthodox methods that include intuition and spiritual wisdom. Mr. C, his violent look-alike, is depicted as a desperado, an archetypal outlaw from the Old West. Cooper and his evil double are costumed according to their moral opposition, a code omnipresent in the Western genre. Nachbar notes, "The good guy wears clean, well-pressed clothes.... The villain dressed sloppily."[23] Mr. C wears cowboy boots, a leather jacket, and an untucked shirt. Combining "nature and artifice," this dress created from animal skins is "adapted to the needs of the wilderness" and underscores "the mediating role of the hero between civilization and savagery."[24] Cooper in his elegant "I am the FBI" suit literally represents order in contrast to Mr. C's disheveled lawlessness. Dougie, with his outdated hair and odd wardrobe (that lime green blazer!) is the entertainingly oafish "ugly" to complete the Leone trio.

Because Westerns often depict settlements and towns under construction, ensemble casts, such as that of *Twin Peaks*, feature numerous smaller roles for allies and townsfolk, the latter of whom position themselves on the side of good or bad. Too numerous to mention in their entirety, some featured in Season 3 include Doctor Jacoby and Nadine, both of whom espouse the former's mantra, "Dig yourself out of the shit!," in order to improve their lives and better society, and Norma, who nurtures the community and holds her own miniature showdown against Walter, the businessman who favors profits over quality while franchising her beloved Double R pies.[25] Ben Horne continues to redeem himself through good deeds, despite the challenges of his dysfunctional family, particularly his outlaw grandson, Richard. In Western terms, Richard is comparable to the "young gun," a junior gunslinger compared to the older and more experienced outlaw, Mr. C. Carl Rodd is depicted as an elderly cowboy who strums a soulful rendition of "Red River Valley" on his guitar and looks out for his neighbors with a compassionate eye.[26] In Las Vegas, where a not-yet-awakened Cooper is masquerading as Dougie Jones, his faithful allies include: Janey-E, who sends a pair of loan sharks packing; Bushnell Mullins, who attempts to unravel the truth behind the fraud at his Lucky 7 insurance firm; and the Mitchum Brothers, who represent the transformation of archetypal villains turned good.

Many of these characters are associated with prominent establishments featured in the Western genre, particularly the casino and the saloon. The former is most obvious via the action that transpires at the Silver Mustang Casino owned by the Mitchum Brothers, who are surrounded by Candy and an entourage of pink-clad young women akin to saloon ladies. The latter are women who were traditionally tasked with brightening the drinking and gambling environment, but have also been associated with prostitution. While the neon gun of the Bang Bang Bar, also known in Twin Peaks as the Roadhouse, evokes images of the gunfights that transpire in Western saloons, the Double R Diner can also be viewed as a modern adaptation of the saloon. Like saloons depicted in Westerns, the Double R is a local watering hole run by a recognizable personality and fulfills an important social function in the town. Just as cowboys and townsfolk meet at the saloon to satiate their thirst for alcohol and news, residents of Twin Peaks come to stimulate their senses with Norma's pies and coffee while sharing the latest gossip. Hotels represent another prominent fixture in Westerns, where the newly-arrived mingle with the locals, creating narrative tension and story arcs. In Season 3, Cooper's room at the Great Northern continues to play a key role in the *Twin Peaks* narrative.

The local sheriff and his jail are another hallmark of the Western genre. At times portrayed as doltish (*Pardners*, 1956) or corrupt (*I Killed Wild Bill Hickok*, 1956), the sheriff may also double as the hero (*High Noon*, 1952), or serve as an important ally for the outsider hero (*Rio Bravo*, 1959). Sheriff Truman of Season 3 (the "new sheriff in town") falls into the latter category. His light-colored cowboy hat and attitude resemble Randolph Scott's character, a righteous sheriff in *Seven Men from Now* (1956). By placing his trust in Cooper, Sheriff Truman provides the hero with the necessary agency to prevail in the fight against dark forces. Earlier in the season, when Cooper is still living Dougie's life in Las Vegas, his child-like attraction to a policeman's badge reflects the fetishized sheriff's star of classic Westerns. Dougie's tactile fascination with this object is illustrated on two separate occasions, underscoring not only his true nature that desires to be a force for order and good, but also recalling his strong association with the Twin Peaks Sheriff's Station, particularly Sheriff Truman of Seasons 1 and 2 (who deputized him) and other officers, such as Andy and Hawk.

Of all the aforementioned Western character types, one of the most striking contrasts between them that resonates strongly in Season 3 of *Twin Peaks* is the distinction between the supporting cast of characters, the settlers; and the outlaw/hero, the drifters: "The townspeople are static and largely incapable of movement, beyond their little settlement. The outlaws or savages can move freely across the landscape. The hero, though a friend of the townspeople, has the lawless power of movement."[27] In John Ford's *The Searchers*, John Wayne portrays Ethan, a character who travels many miles across the landscape of Monument Valley to locate an abducted woman and return her to her family. When he finally succeeds, home is no longer the same and he sets off again.[28] Similarly, Cooper appears doomed to wander, driven by an internal force that propels him continually to embark upon a new quest, even when one showdown has been successful. Perpetually seeking to restore balance by bringing Laura Palmer back home, Cooper is a pioneer of multiple frontiers, crossing diverse geographies and timelines to do so.

Eternal Returns: Western Themes and Mythology

Some studies in popular culture contend that the roots of the Western originate with Homer, a heritage that feels pertinent in the case of *Twin Peaks*' third season.[29] Mark Frost has been particularly forthcoming about its links to *The Odyssey*, reflected in Cooper's epic journey back to Twin Peaks and to himself.[30] Discussing the dramatic origins of the Western, Kathryn C. Esselman underlines the importance of the quest to the genre.[31] Beyond the pioneering spirit that characterizes the mythos of the West, many of the genre's films and serials are constructed around a protagonist who leaves home and then struggles to return after having fought a battle, be it personal or collective. Combining physical threats with metaphysical angst, the odyssey of Cooper's many manifestations contain striking parallels to those of the Western.

As previously mentioned, *The Searchers* depicts multiple quests and returns: a soldier's homecoming at the end of the Civil War; his departure in search of Debbie, a young woman abducted by the Comanches; and his final departure. While Texas has become far more peaceful during Ethan's absence, he no longer has a family of his own, and as a result the cyclical search continues. In *The Dakota Incident* (1956), a bank robber is shot and left for dead in the desert, only to appear in town shortly afterwards. This unexpected resurrection mirrors Mr. C's reappearance at "The Farm." Although Ray shot Cooper's evil double multiple times in an isolated clearing off the road, the supernatural Woodsmen perform a ritual that precipitates his return to the realm of the living. While supernatural elements are not a common trait of the Western genre, trickery, illusions, and dumb luck (in the case of *The Dakota Incident*) fulfill similar plot devices in numerous Westerns.

The gold rush of the American West was a real-life quest to attain prosperity and a new life that "multiplied the number of migrants and altered their destination, their composition, and their ambition. In 1849 and during the next decade, the vast majority of overland travelers went to California."[32] Unsurprisingly, silver and gold are recurring themes in the Western genre, reflected in films such as *The Treasure of the Sierra Madre* (1948), *Seven Cities of Gold* (1955), and *The Lone Ranger and the Lost City of Gold* (1958). In Season 3 this lust for wealth and its negative consequences are underscored in scenes at the Silver Mustang Casino, where somber depictions of income inequality and excessive wealth are brought to the fore. Cooper as Dougie strikes it rich, while an elderly and disheveled character named Lady Slot-Addict stands by in frustration. Until he provides her with a supernatural tip that allows her to cash in her own mega jackpot, Lady Slot-Addict, who suffers from malnutrition and poor hygiene, is visibly jealous of Cooper's good fortune. Similar themes can be traced throughout various Westerns that focus on the search for precious metals, resulting in murder, betrayal, and gross inequalities. The question of who has access to riches and how they are distributed is a theme developed in Season 3, memorably underscored during Janey-E's scolding of two Las Vegas loan sharks. This reflects an interest in the 2008 financial crisis and a leftward leaning political outlook that both Frost and Lynch share. Based on interviews and social media posts, one can observe how the Western framework serves to advance their opinions regarding the socio-political climate in present-day America and a "lawlessness" or injustices that they see as harmful and off balance.[33]

While the above references to gold focus on external wealth, it should be noted that gold also serves a positive purpose in Season 3 that continues to reference the Western gold rush through one of its most iconic tools, the shovel. Symbolically turning shit to gold, Doctor Jacoby promises a gold rush of the psycho-spiritual variety to prospective miners, including Nadine and other followers of his podcast. Under the name of his alter-ego, Doctor Amp, he focuses on inner wealth, advising listeners to shovel their way "out of the shit and into the truth." Preaching the ideals of self-empowerment and independence worthy of any pioneer, Doctor Amp shares a message that reflects the ideals that propelled Frost and Lynch outside mainstream conventions, investing in deeper truths and a quest for the freedom to tell stories that matter. As Lynch would say, "if you want to catch the big fish, you've got to go deeper."[34]

Conclusion: Sinking Suns in Every Town

The setting sun is an archetypal image found at the close of many classic Westerns. Evil has been defeated, the work is done, and a new day dawns. The etymological root of the word "West" in relation to evening and night is well documented, and the overall movement of *Twin Peaks* Season 3 transitions from morning to night, from the opening scene of Doctor Jacoby receiving his delivery of shovels to Cooper/Richard and Laura/Carrie's return to Twin Peaks.[35] The West is, after all, the direction opposite that of the Earth's rotation on its axis. It can be argued that the eighteen parts in Season 3 are really one long cosmological day underscored by the season's cyclical nature, akin to those of the aforementioned Westerns, most notably *The Searchers*. Cooper and Laura are searchers and will remain so until they complete their spiritual quests.

Although not overtly and not solely a neo-Western, the third season of *Twin Peaks* follows the codes and ideals of the classic Western more so than any revisionist Western. The Manichean distinction between right and wrong remains strong in Season 3. While heroes and villains (the many doppelgängers) appear similar on the surface, their resemblance is only skin deep: "For generations, popular entertainment made it easy to explain violence by neatly distinguishing between good guys and bad and by seeing the 'Wild West' as a clash between civilization and savagery, between law and disorder. Recent scholarship has accented broader social, economic, and political causes."[36]

Several subjects related to the Western genre and *Twin Peaks* merit further exploration that fall beyond the scope of this essay, particularly representations of Native Americans and the character of Hawk, the symbolism of horses, the railroad, gun violence, country western music, and the American frontier.[37] There is also a strong argument that Season 3 is in many ways reminiscent of the Acid Western tradition, exemplified by films such as *El Topo* (1970), *Dead Man* (1995), or *Blueberry* (2004). Elements featured throughout Season 3, including a Jungian spiritual quest, dreams, hallucinogenic drugs, and the supernatural, are all traits of this subgenre.

An additional reading of the Western's importance in Season 3 can be found in relationship to dreams and a possible response to Monica Bellucci's question, "Who is the dreamer?" The only person caught in the actual state of dreaming happens to be Sarah Palmer in Part 8.[38] The year is 1956, and after the Frogmoth enters her mouth, the closing credits of the episode depict her sleeping, with rapid eye movements indicative of paradoxical sleep and dreaming. If she is indeed *the* dreamer, arguably the zeitgeist of 1956 is marked by the omnipresence of Westerns, occupying a crucial role in the texture of her dream.

The Western has provided Frost and Lynch with important building blocks upon which a compelling and multilayered eighteen-part quest emerged, drawing on the genre's mythic archetypes and spiritual odysseys. Although the peak of the Western film has passed, the culture of the American West, whether real or imagined, is deeply embedded in the American dream and continues to resonate in the present. Has westward expansion only caused further displacement and sorrow? Frost and Lynch's explorations of the Western's mythology seems to suggest it, as Frost recently noted, "There are untold consequences that attend every act of hubris, and that's where we ended up with our ending."[39]

NOTES

1. A definition of the neo-western outlined in the video essay "The Neo-Western Genre in Movies" on the "Screened" YouTube channel: https://www.youtube.com/watch?v=qLxLLmy5Su4 (April 15, 2020).

2. Stephen Aron, *The American West* (Oxford: Oxford University Press, 2015), 110.

3. Graham Allen, *Intertextuality* (Routledge, 2000), 1. Allen writes, "Texts, whether they be literary or non-literary, are viewed by modern theorists as lacking in any kind of independent meaning. They are what theorists now call intertextual.... Reading thus becomes a process of moving between texts. Meaning becomes something which exists between a text and all the other texts to which it refers and relates, moving out from the independent text into a network of textual relations. The text becomes the intertext." In addition to the Western, another example of intertextuality includes Frost's acknowledgement that Homer's *The Odyssey* was influential regarding Cooper's quest to return to Twin Peaks in Season 3.

4. Lynch was born in 1946 and Frost in 1953.

5. Thomas Schatz, "Cowboy Business," *New York Times Magazine*, accessed March 1, 2020, https://www.nytimes.com/2007/11/10/magazine/11schatz.html.

6. *Focus on the Western*, ed. Jack Nachbar (Eaglewood Cliffs: Prentice Hall, 1974), 4.

7. For an example of how Deadwood became mythologized in contemporary screen culture, see: *Deadwood*, David Milch, et al., HBO, 2004–2006 (television), 2019 (movie); The Black Hills region and its residents inspired numerous Westerns of the mid-20th century, including *The Badlands of Dakota* (1951), *Calamity Jane* (1953), *I Killed Wild Bill Hickok* (1956), and the earlier Western serial *The Great Adventures of Wild Bill Hickok* (1938), to cite only a few.

8. See: *The Westerner* (1940), *Sheriff of Las Vegas* (1944), *Heldorado* (1946), *Night Time in Nevada* (1948), *Carson City* (1952), *City of Bad Men* (1953), and *The Yellow Mountain* (1954), among others.

9. Including *The Northwest Passage* (1940), *The Oregon Passage* (1957), and *The Way West* (1967); Mark Frost, *The Secret History of* Twin Peaks (New York: Flatiron Books, 2016). Even within Frost's expanded narrative of *The Secret History of* Twin Peaks, he further develops intertextual references related to the Western and blurs the lines between fiction and reality through the inclusion of real novels that are said to be the Bookhouse Boys' favorites. These include Wallace Stegner's *Angle of Repose* (1971), described as "an iconic novel of the West" on its back cover. Stephen King's *The Stand* (1978), featured on the same book list, contains scenes set in Las Vegas. One of the novel's protagonists hallucinates that Las Vegas is Cibola, one of the mythic "Seven Cities of Gold." The list also includes Robert M. Pirsig's *Zen and the Art of the Motorcycle Maintenance* (1974), a philosophical motorcycle trip across the American Northwest.

10. Robert Warshaw, "Movie Chronicle: The Westerner," in *Focus on the Western*, ed. Nachbar (Englewood Cliffs, N.J.: Prentice-Hall, 1974), 54.

11. Rob King, "The Horse is the White of the Eye: Pioneering and the American Southwest in *Twin Peaks*," *NANO*, accessed March 1, 2020, https://nanocrit.com/issues/issue15/The-Horse-is-the-White-of-the-Eye-Pioneering-and-the-American-Southwest-in-Twin-Peaks; Bushman, David, *Conversations with Mark Frost:* Twin Peaks, Hill Street Blues, *and the Education of a Writer* (Columbus, Ohio: Fayetteville Mafia Press, 2020), 249.

12. Veruda is the deity of the West in Hinduism, associated with justice and truth; Vedic texts are religious texts from ancient India that are central to Hinduism, as well as additional religious and spiritual practices in the Indo-Iranian region; References to Hinduism and Vedic scriptures are recurrent in Frost's fiction, including his *Paladin Prophecy* Trilogy (Random House, 2012–present), in addition to theosophical beliefs (a spiritual movement that appropriated numerous ideas from Vedic traditions).

13. Bushman, 171; Krishnamurti, "The Core of the Teachings," *J. Krishnamurti*, accessed March 1, 2020, https://jkrishnamurti.org/about-core-teachings.

14. In his book, *The Uses of Enchantment: The Meaning and Importance of Fairy Tales*, Bruno Bettelheim writes, "Since ancient times the near impenetrable forest in which we get lost has symbolized the dark, hidden, near-impenetrable world of our unconscious" (Penguin, 1991, p. 33). The desert is often represented as a place of Jungian individuation, or self-development, out of the unconscious landscape, as Joseph Campbell advances by citing comparative religious and mythological examples in the 1988 television documentary *The Power of Myth*, particularly episodes "Myth and the Modern World" and "The Hero's Adventure" (PBS).

15. Another theme that resonates with Vedic scripture in terms of cycles and rebirth, or as the script of *Twin Peaks* notes, "The past dictates the future" (Season 3, Part 17).

16. Note that the Trinity Test is the oldest historic event depicted in the series and that BOB, the series' physical representation of evil, is ejected from the experiment's mouth following the explosion. The sequence is filmed in black and white, further illustrating the interdependence of light/darkness or good/evil outlined in the spiritual traditions studied by Frost and Lynch.

17. *Twin Peaks*, "Slaves and Masters," Episode 22, Season 2, David Lynch, et al., February 9, 1991. In the Log Lady's introduction to the episode, she states: "Balance is the key. Balance is the key to many things. Do we understand balance? The word 'balance' has seven letters. Seven is difficult to balance, but not impossible—we are able to divide. There are, of course, the pros and cons of division."

18. Carl Jung, *The Complete Works of Carl Jung*, "Psychology and Alchemy," vol. 12 (Princeton: Princeton University Press, 1968). Jung's concept of individuation that influenced the development of analytical psychology asserts that the components of one's personality and experiences become, if integrated successfully, a well-balanced whole. Frost has confirmed that he is a Jungian and comments on this aspect of Cooper's storyline. See: Chris O'Falt, "'Twin Peaks': Mark Frost Takes Us Inside the Four-Year Process of Writing a 500-Page Script Over Skype With David Lynch," *Indie Wire*, accessed March 1, 2020,

https://www.indiewire.com/2018/06/twin-peaks-the-return-mark-frost-david-lynch-writing-collaboration-1201975099/.

19. Richard Talmadge, *I Killed Wild Bill Hickock* (June 16, 1956), film.

20. David Lynch, "The Interfaith Voices/David Lynch Interview," SoundCloud audio, 38 minutes (November 2016), podcast. https://soundcloud.com/listeninspired/the-interfaith-voicesdavid-lynch-interview-uncut.

21. The design was fan-made by Pescapin and available for a limited time on Showtime's official merchandise website.

22. Michael T. Marsden, "Savior in the Saddle: The Sagebrush Testament," in *Focus on the Western*, ed. Nachbar (Englewood Cliffs, NJ: Prentice-Hall, 1974), 94–95.

23. J. G. Cawelti, "Savagery, Civilization, and the Western Hero," in *Focus on the Western*, ed. Nachbar (Englewood Cliffs, NJ: Prentice-Hall, 1974), 61.

24. *Ibid.*, 62.

25. The name of the Double R Diner in Twin Peaks is a reference to the railroad, whose tracks are located nearby. Rancho Rosa is another use of double R letters in season three. This is noteworthy because Western ranches and the Transcontinental Railroad were linked intrinsically through mutual business interests: the transportation of cattle. Both cattle and railroads were formative symbols in the American vision of the West that grew out of the post–Civil War period.

26. The role is played by Harry Dean Stanton, who, in addition to other collaborations with Lynch, portrayed Slim, a ranch foreman in Lynch's short film *The Cowboy and the Frenchman* in 1987. Otto Brower and B. Reeves Eason, *The Phantom Empire* (1935), film serial. The serial stars Gene Autry as a singing cowboy. Autry sings *Red River Valley* in the 1936 eponymous film.

27. *Ibid.*, 59.

28. While the story is set in Texas, it was filmed on location in Monument Valley, located near the Utah-Arizona border within the Navajo Nation Reservation.

29. Examples include: Richard W. Etulain, "Cultural Origins of the Western," in *Focus on the Western*, ed. Nachbar (Englewood Cliffs, NJ: Prentice-Hall, 1974), 19; Martin M. Winkler, "Homeric kleos and the Western Film." *Syllecta Classica* 7 (1996): 43–54. doi:10.1353/syl.1996.0024, and Kirsten Day. "What Makes a Man to Wander?": *The Searchers* as a Western *Odyssey*" (2008). *Classics: Faculty Scholarship & Creative Works.* http://digitalcommons.augustana.edu/clasfaculty/2.

30. Chris O'Falt, "Twin Peaks': Mark Frost Takes Us Inside the Four-Year Process of Writing a 500-Page Script Over Skype With David Lynch," *Indie Wire*, June 14, 2008, accessed March 1, 2020: https://www.indiewire.com/2018/06/twin-peaks-the-return-mark-frost-david-lynch-writing-collaboration-1201975099/; Bushman, 255.

31. Kathryn C. Esselman, "From Camelot to Monument Valley: Dramatic Origins of the Western Film," in *Focus on the Western*, ed. Nachbar (Englewood Cliffs, N.J.: Prentice-Hall, 1974), 9.

32. Aron, *The American West*, 58.

33. O'Falt, "Twin Peaks"; Mark Frost (@mfrost11), Twitter, no date, *twitter.com*; David Lynch (@DAVID_LYNCH), Twitter, no date, *twitter.com*.

34. David Lynch, *Catching the Big Fish* (London: Penguin, 2006), 1.

35. "west," *Online Etymology Dictionary*, accessed March 1, 2020, https://www.etymonline.com/word/west.

36. Aron, *The American West*, 73.

37. The Silver Mustang and the recurring pale horse, appearing in both the series and film, echo the white horse with a personality from *I Killed Wild Bill Hickok*, as well as the Lone Ranger's famous mount, Silver; Beyond the Double R's link to the railroad, the archetypal symbol of the "conquest" of the West, the recurrence in the season of trains carrying intermodal containers towards Judy's diner should be noted. Sonny Jim Jones' bedroom, with its Western figurines and space rockets, exemplifies the way the traditional notion of the Western-related frontier shifted towards space in the 1950s, leading up to the recurring role of the Moon and its conquest in *Twin Peaks*.

38. Mark Frost, *Twin Peaks: The Final Dossier* (New York: Flatiron Books, 2017). The

Final Dossier lists Sarah's full name as Sarah Judith. Is Judith indicative of Joudy's influence and infection? *The Final Dossier* confirms the identity of the teenager depicted in Part 8.
     39. O'Falt, "Twin Peaks."

Works Cited

Allen, Graham. 2000. *Intertextuality*. London: Routledge.
Bushman, David. 2020. *Conversations with Mark Frost*: Twin Peaks, Hill Street Blues, *and the Education of a Writer*. Columbus, OH: Fayetteville Mafia Press.
Cawelti, J. G. 1974. "Savagery, Civilization, and the Western Hero." In Nachbar (ed.), *Focus on the Western*. Englewood Cliffs, NJ: Prentice-Hall.
Day, Kirsten. 2008. "'What Makes a Man to Wander?': *The Searchers* as a Western *Odyssey*." *Classics: Faculty Scholarship & Creative Works*. http://digitalcommons.augustana.edu/clasfaculty/2.
Esselman, Kathryn C. 1974. "From Camelot to Monument Valley: Dramatic Origins of the Western Film," In Nachbar (ed.), *Focus on the Western*. Englewood Cliffs, N.J.: Prentice-Hall.
Etulain, Richard W. 1974. "Cultural Origins of the Western." In Nachbar (ed.), *Focus on the Western*. Englewood Cliffs, NJ: Prentice-Hall.
Frost, Mark. 2016. *The Secret History of Twin Peaks: A Novel*. New York: Flatiron Books.
Frost, Mark. 2017. *Twin Peaks: The Final Dossier*. New York: Flatiron Books.
King, Rob. "The Horse is the White of the Eye: Pioneering and the American Southwest in *Twin Peaks*." *NANO*. https://nanocrit.com/issues/issue15/The-Horse-is-the-White-of-the-Eye-Pioneering-and-the-American-Southwest-in-Twin-Peaks.
Marsden, Michael T. 1974. "Savior in the Saddle: The Sagebrush Testament." In Nachbar (ed.), *Focus on the Western*. Englewood Cliffs, NJ: Prentice-Hall.
Nachbar, Jack, ed. 1974. *Focus on the Western*. Englewood Cliffs, NJ: Prentice Hall.
O'Falt, Chris. "'Twin Peaks': Mark Frost Takes Us Inside the Four-Year Process of Writing a 500-Page Script Over Skype With David Lynch," *Indie Wire* (June 14, 2008). https://www.indiewire.com/2018/06/twin-peaks-the-return-mark-frost-david-lynch-writing-collaboration-1201975099/; Bushman, 255.
Schatz, Thomas. "Cowboy Business." *New York Times Magazine* (November 2007).
Warshaw, Robert. 1974. "Movie Chronicle: The Westerner." In Nachbar (ed.), *Focus on the Western*. Englewood Cliffs, NJ: Prentice-Hall.
Winkler, Martin M. "Homeric kleos and the Western Film." *Syllecta Classica* 7 (1996): 43–54.

I'm Going West, Diane

Masculinity and the Cowboy Archetype in the Works of David Lynch

ANDREW T. BURT

The cowboy is a mythic representation of American society's conception of an ideal, individualistic male, a rugged character living on society's margins and liminally straddling the borders of civilization and lawlessness. His ethical code helps him define right and wrong, and he can use it to obtain justice or move on if problems arise. As one of the last frontier figures before populations increased, the cowboy has a complicated relationship with technology, and he often uses old-fashioned know-how. In David Lynch's universe, characters, such as *Twin Peaks'* (1990–1992, 2017) Agent Dale Cooper (Kyle MacLachlan), Sheriff Harry Truman (Michael Ontkean), and *Mulholland Drive's* (2001) Cowboy (Lafayette Montgomery), borrow from these traditions. Their sense of masculinity mirrors the cowboy's codes and procedures of personal resilience even when they search for the comforts of home and region to provide stability. Lynch's characters maintain their masculinity through reliance on ethical codes and a commitment to their chosen roles in a world of problematic boundaries. The cowboy archetype influences how they traverse liminal zones and strengthens their sense of identity while presenting them with options for personal growth, discovery, and in the case of *Mulholland Drive's* Cowboy, dominance.

The cowboy archetype is integral to American identity and is vital to the mythology surrounding American masculinity. William W. Savage, Jr., writes "that the cowboy is the last sentinel on the parapet of Americanism."[1] He becomes a liminal symbol of untamed individualism and a masculine trailblazer who laid the groundwork for American civilization. Thus, he is a man out of time drawing from the past and present to help people understand their place in the world. Philippa Gates contends that

American men, including the cowboy archetype, are expected to represent values associated with "traditional masculinity—strength, heroism, virility, and violence." However, despite stereotypes, modern cowboys must still exhibit "qualities previously associated with femininity—emotional vulnerability, parental affection, and romantic tendencies."[2] Cooper and Truman utilize values from both categories because their codes transcend traditional ones. Gates argues that since Western society sees the former qualities as representative of masculinity as a whole, it prioritizes the lone heroic male figure. Even as men apart, they conform to expected gender roles and "suppress their personal characteristics in favor of exhibiting the ones allocated to their gender and thereby fulfilling their social roles as prescribed by society."[3]

The cowboy archetype is an arbiter of American values, preparing Americans for how to live because his code of ethics stems from principles relating to the American way of life, particularly as it relates to commercialism and personal ethics. In fact, "he transmits social values, and he sells merchandise."[4] He represents how individualist tendencies are checked in American culture because he cannot exist without society or a marketplace to express his ideas. Ramon F. Adams explains: "...lack of written law made it necessary for him [the cowboy] to frame some of his own, thus developing a rule of behavior which became known as the 'Code of the West' ... though the cowman might break every law of the territory, state and Federal government, he took pride in upholding his own unwritten code." Breaking this code generally resulted in hazing and ostracism rather than legal punishment.[5] Because cowboys were so ubiquitous in television and film, the cowboy's code of ethics was reconfigured for the silver screen and beyond, becoming integral to how to achieve the American Dream. Thus, the cowboy archetype has changed to accommodate cultural values, morphing from 1920s virtuous silent film cowboys, such as William S. Hart, to singing cowboys from the 1930s and 1940s along the lines of Gene Autry who generally express their feelings through song, to the more morally ambiguous cowboys that first appeared in Spaghetti Westerns.

Each period of the cowboy archetype spoke to American expectations of individualism, masculinity, and entertainment. In an interview with NPR's Terry Gross, Douglas B. Green discusses the appeal of singing cowboys and their songs: "A lot of Western music was very escapist and came to flower and fruition in the Depression era ... songs like 'Back In The Saddle' just reminded people of being free, and free of mortgage, and debt, and depression and unemployment."[6] These heroes allowed people an outlet to escape their problems that paralleled the American love of movement and individual freedom. By the 1960s singing cowboys gave way to Spaghetti Western cowboys, a twist on the archetype that privileged the cowboy as a more complex antihero. This shift mirrored the cultural upheaval of the decade because different perceptions of what was good for society challenged the conservative ideas of Hollywood Westerns and conceptions of heroism in the West. Christopher Frayling argues that "in the disillusioned climate of post–Vietnam, post–Watergate America, [Frederick Jackson] Turner and Nash Smith [and his *The Virgin Land*]—with their Puritan emphasis on 'rugged individualism,' 'cultivating your own garden,' and John L. O'Sullivan's concept of 'manifest destiny' as key factors shaping the evolution of American society—can have little credibility"[7]

An arbiter of American values and an amalgamation of different periods, the cowboy's liminality continues to modify his toughness and allows him to present his masculinity and stick to his code in numerous ways. He is the guardian of borders between the past and present, between outmoded and forward ways of thinking, and in some cases in David Lynch's works, between the natural and the supernatural. Rebecca A. Umland describes a liminal space as "an anthropological concept of a threshold between past and future, or between conflicting social values and/or individual experiences and desires."[8] Other theorists like Victor Turner and Ronald Primeau extend this idea to include journeys of self-discovery and freedom from societal expectations. Turner sees the liminal as areas where people "distilled the creativity and energy with which they created and re-created society and culture, and returned to them reinvigorated, preparing to keep giving them another try."[9] Primeau acknowledges that they free travelers from constraining social structures to give them the "opportunity to start over and discover one's inner resources and potential."[10] The various borders surrounding the frontier are liminal, along with the spaces that characters inhabit and the decisions they make to maintain autonomy from a system that constrains their ethical codes. Even when they navigate urban areas, those like *Mulholland Drive*'s Cowboy create spaces away from the city's din. The Cowboy's ranch is seemingly incongruous to those in Hollywood proper, but he finds a way to carve out his niche near the city and never changes his appearance or code when he walks its streets.

The cowboy archetype often poses as a guardian of borders and liminal spaces between borders or thresholds, helping to define and restructure these places. Eric Hobsbawm theorizes that cowboys consist of "two types: explorers or visitors seeking something that cannot be found elsewhere ... and men who have established a symbiosis with nature.... They are not bringing with them the modern world, except in the sense that they come with its self-consciousness and equipment."[11] Of course, Lynch's "cowboys" coolly deal with everything in their way, even divisions between worlds like *Twin Peaks'* Red Room, managing their problems through intuition tempered by years of experience. They borrow from the cowboy archetype to walk between borders, guiding others toward how to act or punishing them if they misbehave.

However, cowboys live on the margins of regular society to protect it, and their failings at maintaining romantic relationships emphasize that they will never be "invited to be one of its normal members," as long as they stick to their codes and professions.[12] Indeed, the comforts of home and region provide a difficult situation for our heroes because they are never able to accept home fully and must spend their days searching for it, even though they understand the importance of liminal boundaries in making personal discoveries and maintaining their principles.

Harry Truman guards various borders but seldom crosses them without Cooper. Cooper is a transgressor who can cross the supernatural liminal lines, while Truman is more concerned with personally protecting his community from outsiders. Cooper crosses these boundaries often, perhaps because of his esoteric methods, discovering clues within liminal regions that help him with cases. Truman maintains some boundaries without transgressing them and even uses Cooper's FBI credentials to help him police the Canadian border. In Episode 12 he and Tommy "Hawk" Hill (Michael Horse) help Cooper rescue Audrey Horne (Sherilyn Fenn) from One Eyed Jacks by disrupting the ransom deal between Ben Horne (Richard Beymer) and Jean Renault (Michael Parks). This mission ultimately leads to Cooper's suspension, but it shows that each man will break some laws to maintain justice.

Both Cooper and Truman borrow from the cowboy archetype in other ways, even though they alter its principles. Cooper is a visitor seeking something that he cannot find elsewhere, but he is also trying to establish a symbiosis with nature. The pine trees and the area's natural surroundings attract him, and he does not want to leave. Truman, on the other hand, is at home in Twin Peaks, and he guides Cooper in the local ways of life and law enforcement. Cooper has searched for years to find a place to belong, performing many esoteric activities in hopes of finding one.[13] Cooper associates food and nature with comfort and belonging, things that cowboys needed to ready themselves to head out for the frontier. In *Twin Peaks*, even comfort can be discomforting because of how liminal the region is, literally and metaphorically. Cooper has been taking trips since he was a child, even deciding not to take a bus home from camp to make his own way and inadvertently prepare himself for liminal life. Cooper attempts to understand his wanderlust, asking Diane, "Do you ever wonder if you were left on your parents' doorstep by Gypsies?"[14] Like historical cowboys, his travels took him west, first to San Francisco, and finally to Twin Peaks. He writes, concerning the U.S.-Mexico border, that "the mess that results when two cultures meet in one place on a common border is food for the imagination. Every imaginable sin, vice, perversion, and degradation is laid out in the open in living color"; an apt description for how the borders between Twin Peaks and neighboring Canada play out, as well as a typical description of a wild west town.[15]

The cowboy archetype is connected to the borders between the East and the West, and he represents the expansion of American thought and an idealized masculinity that is not only connected to class but regional identity. Clint W. Jones claims that cowboys made the "economic booms of Reconstruction possible in the East" through cattle drives, and to many they represented unlimited opportunities to Easterners. He argues that this stems from Theodore Roosevelt's image of the cowboy to "substantiate the 'tough' personae of a rising urban-industrialist class—the class of workers carrying the baton of nation building into the twentieth century."[16] Roosevelt built on Frederick Jackson Turner's concepts concerning expansionism. He used regional identity to emphasize a new type of masculinity by conflating Eastern and Western conceptions of it in order to debunk the mythology of the Eastern "dude" who went west to work on ranches but without the know-how of the Western cowboy and was more concerned with dressing properly than learning how to be a cowboy. Richard A. Hill argues that the "*dude* became synonymous with *dandy*, a term used to designate a sharp dresser in the western territories. From the earliest usage *dude* also carried the taint of 'outsider' or 'uninitiated' in the same sense that greenhorn was applied, though a greenhorn was not necessarily a sharp dresser [emphasis in original]."[17] Other politicians, such as Ronald Reagan, continued to use the cowboy archetype to political advantage, and this sort of political influence affected Cooper's development. Cooper is a convergence of East and West, bringing notions from his East Coast upbringing to the West Coast to help the Twin Peaks community, but he does not represent the "dude." Rather, he is a tough individualist with the character and skill to help Twin Peaks. Despite his family and FBI connections, he is a self-made man who cannot rely on previous wealth or position, but on character and skill. He hones these abilities by continually testing himself through FBI training and esoteric practices, such as testing the limits of his body and mind. As a young man, he performs experiments, including testing the "duration my body can function without sleep and … the minimum amount of sleep required to sustain a high level of operation."[18] Of course, this experiment backfires when he reaches forty-eight hours with no sleep.

Agent Cooper resembles a Philosopher Cowboy, using methods culled from his experience and his appreciation of Buddhist precepts. A man out of time, he is searching for something within and without himself. His philosophy represents how he is an amalgamation of different periods of the cowboy archetype, including the Eastern "dude" and the rugged individualist. He incorporates elements of singing cowboys, the stoic John Wayne types, and the more morally ambiguous Spaghetti Western heroes. In doing so, he realizes the promise of the liminal in helping people reach their potential and can cross thresholds into other worlds in pursuit of justice. In Season 1, Episode 2, Cooper introduces the Tibetan Method, in which he eliminates suspects by throwing stones at bottles labeled with the letter "j." With another method, he narrows down the suspect list and sets his sights on One Eyed Jacks as one of the clues informs him of "The Jack with One Eye."[19] His code appears flexible in direct relationship to his enthusiasm for small-town life and his colleagues, such as Albert Rosenfield (Miguel Ferrer), who is unrelenting in his principles and more skeptical. Cooper has the flexibility and individualism of the white knight detective and the cowboy, and he is willing to make mistakes to help his friends. To exemplify these stalwart qualities, Cooper is open with his feelings and philosophy. In the pilot he tells Truman, "Every day, once a day, give yourself a present. Don't plan it, don't wait for it, just let it happen." This mantra echoes the cowboy code because it prioritizes self-reliance. However, it complicates the cowboy mythology by presenting a reflective element that allows the hero to take a moment instead of engaging in action and validates the complexities of their guardian roles.

Truman is a purer form of the archetypal cowboy since he is a sheriff and a gatekeeper, harkening back to a pre–Spaghetti Western period. Therefore, he is more of a traditional lawman who is not as willing to break the law yet still lives by a personal code. Twin Peaks appears normal on the surface, and his quiet manner and emphasis on quickly cleaning up messes reinforce that appearance, despite supernatural events. His father was the sheriff before him, and because Twin Peaks is a small border town, he has leeway that he might not have if he was closer to a larger city. Tamara Preston relates:

> While Harry could at many times have smudged the line between extracurricular vigilantism and the strict limits of the law—specifically through the offices of the local "social club" he eventually led, known as the Bookhouse Boys—a closer examination of their history has convinced me that the Boys have always acted in accordance with the spirit of the patriotic home guard Truman's father founded during World War II.[20]

In this sense, Truman is Cooper's foil, providing a sensible alternative to the latter's theories. Just like Cooper, he is a man out of time who does not rely on modern technology but relies on his personal sense of justice. He is a true Western lawman, quiet, chivalrous, and patient to a fault, yet he has a breaking point. In Season 1, Episode 2, when Albert challenges him, he puts the man in his place, guarding the borders of what is right in his town. He allows those he believes will defend the community's values but has little time for those who do not. He sees Albert as a consummate outsider, a man who is there to challenge his code and make things tougher for the community. Albert represents the snobby Easterner and the inexorable arm of the Eastern establishment.

Cowboys presented their masculinity in a technologically and often geographically changing world, and technology still configures the changing liminalities of Lynch's worlds. Characters are uncertain of their place and utilize new technologies and theories to reinforce their masculinity against this backdrop of uncertainty. For example, just like in Western films, the gun becomes "part of consumer society wherein men are able to gain status and means of power, and openly demonstrate this power, through their consumer spending and through their skills to use this new technology to its fullest potential."[21] *Twin Peaks* does not obviously indicate this demarcation because law enforcement only draws guns when necessary. Nevertheless, guns are still the symbol of the patriarchy when Cooper and Sheriff Truman are in charge, and they sometimes use technology to do their talking for them. However, technology does not effectively help them deal with supernatural thresholds, and Cooper eventually finds himself trapped and unable to communicate or return to share what he has learned. Even so, in Season 3, Part 18, Cooper shows how guns can help tame the lawlessness of three cowboys who attack a waitress. He quickly uses his gun to disable them before he symbolically destroys their guns in a deep fryer.

In *Twin Peaks* technology does not only serve the status quo but also helps strengthen relationships and understanding. Cooper brings the tools of his trade with him, not just the trappings of civilization but devices from the outside world. His tape recorder is a liminal marker akin to a magical portal between the older natural world that Twin Peaks represents, the 1950s, and the modern world of the 1990s. Even so, it is on the verge of being outdated. It allows Cooper to have one foot in the past and the other in the increasingly uncertain present and reflects his uncertainty about his identity. Nevertheless, even when Cooper uses technology, such as his tape recorder, to address women, he still upholds patriarchal power structures. Diane is not seen or heard until Season 3, despite his insistence on directly addressing her in search of advice: "Diane, I hope you will not mind that I address these tapes to you even when it is clear that I am talking to myself. The knowledge that someone of your insight is standing behind me is comforting."[22]

Cooper and Truman struggle to find romantic relationships, even as their friendship remains strong, thus representing the cowboy archetype's inability entirely to belong. Truman's love affair with Josie Packard (Joan Chen) is doomed to fail. Their secret relationship revolves around his protecting her from a supposed prowler. He swears to defend her but ultimately fails in his task when she suddenly dies in Episode 23 after shooting Thomas Eckhardt (David Warner) and lying to Truman about her criminal activities. Tamara Preston writes that "As badly hurt as he was by Josie's betrayal, I believe Harry may have been even more haunted by the sudden disappearance of his friend Cooper."[23] Truman is more private than Cooper, but he is staunchly loyal and always honors his commitments. Similarly, Cooper makes connections, but they are always doomed to fail, sometimes because of his code to protect and other times because of his inability to make connections with good people. For example, he rejects Audrey because she is too young, and Windom Earle (Kenneth Welsh) abuses their connections to take away all his other romantic relationships. According to Preston in *The Secret History of Twin Peaks*, "Earle not only suspected his wife and partner's budding affinity; he perversely proceeded to do everything in his power to push them together in order to prove that it existed." He loses Annie Blackburn (Heather Graham) to Earle in what Preston believes is an "ingrained impulse to save a troubled woman from herself.... Cooper's obsession with the Laura Palmer (Sheryl Lee) case harbors echoes of this tendency." Although, as Preston expresses, their connection might have more to do with "vicious assaults by dangerous criminals against the core of their being."[24]

Cooper and Truman explore the borders between the natural world and Twin Peak's other dimensions. On the other hand, *Mulholland Drive*'s Cowboy presents a version of the cowboy archetype as guardian between worlds, helping characters to understand their place in the world and restore his personal order. As a doppelganger for various Hollywood cowboy types, he is placed by the film's Los Angeles setting in an urban frontier resembling the Wild West, even though he finds a home that recalls the actual frontier. His stoicism is similar to the post–1950s Hollywood cowboy, as exemplified by Clint Eastwood or John Wayne. Even so, he takes his main precedent from Hollywood's silent cowboy stars, physically resembling Tom Mix or William Hart. His brightly colored duds recall singing cowboys, such as Gene Autry, who adapted the silent cowboy's look and had a powerful presence in early Hollywood. His menacing demeanor stretches the boundaries of fictional cowboys because of its incongruity. The Cowboy is not benevolent or fatherly, but he exudes confidence and an all-knowing yet taciturn demeanor. His ethical code proves he is more aware of his place as a gatekeeper and upholder of specific values. The Cowboy holds the upper hand over Adam Kesher (Justin Theroux) and determines what happens to him. He is a go-between, who resembles a fixer, giving his victim no other options, explaining to Adam what his role is, but not acting as the final hand of fate. In this respect, he creates boundaries between corporate Hollywood and artistic decisions. A.D. Denham and F.D. Worrell argue that he and Mr. Roque (Michael J. Anderson) are "deities that move the film's characters to action and leave them to suffer the consequences alone."[25] A far cry from Cooper or Truman, the Cowboy is a moral arbiter, despite his seeming connections to organized crime, and it is never certain if he is directly answerable to Roque. Although "Roque and the Cowboy seem to be the only figures in *Mulholland Drive* who are properly in control of their own destinies and able to effectively impose their wills on the world."[26] He acts like he is helping Adam, even though he threatens him in the fire and brimstone rhetoric of the Old Testament God. He keeps and restores the order of Diane's dream and sticks to his moral code, which he continually imposes on others and to which he is never held accountable, unlike those he affects, because they cannot reach him.

The Cowboy's speech straddles the borders between menacing and comical, but he controls the situation by controlling Adam and appearing to give him options. When they meet, he responds to Adam's flippant attitude, asking him, "A man's attitude goes some ways the way his life will be. Is that somethin' you might agree with?" He forces Adam to conform to his ideas of what is right. When Adam responds disrespectfully, the Cowboy asks, "Did you answer because you thought that's what you thought I wanted to hear, or did you think about what I said and answer cause you truly believe that to be right?" When Adam responds affirmatively, the Cowboy chastises him: "Since you agree, you must be a person who does not care about the good life." From his response, it appears that Adam is trying to meet the Hollywood ideal, despite his impetuous smashing of the Castaglianes' (Angelo Badalamenti and Dan Hedaya), the mobsters who threaten him that he must cast the right girl, windshield. The Cowboy continues, "You're too busy being a smart aleck to be thinkin.' Now I want ya to think and stop bein' a smart aleck. Can ya try that for me?" He makes it seem like Adam's attitude is the problem and that he has the right attitude: "You were recasting the lead actress…. When you see the girl that was shown to you earlier today, you will say 'This is the girl.' The rest of the cast can stay—that's up to you, but that lead girl is not up to you." Interestingly, his agenda parallels the conservative ethic of personal responsibility, which almost makes him seem like a Hollywood outsider. Adam conforms to the code and chooses commerce over art for a modicum of happiness.

Their exchange ultimately reinforces the Cowboy's liminal nature and need for dominance, adding to his folkloric resonance. He gives Adam an ultimatum that revolves around the number three: "Now, you will see me one more time if you do good. You will see me two more times if you do bad." Adam does what he is told so that he does not have to deal with the Cowboy again, but the threat holds resonance. Indeed, he appears in each act as a liminal connection holding together the various plot threads. In the film's final act, after Betty Elms (Naomi Watts) uses the key and opens the Pandora's Box that reveals her real life as Diane Selwyn, the Cowboy makes several appearances. Perhaps he is judging Diane's horrible life decisions. Even though she helps Rita (Laura Elena Harring) in her dream/fantasy, once they make love, things fall apart when Diane is incapable of following the code, or perhaps is not allowed to because she is a woman. After the "Silencio" performance and her use of the key, the narrative reveals the truth. Diane hired a thug (Mark Pellegrino) to kill Camilla Rhodes (Laura Elena Harring) because she was jealous of her for usurping her Hollywood starlet dreams and breaking her heart. At Adam's party, Camilla and Adam prepare to make a wedding announcement because he had just separated from his wife. Diane is humiliated. The hitman promises her that he will leave a key when he completes the task, although they never directly discuss the true nature of his job. During the party, a different cowboy moves through the frame, perhaps signifying that Adam did well.

However, the film subverts this promise because this cowboy is different, and Diane sees what she wants to see. Diane's subconscious was punishing Adam, but here he gets what he wants, and she is left alone. This sullen cowboy is there to punish Diane for her transgressions because she broke the code. Diane did not hold to what the Cowboy asked because she did not have a "good attitude." When she hired a hitman to kill Camilla, she assures him that she does not care about the "good life." Her actions comment on the urban frontier's femme fatale, yet they also represent the avaricious qualities of Hollywood, the ones that she lampoons and denies in her fantasies. Even though the Cowboy appears to be a cynical and evil figure, he maintains his code and offers life lessons that Diane does not choose to heed. The final time that the Cowboy appears, he acts as a guide, signaling that she should wake up from her dream but also using his masculinity to control her. He tells her with a slight smile, "Hey, pretty girl, time to wake up." His appearance reinforces how the Cowboy uses his personal ethos in negative ways to maintain control. Conceivably, this action also demarcates the realizations to which Diane is slowly coming and prefigures her demise because she broke the rules and will always be the "othered" outsider. His masculine code allows zero room for her indiscretions.

The cowboy archetype is alive and well in Lynch, even though its form is fluid and it allows characters to present their masculinity in complex and contradictory ways. They rely on personal codes and value systems that conform to societal expectations. As guardians and explorers of liminal borders, they search for stability and order, whether that means developing relationships, finding stable homes, or taking comfort in a job well done. The liminal zones and thresholds that they must account for make their efforts difficult but not impossible. They deal with them to uphold their codes and maintain their identities in a world of problematic boundaries. Cooper and Truman uphold the law to the best of their abilities, and their codes help them find justice and personal growth even when the world goes crazy around them. The Cowboy most typically represents the cowboy archetype's guardianship of the much-debated "conflict of art and commerce" because he dominates those around him, in essence using his code to help them understand their codified place in society.[27] Lynch's "cowboys" are in charge of understanding thresholds and boundaries, and they continually help others understand them as well, even if they use unusual methods to restore the status quo.

Notes

1. William W. Savage, Jr., *The Cowboy Hero: His Image in American History & Culture* (Norman: University of Oklahoma Press, 1979), 15.

2. Philippa Gates, *Detecting Men: Masculinity and the Hollywood Detective Film* (Albany: State University of New York Press, 2006), 29.

3. *Ibid.*, 36.

4. Savage, *The Cowboy Hero*, 150.

5. Ramon F. Adams, *The Cowman and His Code of Ethics* (Austin: The Encino Press, 1969), 11.

6. Douglas B. Green, "Western Music Expert Doug Green Revisits the Era of the Singing Cowboy," interview by Terry Gross. *Fresh Air*, NPR, September 25, 2019, audio, 28:05, https://www.npr.org/2019/09/25/764227667/western-music-expert-doug-green-revisits-the-era-of-the-singing-cowboy.

7. Christopher Frayling. *Spaghetti Westerns: Cowboys and Europeans from Karl May to Sergio Leone*. (London: Routledge & Kegan Paul, 1981), 41.

8. Rebecca A. Umland, *Outlaw Heroes as Liminal Figures of Film and Television* (Jefferson, NC: McFarland & Company, Inc., 2016), 1.

9. Nigel Rapport and Joanna Overing, *Social and Cultural Anthropology: The Key Concepts* (London: Routledge, 2000), 234. Their ideas are a paraphrased summary of Frederick Jackson Turner.

10. Ronald Primeau, *Romance of the Road: The Literature of the American Highway* (Bowling Green, OH: Bowling Green State University Popular Press, 1996), 69.

11. Eric Hobsbawm, *Fractured Times: Culture and Society in the Twentieth Century* (New York: The New Press, 2014), 278.

12. Gates, *Detecting Men*, 34.

13. Scott Frost, *Autobiography of F.B.I. Special Agent Dale Cooper: My Life, My Tapes* (New York: Pocket Books, 1991).

14. *Ibid.*, 167.

15. *Ibid.*, 178.

16. Clint W. Jones, "The Enduring Myth of the American Cowboy: Twenty-first Century Transformations of the Western Ideal in *Longmire*," *Journal of the West* 58, no. 1 (2019): 13–14.

17. Richard A. Hill, "You've Come A Long Way, Dude: A History," *American Speech* 69, no. 3 (Autumn 1994): 321.

18. Scott Frost, *Autobiography*, 76.

19. This is an on-the-nose reference to the 1961 Marlon Brando western film.

20. Mark Frost, *Twin Peaks: The Final Dossier* (New York: Flatiron Books, 2017), 99.

21. Emma Hamilton, *Masculinities in American Western Films* (Oxford: Peter Lang, 2016), 153.

22. Scott Frost, *Autobiography,* 126.

23. Mark Frost, *Twin Peaks,* 99.

24. *Ibid.,* 62–63.

25. A. E. Denham and F. D. Worrell, "Identity and Agency in *Mulholland Drive,*" in *Mulholland Drive,* ed. Zina Giannopoulou (London: Routledge, 2013), 27.

26. *Ibid.*

27. Morris B. Holbrook and Michela Adis, "Art Versus Commerce in the Film Industry: A Two-Path Model of Motion Picture Success," *Journal of Cultural Economics* 32, no. 2 (2008): 100.

Works Cited

Adams, Ramon F. 1969. *The Cowman and his Code of Ethics.* Austin: The Encino Press.

Denham, A.E., and F.D. Worrell. 2013. "Identity and Agency in *Mulholland Drive.*" In Zina Giannopoulou (ed.), *Mulholland Drive.* 8–37. London: Routledge.

Frayling, Christopher. 1981. *Spaghetti Westerns: Cowboys and Europeans from Karl May to Sergio Leone.* London: Routledge & Kegan Paul.

Frost, Mark. 2017. *Twin Peaks: The Final Dossier.* New York: Flatiron Books.

Frost, Scott. 1991. *The Autobiography of F.B.I. Special Agent Dale Cooper: My Life, My Tapes.* New York: Pocket Books.

Gates, Philippa. 2006. *Detecting Men: Masculinity and the Hollywood Detective Film.* Albany: State University of New York Press.

Green, Douglas B. 2019. "Western Music Expert Doug Green Revisits the Era of the Singing Cowboy." Interview by Terry Gross. *Fresh Air,* NPR, September 25. Audio, 28:05. https://www.npr.org/2019/09/25/764227667/western-music-expert-doug-green-revisits-the-era-of-the-singing-cowboy.

Hamilton, Emma. 2016. *Masculinities in American Western Films.* Oxford: Peter Lang.

Hill, Richard A. 1994. "You've Come a Long Way, Dude: A History," *American Speech* 69, no. 3 (Autumn): 321–327.

Hobsbawm, Eric. 2013. *Fractured Times: Culture and Society in the Twentieth Century.* New York: The New Press.

Holbrook, Morris B., and Michela Adis. 2008. "Art versus Commerce in the Film Industry: A Two-Path Model of Motion Picture Success," *Journal of Cultural Economics* 32, no. 2 (December): 87–107.

Jones, Clint W. 2019. "The Enduring Myth of the American Cowboy: Twenty-First Century Transformations of the Western Ideal in *Longmire.*" *Journal of the West* 58, no. 1 (Winter): 11–28.

Lynch, David, dir. *Mulholland Drive.* (2001; Universal City, CA: Universal Pictures. 2002), DVD.

_____, dir. *Twin Peaks,* Season 1, pilot, "The Northwest Passage." Produced by Lynch/Frost Productions. Aired April 8, 1990, on ABC Television.

Primeau, Ronald. 1996. *Romance of the Road: The Literature of the American Highway.* Bowling Green, OH: Bowling Green State University Popular Press.

Rapport, Nigel, and Joanna Overing. 2000. *Social and Cultural Anthropology: The Key Concepts.* London: Routledge.

Savage, Jr., William W. 1979. *The Cowboy Hero: His Image in American History & Culture.* Norman: University of Oklahoma Press.

Umland, Rebecca A. 2016. *Outlaw Heroes as Liminal Figures of Film and Television.* Jefferson, NC: McFarland.

David Lynch's Desert Frontier

Road Movie, Desert Horror and Western Liminality

Thomas Britt

David Lynch's vision of the American West is defined, in part, by conquest and staking claim, actions that correspond to attitudes from American history, but which Lynch renders with a critical view of the civilization
that is the product of individual conquest. One recurring narrative relationship, linked to acts of taking and becoming in Lynch's films, is that
between physical settings and spiritual, supernatural, or psychic transitions. The topic of Western liminality is central to Lynch's work, as it is
a canvas for these dual processes. Largely as the result of their excessive
drives and identities in crisis, Lynch's protagonists fall victim to transfor-
mative frontiers that go far beyond mere thresholds or lines in the sand.
Repeated locations such as homes, roads, motel rooms, prison cells, and
deserts, concretize the drama.

Two movie genres that significantly inform Lynch's approach to such
western frontier narratives are the road movie and the desert horror film.
This essay acknowledges the influence of these setting-focused genres in
Wild at Heart (1990), *Lost Highway* (1997), and *Twin Peaks* Season 3 (2017).
These works progress from *Wild at Heart*'s westbound protagonist crossing into a freer landscape, to *Lost Highway*'s distrusting husband who
becomes a new man after his wife is murdered, to *Twin Peaks*' FBI agent
whose manifold fragmentation carves up the Western United States (and
beyond) when he travels to times and places beyond mortal understanding. The road and the desert offer these men a double-edged agency. They
are free to cross boundaries and attempt to conquer their objectives, but
they are also haunted by the road's limited vista and the desert's limitless
void.

Many volumes have been written about road movies, and several
in recent years have devoted scholarly attention to Lynch's films as road

movies, beginning with *Wild at Heart*. In *Driving Visions: Exploring the Road Movie*, David Laderman writes that *Wild at Heart* "seems a road movie watershed, cutting loose the popular 1990s road movie trend of ever more graphic high-tech spectacles of violence."[1] In contrast to this postmodern view, critic Roger Ebert observes the road movie classicism of *Wild at Heart*, calling it "a road picture, with a 1950s T-Bird convertible as the chariot, and lots of throwaway gags about Ripley's snakeskin jacket."[2] However, Lynch scholar Martha P. Nochimson writes in a more qualified way about Lynch's adherence to the road movie within the same film, specifying that "*Wild at Heart* is actually closer to the genre of the maternal melodrama."[3] *Wild at Heart* could be seen as both a road movie and a "maternal melodrama" in part because a significant portion of the narrative juxtaposes an attempt at freedom on the road with emotional and existential damage caused by a villainous mother. Later Lynch works such as *Lost Highway* and *The Straight Story* (1999) have also been explicitly read as road movies. Concerning an understanding of the road movie's main features, Laderman provides a description of the road movie genre that undergirds the present essay's view of Lynch's combination of internal/spiritual transformations with quotidian places and objectives, in stories about characters undergoing conquest and transformation:

> …we can appreciate the road movie's repeated venture beyond familiar culture as a rejuvenating hegira through some emptiness imagined as more primal. Freedom becomes rediscovered as a movement across open space. However, we should emphasize that most road movies do not take place entirely in a so-called wilderness. In fact, road movies exaggerate cultural isolation with vestiges—like the car itself—of that culture. Most often the sense of some wilderness beyond culture becomes heightened in road movies with sundry detours, motels, diners, and gas stations.[4]

Indeed, the narrative and visual designs of *Wild at Heart* foreground such locations that simultaneously express the characters' quest for freedom with the persistent, isolating realities and demands of the culture from which they are trying to escape.

Within Lynch's work, the desert horror subgenre contributes the site of "primal emptiness" or "wilderness" only partially present in road movies. Deserts and wildernesses appear as final frontiers in *Wild at Heart*, *Lost Highway*, and *Twin Peaks* Season 3. In all of these works, such settings within the American West combine the potential for opportunity and renewal with the threat of dissociation and annihilation. Historically, however, it is Australian Outback stories (real and imagined) that have influenced the way desert horror functions as a mode of narrative cinema, including notable works such as Peter Weir's *Picnic at Hanging Rock* (1975). In "The Imagined Desert," Tom Drahos observes that "the Outback has received attention as the site of isolated and infrequent horror stories" depicting "societal outsiders attacking passive agents seeking to consume the space.... Travelers in the 'Dead Heart' are likely to come under attack, from the landscape, from its creatures, from the 'other.'"[5] Within the context of global cinema, the influence of desert horror rooted in the history and imagination of Australia has since extended to other places and times. Films such as Gus Van Sant's *Gerry* (2003) and Jonás Cuarón's *Desierto* (2015) have contributed to a widening of the desert horror boundaries and subjects well beyond the Outback.[6]

Two key works outside of narrative and film studies regarding roads and deserts are Frederick Jackson Turner's "The Significance of the Frontier in American History" (1893) and Arnold van Gennep's *The Rites of Passage* (1960). Turner's work defined and detailed historical frontiers according to a theory that American identity could be understood through the process of westward expansion. The characters in Lynch's narratives encounter a negation of Turner's explication of Manifest Destiny and American exceptionalism, insofar as *Wild at Heart, Lost Highway,* and *Twin Peaks* Season 3 reframe Turner's ideas about the quest for triumphant self-identity with characters who have lost their way and who are quickly engulfed by competing forces.[7] Van Gennep's work is noteworthy for its elucidation of liminality and the phases of "separation, transition, and incorporation" connected to "life crises."[8] However, as Lynch has already been widely interpreted through van Gennep's theories of liminality as well as threshold experiences, it is instead van Gennep's attention to sacred, neutral, and profane zones that partially guides this essay's attention to Lynch in the context of the American West.

Lastly, in the promotion for *Twin Peaks* Season 3, Lynch reiterated his advice to "keep your eye on the donut" rather than the hole.[9] This essay is written in that exegetical spirit, an approach that van Gennep is also said to have insisted upon in research. In the introduction to *Rites of Passage,* Solon T. Kimball writes that van Gennep "was vehement in his protest against those who extracted from 'context' data which supported their theses. He was insistent that ceremonies needed to be examined in their entirety and in the social setting in which they were found."[10] Thus despite the heavy presence of the metaphysical and transcendental in Lynch's works, this study mostly tracks the observable, ordinary physical places and events that reveal the protagonists' conquests and identity developments. In *Wild at Heart, Lost Highway,* and *Twin Peaks* Season 3, three categories, including private homes, temporary accommodations (hotels, motels, bars, and prison cells), and the desert/wilderness, constitute the sites of conquest and transformation. Within the context of American frontier history, these categories involve what Turner refers to as a "fluidity" of establishing land ownership, the law of the land, and other aspects of civilization being worked out in time and space. For characters on the road, these zones are the "donuts" that ground viewers, despite the presence of so many "holes."

The road movie, filtered through Lynch's imagination, is one in which a domestic rupture prompts a departure from the private home and may sometimes involve a return to it. Generally, the private home in Lynch's works features collisions between the sacred and profane, in the tradition identified by van Gennep in *Rites of Passage*: "...whoever passes through the positions of a lifetime one day sees the sacred where before he has seen the profane, or vice versa. Such changes of condition do not occur without disturbing the life of society and the individual, and it is the function of rites of passage to reduce their harmful effects."[11] In Lynch's road narratives, disturbed characters leave private homes for the desert.

In *Wild at Heart* (adapted from Barry Gifford's novel *Wild at Heart: The Story of Sailor and Lula* [1990]) Lynch dramatizes private homes as being beset by trauma and malevolent forces. The film pays little attention to Sailor Ripley's (Nicolas Cage) past or present life in a private home, beyond dialogue describing how death and dysfunction within his family set him up as an outlaw from a young age. However, Lynch provides several visually and aurally illustrated flashbacks to the former home life of Sailor's romantic partner, Lula Pace Fortune (Laura Dern).

One of these scenes, recounted while on the road/on the run, is the rape of young teenage Lula by her Uncle Pooch (Marvin Kaplan). This is a flashback scene that focuses on the aftermath of the rape, with Lula on a bed, bloody and crying. Within Gifford's novel and Lynch's film, there is an intentionally unreliable or inconsistent account of how aware Lula's mother Marietta Fortune (Diane Ladd) is of her young daughter's rape. As Lynch's film renders the rape flashback in active terms rather than simply as a story Lula tells, as in the novel, the viewer takes on a more direct awareness of the circumstances that Sailor, by contrast, can only imagine. This is one of many moments in the film in which Sailor is comparatively blunted to the horrors that Lula has experienced, relative to the viewing audience's experience of the vividly dramatized past scenes. The fractured structure of the film contributes another layer of irony regarding the outlaw couple's awareness of the malevolent forces pursuing them as they flee for a new frontier. Marietta is evil, and her actions abruptly interrupt the flow of the road movie narrative that houses Sailor and Lula. Lynch's adaptation of Gifford's novel plays up Lynch's preoccupation with *The Wizard of Oz* to such an extent that Marietta represents the Wicked Witch of the East as she plots to kill Sailor and abduct Lula from her home.[12]

The second act of the film begins with Sailor "thinking of breaking parole and taking [Lula] out to sunny California." Sailor and Lula's journey toward ostensible freedom remains anchored in the evil of the private home, insofar as the film cuts jarringly to the machinations of Marietta back at home in North Carolina, and then later as she pursues them westward. Marietta embodies Turner's observation that "The East has always feared the result of an unregulated advance of the frontier, and has tried to check and guide it."[13] Additional flashbacks, cross-cut with the ongoing road movie narrative, illustrate that the Fortune home was always a dangerous place. The structure of *Wild at Heart* provides regular reminders that Sailor's road-bound rescue of Lula is an attempt to move her out of a profane and evil home, even as she is susceptible to evil on a level that he cannot fully comprehend.

Lost Highway is a film whose narrative is often described as incomprehensible or irreconcilable. Lynch co-wrote the script with Gifford, and in many ways the film complements the narrative of *Wild at Heart*, though the film style is markedly different. The mood of *Lost Highway* is much more unified by a potent neo-noir influence, and the fractured structure in this case occurs within the character and psychology of the protagonist, not outside of them. There is no wicked witch. The would-be sacredness of the private home of *Lost Highway* is initially profaned in two ways, and these occur in quick succession within the first act of the film. First, protagonist Fred Madison (Bill Pullman) suspects that his wife Renee (Patricia Arquette) is being dishonest or unfaithful when she does not answer the phone when he calls her after playing a jazz gig that Renee did not attend. Second, the couple begins to receive videotapes of their house, which progress from images of exterior shots to interior shots of them in bed, suggesting that someone has entered their private home unbidden to record them.

While the road movie journey of *Lost Highway* is somewhat more tangential to its plot than the literal cross-country pursuit of *Wild at Heart*, the second act of *Lost Highway* shares *Wild at Heart*'s horrific ruptures within the private home. Fred encounters a Mystery Man (Robert Blake) at a party. This man insists that he met Fred before at Fred's house. Further, he says he is also at Fred's house at that very moment. When Fred calls his house to substantiate this "absurd" claim, the Mystery Man answers Fred's phone and says, "You invited me. It's not my habit to go where I'm not wanted." Associated with this event is a videotape in which Fred appears to mutilate and murder Renee. Together these events establish that something evil has entered Fred's private home and forever changed it.

Another complicating layer of the narrative involves Fred's penchant for subjectivity. Before Renee's murder occurs, he says to two detectives investigating the videotaped home invasion, "I like to remember things my own way.... How *I* remember them. Not necessarily the way they happened." The visual design of Fred and Renee's house coheres with his psychological subjectivity, as the space is evocative of the production design within German Expressionism and associated cinema styles, wherein the physical features of the home appear to be illustrations of a troubled mind state. Beyond the way in which the physical features of the home indicate Fred's state of mind, the Madison home also features windows shaped like the holes of an electrical receptacle, an architectural detail also present in the Fortress/Fireman's home in *Twin Peaks* Season 3; windows neutral or hot, corresponding to van Gennep's theory of alternating zones.

In many ways, *Twin Peaks* Season 3 amplifies the current of subjectivity that exists within *Lost Highway*, arguably framing all events of *Twin Peaks* within a quasi-mantra spoken by multiple characters within the season: "We are like the dreamer who dreams and lives inside the dream. But who is the dreamer?" There is an abundance of evidence within the season to answer that question, pointing convincingly toward several characters as potential sources and inhabitants of dreams. However, for this exegetical approach to Lynch, the more pertinent question is: who is the protagonist that best illustrates the Lynchian view of the American West? Said protagonist begins with FBI Special Agent Dale Cooper (Kyle MacLachlan), though he is only one of a multiplicity of protagonist variations. In Season 3, Cooper also exists in the form of evil doppelganger Mr. C; a tulpa in the form of insurance agent Dougie Jones, Cooper having returned as a blank slate within the home and family of Jones; a galvanized Cooper shedding the Jones persona; and the mysterious concluding incarnation, likely a man known as Richard. These many identities result in a much more complicated trajectory than Sailor and Fred's journeys. Yet the Cooper variants interact with the private home in a way that upholds the domestic collision of sacred and profane within the Lynch filmography.

In *Twin Peaks* the foundational rupture within the private home is the abuse and later killing of Laura Palmer (Sheryl Lee) by her father Leland (Ray Wise), facts that are revealed in the second season of the original series and elaborated on in the feature film *Fire Walk with Me* (1992). Leland, possessed by BOB (Frank Silva), permanently profanes his home with these acts. As a result, in Season 3, his widow, Laura's mother Sarah (Grace Zabriskie), exists within a damned loop on a couch that forms part of an apparent hell within her private home. This motif is cyclical, as we discover in Season 3 during a flashback to young Sarah in 1956, in which her home and body are invaded by a frogmoth.

For the various Coopers of *Twin Peaks* Season 3, the framework for sacred and profane treatments of private homes involves the formalities with which one respects (or fails to respect) the sacredness of the homes.

For example, using both dialogue and visuals, Lynch and co-writer Mark Frost pay conspicuous attention to the formality of knocking on a door to announce oneself and to request permission to enter. Within *Twin Peaks*, this is a central formality that separates the civilized from the savage, to paraphrase Turner.[14] The evil Mr. C regularly ignores this gesture, physically invading homes throughout the narrative. His son, Richard Horne (Eamon Farren), displays a similar lack of respect by forcing his way into homes of others, including family members, to assault and rob them. FBI Special Agent Dale Cooper, on the other hand, knocks and exhibits respect for the owners of private homes, even when his being has seemingly shifted to "Richard" late within the narrative. As a tabula rasa, Cooper-as-Dougie is defined in part by not knowing what to do with doors at home or at work, other than repeating the information that the door of Dougie's home is red.

Within *Twin Peaks* Season 3, Cooper's experience adrift in Dougie's life begins and ends in temporary spaces, which are a second category of zones (following private homes) through which Lynch's western frontier narratives could be tracked.[15] We first see Dougie in an empty home in a housing development, a temporary zone the unaware tulpa is using for a tryst. He is spirited back to the Red Room, and Cooper returns through the electrical socket to begin his journey back towards self-identifying as Agent Cooper.

It is Mr. C, however, whose conquest is particularly defined with transitional or temporary spaces. Often seen driving at night, Mr. C spends time in motels, a prison cell, and an especially liminal convenience store, among other settings, in his attempt to destroy everything that would draw him back into the Red Room and out of corporeal existence. In *Wild at Heart*, Sailor's road trip involves a different set of objectives (chiefly his own individuality and freedom), but he exhibits a similarly outsized confidence in his ability to control circumstances. Sailor, like Mr. C, experiences prison as a minor inconvenience that he shakes off without consequence. Within the context of American road narratives, this treatment of prisons is perhaps a critique of the function of prisons as places that merely stall individuals and kill time but have no rehabilitative effect. And in some in-between settings, such as a roadhouse, Sailor appears to control the world around him, refashioning a wild rock and roll show into a sensitive, performative declaration of love for Lula. On the other hand, Sailor's limited awareness of Lula's vulnerability prevents him from seeing how easily he exposes her to victimization by would-be rapist Bobby Peru (Willem Dafoe), who breaches the temporary sacredness of the motel room.

In *Lost Highway*, Fred Madison also loses his way in conjunction with prison cells and motel/hotel rooms. Convicted and sentenced to death for murdering Renee, Fred becomes Pete Dayton (Balthazar Getty) while in prison. Released as a result of becoming a new man, Pete appears to have a new start (in a way that prefigures Cooper-as-Dougie), though he is outmatched by the femme fatale Alice Wakefield (a double of Renee also played by Arquette). Pete and Fred both struggle to possess Renee/Alice (or "have" her, in Alice's parlance), pursuing her through hotels, motels, homes, and cars as her participation in pornographic films becomes more evident. *Lost Highway* also establishes a liminality of setting, in which protagonists in crisis have visions of other settings from the narrative via impossible portals. While in his prison cell, Fred has a vision of a cabin in the desert, a location that is his alternate body's destination and the eventual site of his rebirth. While in his bedroom, Pete has a vision of a prison cell. Within the oblique narrative, the prison is simultaneously the place from which he came, a location where some aspect of his self might presently be, and a future to which he could return.

The temporary settings of these works occupy most of the running times, which is consistent with the form of the road movie. Corey K. Creekmur observes that "despite the strong emphasis given to departures and arrivals, the road trip is largely defined by its extended middle."[16] Yet the desert is the terminus that ends the road journey. In Lynch, Gifford, and Frost's narratives, with the private home being profaned and temporary zones by their very nature not ultimately sustaining, the desert is the final site to conquer or be annihilated. Though as with other aspects of Lynch's works, the outcomes are rarely certain.

Sailor and Lula reach the desert setting of Big Tuna, Texas, tentatively joining a group of "strandees of the economic variety." Yet this temporary status is as close as they will come, for now, to fulfilling the westward journey to California promised by Sailor. Bobby Peru is eager to manipulate both of them, and Marietta's plotting has positioned Sailor for destruction. Even Sailor's multiplicative existence, in the form of Lula's unborn baby, is threatened by the ominous forces that seem to rule this desert setting. Finally, just before Bobby tempts Sailor to participate in a robbery, Lynch inserts a shot of Sailor's head physically distorting in a reflective surface at a bar. The image of a distorted head runs throughout Lynch's art and film/television work, and here the impression is that of a man pulled between his criminal past and his desired straight future, if only he could get back on the road. Sailor and Lula do eventually enjoy a happy ending, though only after Sailor takes several more lumps.

In *Lost Highway*, Alice similarly tempts Pete into a criminal plot, with the promise that the money they get will enable them to "go anywhere." The one catch is that Pete will have to go to the desert with Alice to meet a fence. Their trip to the desert climaxes with Pete's realization in no uncertain terms that he will never possess Alice. Fred returns, is forced to face Renee's infidelity anew, and with the Mystery Man murders his rival Dick Laurent (Robert Loggia). In the end, Fred ends up at the home where the journey started, though he too has multiplied and fragmented. His head and face distort as he escapes from the home toward an unknown future.

Though FBI Special Agent Dale Cooper is unlike Sailor and Fred by virtue of his distinct relationship to the law, his actions to attempt Laura's rescue, likewise result in being thwarted in the desert. He and Diane (Laura Dern) drive 430 miles into a desert setting after which their lives radically change. Just as the supposedly neutral zone of the desert redirected Sailor back to prison and Fred back to the hotels and homes of his wife's infidelity, the desert (and the all-powerful electricity that runs throughout) sends Agent Cooper into another branch of existence. In a motel with Diane, he becomes Richard, too confident to realize he is unmoored. In Texas, at the private home of Carrie Page (Sheryl Lee), he ignores a profane omen (a dead body), so strong is his instinct to rescue Laura and return her to her home in Twin Peaks, Washington. Driving Carrie northwest, Richard literally reaches the threshold of accomplishing his mission before realizing that Jowday (a threat far greater than Marietta Fortune or Renee Madison) has destroyed his goal of a fresh start with Laura, the woman he wants to save.

One could conclude from the narrative formula identified here that Lynch views the journey from the private home through temporary settings on the road and toward the desert as a futile attempt at conquest; that the primordial evil the protagonists face can never be conquered. There is within this formula an implicit commentary about historical westward advancement. However, Lynch's words in a 1990 interview with David Breskin suggest that the frontier advancement he explores in film and television has a higher, though quixotic, moral purpose. Breskin asserts that audiences are attracted to evil characters in Lynch's works because they "free us from the bounds of our own civility." Lynch responds, "I think we want to understand it so we can conquer it."[17] Such is the position of the frontiersman in American history: to forge an identity that might be annihilated in the face of the unconquerable unknown.

Notes

1. David Laderman, *Driving Visions* (Austin: University of Texas Press, 2002), 166.

2. Roger Ebert, "Wild at Heart," *RogerEbert.com*, accessed March 1, 2020, https://www.rogerebert.com /reviews/wild-at-heart-1990.

3. Martha P. Nochimson, *The Passion of David Lynch* (Austin: University of Texas Press, 1997), 48.

4. Laderman, *Driving Visions*, 15.

5. Tom Drahos, "The Imagined Desert," *Coolabah* (2013): 11, doi: 10.1344/co201311148–161.

6. Other popular desert horror films readers will recognize include *The Hills Have Eyes* (1977) and *Tremors* (1990).

7. Frederick J. Turner, "The Significance of the Frontier in American History," *Annual Report of the American Historical Association for the Year 1893* (1894): 199–227.

8. Solon T. Kimball, "Introduction," in *The Rites of Passage*, by Arnold van Gennep (Chicago: The University of Chicago Press, 1960), vii.

9. David Lynch and Kristine McKenna, *Room to Dream* (Random House, 2018).

10. Kimball, "Introduction," vi–vii.

11. Arnold van Gennep, *The Rites of Passage* (Chicago: The University of Chicago Press, 1960), 13.

12. Brian Hoyle, "*Wizard of Oz*: Why This Extraordinary Movie Has Been So Influential," *The Conversation*, accessed July 25, 2020, https://theconversation.com/wizard-of-oz-why-this-extraordinary-movie-has-been-so-influential-108098.

13. Turner, "The Significance."

14. Turner, "The Significance."

15. van Gennep, "The Rites of Passage."

16. Corey K. Creekmur, "On the Run and on the Road: Fame and the Outlaw Couple in American Cinema," in *The Road Movie Book,* ed. Steven Cohan and Ina Rae Hark (London: Routledge, 1997), 90.

17. David Lynch, interview by David Breskin, "David Lynch," *Rolling Stone*, 1990, http://davidbreskin.com /magazines/1-interviews/david-lynch-2/.

WORKS CITED

Creekmur, Corey K. 1997. "On the Run and on the Road: Fame and the Outlaw Couple in American Cinema." In Steven Cohan and Ina Rae Hark (eds.), *The Road Movie Book*. London: Routledge, 90–109.

Drahos, Tom. "The Imagined Desert," *Coolabah* (2013): 11, doi: 10.1344/co201311148-161.

Hoyle, Brian. 2018. "*Wizard of Oz*: Why This Extraordinary Movie Has Been So Influential." *The Conversation*. https://theconversation.com/wizard-of-oz-why-this-extraordinary-movie-has-been-so-influential-108098.

Kimball, Solon T. 1960. "Introduction." In Arnold van Gennep, *The Rites of Passage*. Chicago: The University of Chicago Press, v–xix.

Laderman, David. 2002. *Driving Visions*. Austin: University of Texas Press.

Lynch, David, and Kristine McKenna. 2018. *Room to Dream*. New York: Random House.

Nochimson, Martha P. *The Passion of David Lynch*. Austin: University of Texas Press.

Turner, Frederick Jackson. 1894. "The Significance of the Frontier in American History." *Annual Report of the American Historical Association for the Year 1893*. Washington, DC: Government Printing Office, 199–227.

van Gennep, Arnold. 1960. *The Rites of Passage*. Chicago: The University of Chicago Press.

The Western Road as Metaphor for American Instability in David Lynch's *Lost Highway*

Mark Henderson

The American Gothic is the darker twin of the American Dream—two sides of the same coin of American identity. The latter is the dominant, popular, national narrative, white-washed and simplified—of the rugged, self-reliant, persevering individualism that leads to personal freedom and success. The former is the countering, artistic sensibility that complicates the popular narrative by exploring its ugly, historical underbelly. Historically as well as symbolically, both the Dream and the Gothic have been given a direction—the American West; for, if the first mainland European settlers had arrived on the Atlantic coast, the ultimate realization of colonizing the continent would necessitate a grand push westward, toward the Pacific coast. Driven by the American Dream, this American frontierism would also involve a stunning repetition of atrocities—against Native Americans, African Americans, and Mexican Americans. Such atrocities and other unpleasant truths are the stuff of the American Gothic. A a retroactive, twentieth-century awareness of these truths finds recent artistic expression in the so-called "neo-noir" genre of filmmaking—a later, even more cynical and violent revisiting of early- and mid-twentieth-century *film noir*, whose shadowy and uncertain environments effectively correspond to their anti-hero protagonists' (typically detectives or wrongly-accused everymen) moral ambiguity and unstable sense of identity. David Lynch creates what is perhaps the most encapsulating neo-noir metaphor for this American sense of unstable identity in his 2000 film *Lost Highway*: the western road.

The instability of identity has been a consistent trope throughout David Lynch's work as a film director—from Henry Spencer's terrified uncertainty of all that is considered normal and his place within that normality in *Eraserhead* (1977) to Jeffrey Beaumont's nightmarish uncovering of idyllic suburbia's dark underbelly and criminal underworld in *Blue Velvet* (1986). However, anticipating a trend that he would continue in terms of both narrative device and setting with *Mulholland Drive* (2001), Lynch employs a rather literal representation of an unstable identity in 1997's *Lost Highway*. It occurs when Fred Madison (Bill Pullman) actually and inexplicably transforms into a younger man named Pete Dayton (Balthasar Getty) after being imprisoned for allegedly murdering his wife Renee (Patricia Arquette), leading to his release from prison and living a new life. Also, present throughout the film, and coexisting with its surreal and even magically realistic plotline, is the motif of the speeding highway. Furthermore, *Lost Highway* takes place in Los Angeles (as opposed to the anonymous, representative cityscape of *Eraserhead*, or the unnamed North Carolina suburb in *Blue Velvet*), so this is a specifically *western* American highway, resonating with the sinister aura left by the history of American westward expansion.

American film is an extension of American literature, and thus inherits the sensibility of what has come to be known as the American Gothic. According to Leslie Fiedler, of all the fiction of the West, American literature is "bewilderingly and embarrassingly, a gothic fiction, nonrealistic and negative, sadist and melodramatic—a literature of darkness and the grotesque in a land of light and affirmation."[1] From literature to film, one sees the heritage and further perpetuation of American mythology—a mythology historically established, due to accident of geography, along a *westward* trajectory. The West has a long-standing significance as a symbol within the American mythos contextualized in frontierism and the problematic doctrine of Manifest Destiny. Roads and highways have also become symbols of the American individualistic need to self-actualize through a seemingly infinite mobility and to strike out on one's own. This is especially true in the case of *Lost Highway*. Consistent with Slavoj Žižek's interpretation of the film as an exploitation of the opposition between the two horrors of fantastic perversion and alienating drabness, the film's manipulation and interweaving of the extraordinary and the mundane within an American western setting can be seen as a commentary on the confusion and alienation that seems to plague the modern American identity as formed by the American mythos.[2] Again, as a cinematic continuation of the American Gothic literary tradition, the film exemplifies what Alan Lloyd-Smith calls "negative Romanticism"—"the blackness of vision when Romantic inspiration succumbs to an equally overwhelming but far bleaker subjectivity, [an] agonized introspection concerning the evil that lies within the self."[3] The American Dream, the beacon of that mythic drive which spurs the archetypal American ever westward, is therefore counterbalanced by its gloomier and more sober twin in the American Gothic—a tradition that is palpable throughout Lynch's film.

Throughout the film, the recurring motif of a front-seat perspective shot of a rushing-by highway suggests circularity and repetition, both of which calling to mind that Freudian concept and descriptor which has become so virtually synonymous with the gothic, the uncanny—"that class of the frightening which leads back to what is known of old and long familiar."[4] The uncanniness of this highway also suggests a pattern of damnation that calls to mind the Flying Dutchman and the torments of Sisyphus and Tantalus in Hades. Such a structure appropriately reflects the uncertainty and instability within the American identity. If a significant component of the American identity is expansion and exploration, mythically defined by the direction of the American West, a troubling question remains. What is there left to do when one runs out of literal western space but madly speed around in circles on a nightmarishly endless western highway in search of more frontier that is simply not there? *Lost Highway*, then, is an artistic interpretation of this particular American hell—self-created and self-fulfilled through the uncanny perpetuation of American myth's questionable promises and bases in fact. Aesthetically, *Lost Highway* recalls the near-phantasmagoria and the deliberately confusing, labyrinthine plots of prototypical American Gothic literature—in particular, the fiction of Charles Brockden Brown, arguably the creator of the American Gothic, and especially in his novel *Arthur Mervyn* (1799). Even a brief plot summary of the film is sufficient to convey how the film, in typical Lynch fashion, is extraordinary to a degree that calling it merely surreal seems inadequate. From Fred's encounter with the Mystery Man to his transformation into Pete, evidence of the American Gothic is present

Early in the film, Fred explains his hatred of cameras to the detectives to whom he has reported the regularly arriving tapes, saying, "I like to remember things my own way…. How I remember them. Not necessarily the way they happened." This statement sums up the troubled conclusions surrounding identity, memory, and the past that permeate the film. Lynch seems to work through these issues on the metafictional level, allowing the conventions of the American neo-noir genre—of which *Lost Highway* is a transparently obvious pastiche—to collapse in upon themselves, reflecting a similar fragility in the national myths that such attributes represent. The film is a veritable stew of neo-noir conventions: fast and/or expensive cars, gorgeous femme fatales, powerful but sleazy men who ruthlessly exploit the vulnerable, and outlaws. This matrix of mythology can be interpreted as both the fuel and the symptom of the magically realistic representations of unstable identity and circular time that are central to the film, both of which leaving the viewer with the unsettling sense of being trapped in an existential prison. Cars are prevalent throughout the film. Many pivotal scenes revolve around them. Even Pete's job is that of an auto mechanic, and one of the many marks of Mr. Eddy's success and influence is the Cadillac that he brings to Pete for repairs. Even before this, Pete's parents, upon picking him up from the prison, are both strikingly dressed in blue jeans, leather jackets, and dark sunglasses, recalling the rebellious, rock 'n' roll, high-speed 1950s universe of *Rebel Without a Cause* (1955) and *The Wild One* (1953). And what is perhaps one of the film's most darkly amusing scenes involves a testosterone-fueled conflict between two drivers. While taking Pete for a drive to show him how his Cadillac handles, Mr. Eddy signals an impatient tailgater to drive around him; but when that tailgater gives him the middle finger, Mr. Eddy rams him from behind, drags him from his car, and pistol whips him while profanely screaming automotive accident and death statistics into his face, finally ordering him to get a driver's manual and read it thoroughly before leaving him on the ground sobbing.

It is clear from this episode in particular that Mr. Eddy is, as Marek Wieczorek describes, "one of those Lynchean characters who embodies both [the ridiculous and the sublime]: on the one hand, he strictly enforces the rules, representing the enactment of the socio-symbolic Law, but on the other, he does so in such an exaggerated, excessively violent manner that his role exposes the inherently violent and arbitrary nature of [that] law."[5] Such a paradox of "lawless law" is ostensibly neo-western in terms of both genre and aesthetic; and it is emblematic of both Richard Slotkin's expansionist "regeneration through violence" and D.H. Lawrence's summation of the "essential American soul" as "hard, isolate, stoic, and a killer" as confessional representations of the dark underbelly of America's history of westward frontierism (especially with its atrocious exploitation and destruction of both the environment and indigenous peoples).[6]

Pete's first object of identification with power and success is this outlaw gangster, whose rule of law is his own, sanctioned only through the might-makes-right influence of violence and intimidation. For him, Mr. Eddy is the essential, all-American man—an accidental, darkly father-like role model. Coexisting with Mr. Eddy's violently American masculinity is Pete's other object, the trophy-femininity of Alice, the sensuous and assertive, blonde femme fatale doppelganger of Fred's wife, the darker-haired and more subdued Renee. The scene of her first appearance to Pete is resplendent with Hollywood love-at-first-sight clichés—including slow-motion hair-tossing and side-glancing to a soundtrack of Lou Reed singing "This Magic Moment." The sex they have is also intentionally and diametrically opposed to that between Fred and Renee—virile, passionate, and mutually satisfying versus impotent, charitable, and frustrating. Whereas Renee is the sad and disappointed, post-honeymoon trophy of the struggling and older Fred, Alice appears for the younger Pete as the new, eager, and rejuvenating lover. However, consistent with the transparently false comforts provided by the superficialities of the film's pastiche, Alice's initial front as dream-girl and sexual angel gradually melts away to reveal something less innocent and more disillusioning.

The ideal-shattering disenchantments are revealed in succession: Alice's plot to steal from Andy, her forced recruitment into Mr. Eddy's amateur world of pornography, a visceral discrepancy between actually seeing evidence of the less romantic side of her sexuality and merely hearing about it, and her overall demeanor becoming more confident and menacing. But her ultimate and defining betrayal of Pete's romanticism comes in how, after having sex with him on the desert ground in front of the cabin (from his dreams!), her response to his ecstatic repetition of "I want you" is a cold-hearted "You'll never have me." She then gets up and walks, naked, into the cabin, disappearing inside.

Her role as neo-noir femme fatale functions to intercept and betray Pete's need for validation or renewal of his American persona, his western masculinity. For Žižek, Alice is an example of the femme fatale of the neo-noir, versus that of the traditional noir—who, rather than suffer the punishment or redemption typical of that archetype in the traditional noir, betrays the patriarchal fantasy of such punishment and redemption through a brutal "self-commodification," giving the male lover/suitor exactly what he wants, sexually, in gross, hyper-objectified, and non-romanticized fashion.[7] Paradoxically, the validation and/or renewal of masculinity sought after through sexual conquest of this neo-noir femme fatale is "thwarted in its efficiency as the support of desire"; she seems to say, "I'll thwart your desire by directly gratifying it … you'll get me, but deprived of the fantasmic support-background that made me an object of fascination."[8] Her triumph is how, through that self-commodification, what is ultimately sacrificed is not herself, but the "fantasmic image-support" of the male's desire—the residue of which leaving not the dream-girl/sexual angel, or even the damsel-in-distress, but a "vulgar, cold, manipulative 'bitch' deprived of any aura."[9] The lover/suitor is thus left with the humiliating and emasculating reality of his own delusion.

However, Žižek's observations can be further extrapolated toward a more specifically American metaphorical commentary. The final sex scene between Pete and Alice, in fact, makes clear all of the components of the film's apparent commentary on American nationalistic myth. They have sex on the ground in the western desert, are illuminated by the headlights of Pete's car, and Alice walks away naked to disappear inside of the cabin—an enduring symbol of American frontier myth, with its promises of ruggedly individualistic (and yes, masculine) self-actualization and autonomy. The sex taking place on the ground recalls the traditional, patriarchal gendering of colonial land-settling—the masculine "drive" penetrating and taming the wild, "virgin" land.[10] Pete's/Fred's ultimate disillusionment at the hands of Alice/Renee is also, then, a disillusionment at the hands of the American Dream and all of its mythological components (women, cars, land, and rugged masculinity among them).

However, the thwarted ambitions of Pete/Fred surprisingly share the beautiful femme fatale as Fitzgeraldian beacon-object of ambitious inspiration (best exemplified through the character of Daisy Buchanan in Fitzgerald's *The Great Gatsby*), even with the realized success of Mr. Eddy/Dick Laurent. To Pete's face, Mr. Eddy alludes to killing anyone with whom Alice had messed around with on him, hinting at the actual, continuing psychological burden of keeping such a trophy-acquisition—and, by symbolic extension, the actual psychological burden of trying to maintain appearances and delusions that are grounded in myth. Mr. Eddy does, after all, ultimately die for it. Also, reference to the apparently alarming frequency and prevalence of similar dreams and romances ending on a tragic note can be found earlier in the film, while Fred/Pete is still on death row, when one of the guards (Henry Rollins) says, "That wife-killer's looking pretty fucked up," only to darkly laugh with the other guard after he replies, "Which one?" Based on the guards' gallows cynicism, such prisoners are apparently not uncommon.

The success, power, and virility associated with the masculinized expansionist drive that the American Dream inspires is also linked to individual autonomy—not only as self-reliance and self-sufficiency but also privacy, which is repeatedly thwarted from the start of the film. The first scene emerges from the darkness of Fred's home, seemingly illuminated only by the lighting of his cigarette. One is stricken not only by the home's sparse lighting (evidence of a need to keep the electricity bill down), but by the irritating, extreme quiet of Fred and Renee's timid dialogue. And this quietness is intentional; just as one cranks the volume to hear that dialogue, a deafening difference between the scenes inside the home and that of Fred playing a loud, impassioned sax solo at a gig is made startlingly obvious. One thus gets the sense that Fred is hiding and embarrassed within his own appearance-keeping and status-validating suburban home—and that Renee is aware enough of this to humor him, maternally nurture him, and walk on the proverbial eggshells. Fred's privacy is thus immediately undermined as one not of power and success, but of shame and impotence. The ensuing infiltrations, evidenced by the multiple VHS tapes, add insult to injury through the actual penetration of that privacy—a penetration that is both violating and emasculating. It is through these mysterious infiltrations that the central issues of mythology and identity are both introduced and sustained throughout *Lost Highway*—rather, how American identity is inherently unstable due to the shaky mythological foundations that attempt to define it (i.e., Manifest Destiny, heroic masculinity, and righteous conquest).

Lynch's fictional, pastiche universe, according to Wieczorek, typically calls self-reflexive attention to the instability of myths and ideals by pushing "the minimum of idealization ... to the limits of believability, indeed to the level of the ridiculous and thus exposed as fantasmatic."[11] He further defines the dynamic of Lynch's universe as a tension between the Lacanian Symbolic and the Lacanian Real—or between the surface realms of appearances and clichés and "the hidden/traumatic underside of our existence or sense of reality," with the Symbolic being a hopelessly flimsy, "fantasmatic" defense against intrusions of extreme and shocking disillusionments.[12] Indeed, for Lacan, the Real is *the* momentous "trauma" that "split[s] ... the subject in relation to the encounter," with the Symbolic being a delusional one-sidedness, a viewing of one's self as merely an "opposite" rather than a multifaceted totality.[13] Such intrusions include a giant projection of Alice's porno scene at Laurant's mansion, as well as the apparent mutilation of Renee that Fred sees on the final VHS tape before his arrest and sentencing for her murder—both of which violently strip away the naïve veneer of male fantasy (the happy marriage/home and the gratefully, sexually rewarding damsel).

But if there is a single presence in the film acting as the uncanny harbinger of these disillusionments and resulting crises of identity, a sort of American Gothic incarnate, it is the Mystery Man, whose initial appearance foreshadows the extraordinary destabilizations—in the form of dual identities, of Fred/Pete, Renee/Alice, and Mr. Eddy/Dick Laurent.[14] Žižek refers to the Mystery Man's "timelessness and spacelessness"—his ability to apparently be in two places at once—as well as his functioning as a "blank screen ... 'objectively' register[ing] Fred's unacknowledged fantasmatic urges," therefore introducing the likelihood of this enigmatic character's being a symbolic, psychic projection.[15] The chief horror of the Mystery Man's uncanny nature lies in how he is Fred's deepest, darkest, most unconscious fantasies made Other, smiling and staring at him with cold and deathly disinterest.

The Mystery Man is linked with three unstable identities. He is, as Andy tells Fred, a friend of Dick Laurent's. During the eerie, in-two-places-at-once phone call at Andy's party, he tells Fred that he is in his home because Fred had invited him in. Before the meeting at Andy's party, Fred had seen a momentary apparition of the Mystery Man's face over Renee's after he has sex with her. So the Mystery Man is linked not only with these three particular unstable identities, but also with Fred/Pete's archetypal relationship among them—as part of a hero-fatale/damsel-nemesis triad. His parting shot with Fred (having transformed back from Pete after Alice had walked away into the cabin) involves confrontationally filming him (both reminding us of how Fred hates cameras and revealing the Mystery Man as the source of the VHS tapes) and saying, "Alice who? Her name is Renee.... What the fuck is *your* name?" This immediately undermines the likelihood of Fred's killing her in the first place; Alice's mythic, archetypal status; and, by extension, the mythological import behind all of Fred's disillusionments and crises of identity. With no actual femme fatale, the entire archetypal construct of the pastiche collapses, calling into earth-shattering question its mythic foundation.

During the shared phone call with Eddy/Laurent to Pete, the Mystery Man cryptically tells Pete: "In the East, the far East, when a person is sentenced to death, they're sent to a place they can't escape, never knowing when an executioner may step up behind them and fire a bullet in the back of their head." This statement, both odd and ominous, foreshadows the film's conclusion, which reveals a circular and inescapable structure to the narrative: the source of the "Dick Laurent is dead" message to Fred is none other than Fred himself, fracturing the narrative's natural laws of time and space, along with further fracturing Fred's identity and his sense of history as a representative American. He is damned, trapped and ever-lost outside of linear space and time, to a seemingly endless, cyclical repetition for some obscure and unnamed sin. Again, the setting of the American West and the ever-present image of the speeding highway point not only toward the historical sins behind the idealized American mythos, but also toward the blind-eyed delusions upon which that mythos is based. This damnation is the logical outcome of, as Fiedler describes, the "Faustian" nature at the core of the American individual, "the individual, who, in the pursuit of 'knowledge' or 'experience' or just 'happiness' places himself outside the sanctions and protections of society."[16] Out of pride, ambition, and desire, Fred/Pete has committed a metaphorically Oedipal murder of the dark father-figure Eddy/Laurent, echoing proto-America's symbolic, revolutionary murder of father-Britain for the sake of its own independence, and has found himself eternally on the run, initiated into the potential for further crimes committed for the sake of self-preservation.

Also in keeping with the circularity of the film's narrative is its both opening and concluding with the telling soundtrack of David Bowie's "I'm Deranged," the title and frantic percussion of which hinting at a break with sanity and stability of identity. In spite of any lessons Fred may or may not have learned through his extraordinary ordeal, he is (as the typical and representative American) incorrigible, stuck on idiocy and madness and doomed to perpetuity in spite of his frustrated dreams (that is, the American Dream). And, thanks to the further metafictional commentary inherent within and provided by the pastiche, even Hollywood conventions and the very medium of Lynch's artistic expression, American cinema, are revealed to be, in fact, the pinnacle expression of America's damned post-frontier delirium. With no more literal land to settle in the West to satisfy the expansionist drive, the American identity must drive around in circles, breaking itself up to manufacture further and more shameless illusions and manufacturing dreams to spread globally, while ironically staying in place, through the industry of American cinema, further altering reality and destabilizing identity through the contaminating effects of myth-laden entertainment. *Lost Highway* can then be viewed, ironically, as both a celebration and a bitter acknowledgment of this fractured national character. It is a truly American Gothic cinematic work.

NOTES

1. Leslie Fiedler, *Love and Death in the American Novel* (Normal, IL: Dalkey Archive, 1966), 29.

2. Slavoj Žižek, *The Art of the Ridiculous Sublime: On David Lynch's* Lost Highway (Seattle: University of Washington Press, 2000), 7.

3. Alan Lloyd-Smith, *American Gothic Fiction: An Introduction* (New York: Continuum, 2004), 34.

4. Sigmund Freud, "The Uncanny," trans. Alix Strachey, *The Norton Anthology of Theory and Criticism* (New York: Norton, 2001), 930.

5. Marek Wieczorek, introduction, in Žižek *The Art of the Ridiculous Sublime*, x.

6. Richard Slotkin, *Regeneration Through Violence: The Mythology of the American Frontier, 1600–1860* (Norman: University of Oklahoma Press, 1973), 5; D. H. Lawrence, *Studies in Classic American Literature* (New York: Viking, 1961), 62.

7. Žižek, *The Art of the Ridiculous Sublime*, 9.

8. *Ibid.*, 11.

9. *Ibid.*

10. *Virgin Land* being, after all, the title of Henry Nash Smith's work on the symbolism and mythology of the American West and westward expansionism.

11. Wieczorek, introduction, x.

12. *Ibid.*, viii.

13. Jacques Lacan, *The Four Fundamental Concepts of Psychoanalysis*, trans. Alan Sheridan (New York: Norton, 1988), 69. Jane Gallop, *Reading Lacan* (Ithaca, NY: Cornell University Press, 1985), 60.

14. Granted, Mr. Eddy is merely the alter ego of Dick Laurent, and it is never clearly answered whether or not Renee was actually murdered or if Renee and Alice are the same person; but both of these dualities relate directly to the outright magically realistic one of Fred/Pete.

15. Žižek, *The Art of the Ridiculous Sublime*, 19–20.

16. Fiedler, *Love and Death*, 440.

WORKS CITED

Fiedler, Leslie. 1966. *Love and Death in the American Novel.* Normal, IL: Dalkey Archive.

Freud, Sigmund. 2001. "The Uncanny." Trans. Alix Strachey. In William E. Cain, Laurie Finke, Barbara Johnson, Vincent B. Leitch, John McGowan, and Jeffrey J. Williams (eds.), *The Norton Anthology of Theory and Criticism.* 929, 952. New York: W.W. Norton.

Gallop, Jane. 1985. *Reading Lacan.* Ithaca, NY: Cornell University Press.

Lacan, Jacques. 1988. *The Four Fundamental Concepts of Psychoanalysis.* Trans. Alan Sheridan. Edited by Jacques-Alain Miller. New York: W.W. Norton.

Lawrence, D.H. 1961. *Studies in Classic American Literature.* New York: Viking.

Lloyd-Smith, Alan. 2004. *American Gothic Fiction: An Introduction.* New York: Continuum.

Lost Highway. 1997. Dir. David Lynch. Perf. Bill Pullman, Patricia Arquette, and Balthazar Getty. Ciby 2000, Asymmetrical Productions, 1997.

Slotkin, Richard. 1973. *Regeneration Through Violence: The Mythology of the American Frontier, 1600–1860.* Norman: University of Oklahoma Press.

Smith, Henry Nash. 1978. *Virgin Land: The American West as Symbol and Myth.* Cambridge: Harvard University Press.

Wieczorek, Marek. 2000. "Introduction." *The Art of the Ridiculous Sublime: On David Lynch's* Lost Highway. By Slavoj Žižek. Seattle: University of Washington Press. viii-xiii.

Žižek, Slavoj. 2000. *The Art of the Ridiculous Sublime: On David Lynch's* Lost Highway. Seattle: University of Washington Press.

Re-Imagined West in the L.A. Trilogy

A Heritage of California Fiction and American Trauma

ROB E. KING

When genre westerns began to fade in popularity, their conventions remained in re-imagined frontier narratives, a combination of noir,
regional, and contemporary stories engaged in new realities of the West.
David Lynch's *Twin Peaks* and his L.A. Trilogy (*Lost Highway*, *Mulholland Drive*, and *INLAND EMPIRE*) all take place primarily in the American West and can be read as re-imagined frontier narratives. Re-imagined
frontier narratives find their origins in Depression-era California noir
and communicate a traumatized American Dream at the terminus of the
mythic and geographic American West. The Lynch-directed narratives are
an extension of this fictional expression with their own specific reactions
and statements on the aftermath of western expansion and its implied
promises. It is through his films' neo-noir styling and incorporation of
nostalgia that Lynch and his collaborators create innovative, re-imagined
frontier narratives, inviting audiences to become voyeurs of their perspectives on American lives in the contemporary West.

The early chapters of *Twin Peaks* arrived in 1989–1992, years that
Michael Craig Gibbs claims as "[T]he tail-end of postmodernism (if one
accepts the notion that we have moved on to a new artistic paradigm in
the twenty-first century)."[1] This is a time, Gibbs goes on to state, when
the traditional Western as a literary form would begin to disappear with
some last efforts by writers like Larry McMurtry and Cormac McCar-
thy to deconstruct and reimagine it.[2] For added historical context, these
are also years at the end of the Cold War. As Alexandra Keller identifies,
"The Western's near disappearance after the critical and financial disaster

of *Heaven's Gate* in 1980 ... and its resurgence with the Oscar-winning *Dances with Wolves* in 1990 and *Unforgiven* in 1992, coincide with the seismic shifts in American culture that were the Reagan-Bush I years (1980–1992)."[3] The introduction of *Twin Peaks* in 1989 with its initial closing in the film *Twin Peaks: Fire Walk with Me* in 1992—the tail-end of the Reagan-Bush I years—is, then, historically timely and telling.

It is also valuable to note that Lynch and Gifford's *Lost Highway* is an exploratory reaction to the O.J. Simpson murder trial and that *Mulholland Drive* premiered short of a month following the September 11, 2001, World Trade Center attack.[4] All these premieres occurred during major signposts of American trauma. Additionally, Mark Frost and David Lynch wrote the continuation of the transmedia of *Twin Peaks* in script and in novel in 2012 with the context of the 2008 recession and their generation's late-age, post-nuclear trauma clearly in mind.[5] In the company of California fiction, Lynch's narratives are also updates on regional American western narratives as their noir conventions reflect a heritage of the urban cowboy. Josh Garrett-Davis notes in *What Is a Western?: Region, Genre, Imagination*, "It seems that frequently western regional art evokes the genre Western, which itself depends on (and is inspired by) the reality of the West, such that the two cannot be cleanly distinguished."[6] While Lynch is not a director of contemporary or neo-westerns, the traumas he engages with his regional western narratives and characters communicate the American's conflicted interiority following nineteenth-century westward expansion.

Lynch had a journey to the American west in his art, one that winds through his neo-noir films with regional as well as spiritual importance. Of his move to California in 1970, Lynch says, "the drive west was beautiful. I remember one point when we were driving down into this gigantic valley and the sky was so big that when you came up over the ridge you could see four different kinds of weather at the same time. There was sunshine in one part of the sky and a violent storm in another part."[7] He could have been describing the context of his characters' settings, sunshine in one part and violent storm in the other, a dichotomy he consistently brings to his American narratives with emphasized distinction. California as a destination for David Lynch's career and his narratives fits a historical precedent when examining the region's history of art and allure for spiritual groups. Furthermore, Lynch's regional western narratives are kin to California fiction of the 1930s in that they capture the story of the American Dream proven false.

American cultural studies recognize the complexities in defining the American Dream. "The American Dream is a complex concept: We can call it an ethos or, in the terms of the Myth and Symbol School in American Studies ... a modern myth. It includes the idea of freedom as the opportunity for prosperity and success, usually in the form of class mobility through hard work."[8] Ideologically, the American Dream includes self-made solvency, rugged individualism, wealth through capitalist, melting-pot unity, and comfort in armed religious piety. Today's traumatized dream encompasses perspectives on those original ideals as tested by civil war, depressions and recessions, civil rights struggles, nuclear warfare, growing minority and diversity movements, and terrorism domestic and international. Yet the struggling dream remains stubbornly hegemonic, disillusioned by its failed promises, a blurring of church and state separations, and catalyst for poisonous nationalism. Lynch's narratives and protagonists are reactionary to this environment. The dream is fragmented, more so resembling a nightmare, but a nightmare through which Lynch looks to Transcendental Meditation (TM) in order to suggest healing beyond all borders.

In a recent interview, Lynch responded to a question about the 2020 pandemic, stating "For some reason, we were going down the wrong path and Mother Nature just said, 'Enough already, we've got to stop everything.' This is going to last long enough to lead to some kind of new way of thinking.... I think it's going to be much more spiritual and much kinder and it's going to bring us all closer together in a really strong and beautiful way."[9] This "new way of thinking" as a response to American trauma is a notion that was popularly evident in California in the 1960s and 1970s with the formation of protests and cults. Still, the basis for spiritual response in California began much earlier. Theosophist leaders had identified the American West as a site for spiritual renewal as early as 1888, when leader Helena Petrovna Blavatsky specifically located it in her *The Secret Doctrine.* "It is in America that the transformation will take place, and has already silently commenced."[10] The heritage of radical spiritualism in California includes pioneering theosophists at Point Loma as early as the late 1800s; charismatic faith healer and radio preacher Aimee Semple McPherson in the '20s and '30s; Jack Parsons's participation in Crowley's Ordo Templi Orientis through Pasadena's Agape Lodge in the '30s and '40s; then, the myriad of perceived cults and religions that proliferate to the present day. One reason, according to Ashcraft, is:

The availability of cheap land in the American West lured numerous communities of various religious and political persuasions to settle there. Beginning in the 1880s, California was an exceptionally attractive haven for those who found more established parts of the nation too constrictive or oppressive. It offered abundant land, a mild climate, and long growing seasons. It also had an Anglo-Protestant minority who competed with other religious groups rather than determining mainstream culture as they did elsewhere in the United States.[11]

Hence, Lynch's introduction to TM and Vedic religion in Los Angeles in 1973 was unsurprising in the region. The land where radical American hope landed at the end of its colonial expansion was not just the end of the West but a stage for efforts at spiritual regeneration. Gibbs defines this stage, writing "Los Angeles represented the terminus of Westward Expansion mere decades before and is now a place where echoes of the Old West continue to haunt the landscape."[12] Greg Grandin adds: "And when the physical frontier was closed, its imagery could easily be applied to other arenas of expansion, to markets, war, culture, technology, science, the psyche, and politics."[13] These ideals and emotions are at the center of the darkness and spiritual thirst portrayed in Lynch's films—industrial nightmares, *Lost Highway* as a reaction to the O.J. trial, Hollywood betrayals, and small towns hidden in the woods of the west where a murder is not a simple statistic and a yellow light still means slow down. The following examines some narrative nostalgia in Lynch's films.

Los Angeles Noir and Detectives—The Urban Cowboy

Film noir is a narrative genre that burgeoned in America with the ultimate cast of urban cowboys: detectives, private eyes, and lone agents. Critically unidentified as such until the 1970s, film noirs were prominent in the 1940s and '50s. Many were based on novels written by California authors during the Great Depression. David Fine, author of *Imaging Los Angeles: A City in Fiction* claims that "These Depression-crazed middle classes of Southern California became, in one mode or another, the original protagonists of that great anti-myth usually known as noir."[14] Still hardened by their environments, these film and literature cowboys were up against odds that continued to require a personal code for survival. He is the "urban cowboy—complete with codes governing behavior, speech, etc.—but this character must still operate in a steel, concrete and glass 'frontier,' a place where crime, corruption, and over-population dominate, and the natural environment has receded into mere pockets ... wilderness pockets."[15] The streets are lined with fire hydrants instead of cactus and lobby ashtrays instead of spittoons. Only the train stations and bar tops remain familiar in this landscape of skyscrapers instead of mountains.

The expansion on these tropes, encompassing films such as 1974's *Chinatown*, 1981's *Body Heat*, and 1997's *Lost Highway*, has been titled Neo-Noir, a genre label with which Lynch is most firmly associated. According to Douglas Keesey, "[I]n neo-noirs ... the city/country distinction breaks down as crime and corruption are shown to be present even in sunny climes ('white' noir) and agrarian locales ('country noir')."[16] Lynch first revealed to audiences a fascination with the young detective in *Blue Velvet* (1986). Kyle McLachlan fulfilled his Hardy Boys–like detective and voyeur in that film as well as the Boy Scout–like FBI man in *Twin Peaks*. Equally, Naomi Watts becomes a Nancy Drew in seeking her lover Rita's identity in *Mulholland Drive*, noting that the character of Audrey Horne was staged as such a sleuth in the early scripting for *Twin Peaks*.[17] The evidence of those vitally American pre-teen texts—The Hardy Boys series and the Nancy Drew series—in David Lynch's work are referenced here as he utilizes their essence in his world building to harken back to a nostalgic period in America. The Hardy Boys book series arrived in 1927 and Nancy Drew in 1930, instilling young minds with a sense of mystery. The characters of each would evolve in tone and style alongside U.S. culture and tastes. Born in 1946, David Lynch came of age in an era where such series, as well as the presence of James Dean and Marlon Brando, might influence one on-screen. This was also the most popular era for Westerns in film and literature. Jane Tompkins notes that "In 1959 there were no fewer than thirty-five Westerns running concurrently on television, and out of the top ten programs eight were Westerns."[18] In a study of movies released by genre from 1995 to 2019—the years encompassing the releases of Lynch's L.A. Trilogy—out of fourteen genres examined, Westerns were in the bottom four with eighty-one releases.[19] Dramas hold the top spot with 5,266 releases. So, it is once again through the neo-noir styling and nostalgia that Lynch creates re-imagined frontier narratives.

Hollywood as Re-Imagined Frontier

The Western genre appeared in Hollywood at the outset. Some of the earliest films produced by Edison Studios were Westerns. This is not surprising as myths and legends of pioneering were still the recent memories of grandparents' stories in the early 1900s. Hollywood was established in 1853 as an agricultural area.[20] According to Gary Krist:

> Incorporated in 1903 as a dry Christian community, it would vote to annex itself to Los Angeles in 1910 to gain access to the water brought by Mulholland's aqueduct, still under construction…. Not until October 1911 would the first movie studio come to Hollywood proper, when two Englishmen, William and David Horsely, began making movies under the name Nestor in a decrepit roadhouse off Sunset Boulevard.[21]

Corruption and wars over water rights in 1920 later became the subject matter of Polanski's *Chinatown*, a modern film noir that borrowed from the re-imagined frontier as defined by Raymond Chandler.

Traditional genre westerns represent the heroes and struggles of pioneering on the frontier, while re-imagined frontier narratives continue the story of what the settled West became and is today—in much of it, more disillusioning than promising. *Mulholland Drive* incorporates this kind of re-imagined frontier narrative. It is more akin to Los Angeles fiction such as Nathanael West's regional *Day of the Locust* than it is with traditional westerns first represented by Owen Wister's *The Virginian*. Like the California fiction of West, Chandler, and McCoy, *Mulholland Drive* includes residues of an Old West mixed into ultimate disillusionment with stardom that the region promised at the end of America's westward expansion. *Mulholland Drive* opens with a dance montage harkening back to happier displays of Hollywood innocence as it was depicted in the 1950s. By the film's tragic end, audiences can see it as Betty's deluded imagination of Hollywood. It can then be compared with the earlier depiction of Hollywood dance competition in Horace McCoy's California novel *They Shoot Horses, Don't They?* Joining a grueling dance competition as a last grasp at hope in Hollywood, Texas, native Gloria Beatty, partner of protagonist Robert Syverten, finally begs for suicide amid her disillusionment with the promise of westward migration and Hollywood.

Gibbs speaks to the elements of California fictions that were the earliest re-imagined frontier narratives as seen in *The Day of the Locust*. "Besides establishing ties to the frontier, *The Day of the Locust* is … the antithesis of the traditional Western setting in many ways: it is urban, it is dark, it possesses a seedy underbelly of crime and corruption, and, to reiterate, it is the place where the Dream proves false." That definition applies the same to Lynch's L.A. Trilogy films. Fine affirms this symbolic Los Angeles as westward expansion terminus:

> [Los Angeles] has become the capital of American noir. The identification of the city with dark imaginings and violent endings began in earnest in the 1930s in the fiction of Raymond Chandler, James M. Cain, Horace McCoy, and Nathanael West. Today the ghosts of these writers are haunting the contemporary narrative landscape of the city—in both fiction and film, in recyclings and resurrections of the hard-boiled style, the tough-guy detective story, and the dark, satiric Hollywood narrative.[22]

Again, Lynch's L.A. Trilogy exemplifies this tradition of L.A. narrative. Replacing the hard-boiled, tough-guy—making exception for Dick Laurent in *Lost Highway*—with characterizations closer to James Dean's jaded, 1950s cool in *Rebel Without a Cause*, creates an amalgamation seen in Lynch's films of all the elements mentioned above. Just as the authors mentioned by Gibbs reflect the outcome of the western narrative in their works, Lynch explores humankind's dark impulses, peripherally examining white guilt, western disillusionment, and corrupt power dynamics in the twentieth and twenty-first centuries.

A Narrative Journey to the Traumatized Post-West

The West in Lynch's films is a destination for traumas. *Lost Highway*'s Fred Madison has a destiny of violence. As he reconciles his murder of his wife, Renee, through the dreamed persona of Pete Dayton, the destination is always the same. Fred is a murderer.[23] In Fred's dream, his destiny of wielding a gunman's pistol involves a very specific setting: "We're floating down an old two-lane highway through a desolate, desert landscape."[24] While it appears that the Mystery Man is the one who shoots Mr. Eddy/Laurent, "[t]he camera cuts back wide to reveal Fred holding the gun. He is standing alone—there is no Mystery Man." He is a lone gunman who has lodged at the Lost Highway Hotel out in the desolate, desert landscape. This scenario is both Old West and neo-noir because Lynch relocates Madison's Los Angeles murder to the western desert, beyond the city in Madison's dream. The Lost Highway Hotel additionally situates a western hotel trope, where the hotel's image is iconic in establishing new society in western settlements. Monica Montelongo Flores tells us that "[E]xamples from cinema and television studied from 1996 to the present join the hotel iconography with themes concerning race, crime, violence, and sexuality. In this period, there is a re-establishing of the icon and a new reliance on the mutability of the hotel as a symbol."[25] This is hotel iconography as it appears in neo-noirs and re-imagined frontier narratives, and the violence associated with the hotel in *Lost Highway* is emblematic of this paradigm. In *Twin Peaks*, The Great Northern Hotel is central and a space of violence, colonization, crime, and sex. Regarding *Twin Peaks'* use of The Great Northern Hotel, Flores writes: "What is critical in *Twin Peaks'* recasting of the hotel is that the site signifies a supernatural doorway, fusing the Western's gateway to civilization with the horror genre's place for paranormal activities. This postmodern approach encourages viewers to compare the site's treatment within and without the Western genre."[26] This is a transition that can aid in our understanding of re-imagined frontier narratives—with and without the western genre—a modern narrative inseparable of the larger persisting myth as it relates to American identity.

The Cowboy Shot

This re-imagined frontier narrative is furthered as Agent Cooper rides a similar two-lane highway as that of Fred Madison and Pete Dayton en route to the Pearlblossom Motel in a desolate, desert landscape in *Twin Peaks* Season 3, Part 18. His road literally leads him to an Old West gun standoff for a woman's honor in an Odessa, Texas, diner. The central action in the Judy's Dinner scene occurs from minutes 28:00–30:00 of Part 18. I outlined thirty-three edits in that timeframe of which I would like to focus on the first four, where the mise-en-scène grounds the western genre. Then, we can note the cinematographic intentionality of including a "cowboy shot."

      1. Over the shoulder, high angle, medium—over waitress shoulder onto FBI Special Agent Dale Cooper in booth (shot "a")

      2. Cut Over the shoulder, eye-level, medium long—back of Cooper's head in lower left-hand corner, Waitress pours coffee, can see extended café and three men in a booth (shot "b")

      3. Cut Over the shoulder, high angle, medium—over waitress's shoulder, onto FBI Special Agent Dale Cooper (shot "a")

      4. Cut Over the shoulder, high angle, medium long—Waitress walks away toward the three men in a further booth mid-room, camera pulls slowly downward left as if to pull Cooper back into focus (shot "b")

The second cut is the establishing shot of this entire scene (shot "b"). Most of action occurs from this point of view (POV). The mise-en-scène in these establishing shots tell us a lot about where Cooper has arrived in his journey and add to the functionality of his role as modern cowboy in a neo-noir shootout. It is over-the-shoulder, eye-level, and framed medium long following Cooper's seated POV, allowing audiences full view of the wood-floored, sparsely seated café decorated with steer horns and horse-shoes on the back wall. The wooden beams and set decoration could infer a corral. The café booths compose most of the seating and line the left-hand side wall in front of Cooper. There are very few distractions in the block-ing, which focuses audiences' eyes on the characters in the frame. The back of Cooper's head is dominant in the lower left-hand corner, where he is dressed in the professional black suit of an FBI agent (could be twenti-eth or twenty-first century)—his traditional hero costume. Also dom-inant is the waitress (Francesca Eastwood) in a standard twentieth- or twenty-first-century waitress uniform. Two patrons in the far back-ground are dressed rural casual while three men mid-room are dressed cowboy-style, Stetson hats and contemporary button up shirts. Without audiences knowing where Cooper is (the setting was previously indicated as Odessa, Texas), the elements of mise-en-scène in the establishing shot communicate a rural setting and stage a western interpretation.

Then, looking to my outlined notes for edits ten through thirteen, we can note the one more instance of intentionality in the inclusion of a "cow-boy shot," a cowboy shot being defined as medium profile framing from mid-thigh up. This would center the protagonist or antagonist from gun belt upward. The storytelling introduces a damsel in distress and western hero response narrative. The antagonists—I label them "cowboys"—of this scene are clearly established.

> 1. Cut Over the shoulder, medium long, eye-level—back of Cooper's head lower left-hand corner—Cowboys # 1–3 walk toward camera and Cooper, camera pulls slightly down left to position low angle (shot "a")
> 2. Cut Medium, eye-level, Cook (spectator) in kitchen (shot "c")
> 3. Cut Over the shoulder, low angle, cowboy shot—Cowboy #1 attempts to intimidate Cooper, who is seated in booth. Low angle expresses cowboy's imposing presence (shot "b")
> 4. Cut Over the shoulder (vanguard of arm, actually), medium, high angle—Cooper in booth responding (shot "d")

The shot in edit number twelve establishes the power dynamic between the antagonists (cowboys) and the protagonist (Cooper/hero). The conflict has been brought to the forefront of the camera and made dominant in shot "b." I suggest that edit number twelve from a low angle could also be considered a low angle "cowboy cut" of Cowboy #1. While Fred Madison's narrative asked questions about the soul of the contemporary Los Angeles man, the Cooper/Richard standoff asks the same question of the contemporary fiction detective, exposing its western roots.

When David Lynch reveals his first "traditional" cowboy since his short *The Cowboy and the Frenchman*, he is a figure on the periphery of Diane Selwyn's Los Angeles in *Mulholland Drive*. He is a wise cowboy, albeit a menacing one. A gun is not his menace, but his word is. He is wrapped up in a mythology altogether different from the frontier American West. Here he is a mystical tool for the corrupt machinations of Diane Selwyn's dream of Hollywood. Again, the harsh reality of Los Angeles for Betty (Selwyn in the dream) is the same as that of Robert and Gloria in *They Shoot Horses, Don't They?* Hollywood is rigged against them. The horrors behind the truth of a Hollywood studio conspiracy—her desires are never reciprocated—have corrupted Betty, leading to her suicide. The same disillusionment leads Gloria to convince Robert, tragically, to shoot her in the head. Each can be read as traumatic reactions to the reality of westward expansion's end, its stark terminus and unfulfilled promise. Los Angeles comes to represent a wall where pressures of expansionism's momentum continues to build pressures to tragic ends.

As stated at the beginning of this essay, *INLAND EMPIRE* completes what has become known as Lynch's L.A. Trilogy. With its inclusion of metanarratives about the Hollywood industry and process, it extends Lynch's engagement with the blurring of fiction, life, and personal narratives as

they exist at the terminus of the American West. He began this in *Mulholland Drive*. *INLAND EMPIRE*'s statements on American trauma, appearing in its subtitle: "A Woman in Trouble" form the most dire in his Los
Angeles narratives. It is the culmination of his explorations from *Lost
Highway* as a reaction to the Simpson trial to *Mulholland Drive* as a story
of the Other corrupted and disillusioned by the failed promise of the West.
Hollywood, of course, remains at the center of *INLAND EMPIRE*, with
precepts of Lynch's TM beliefs proliferating. Perhaps the film is best read
here as expressing a karmic bill of consequences for who the American
has become. As Greg Olson points out, "More than ever, [Lynch] would
express his spiritual beliefs in his art, for *INLAND EMPIRE*'s organiz-
ing principle would be reincarnation and past lives, and a recurring karmic reminder would proclaim, 'There's a bill that must be paid.'"[27] In this
Los Angeles re-imagined frontier narrative, the protagonist, "a woman in
trouble," is not a detective or a cowboy. She is the traumatized American at
the precipice of the destabilized frontier. With nowhere else to go, Lynch
introduces the idea of the marketplace, which has been explained by Martha Nochimson thusly: "Lynch's term 'marketplace' refers to the problematic limits of ordinary domestic and public transactions … 'marketplace'
refers to a level of reality at which illusions of stability are promoted by
culture."[28] Lynch's use of the marketplace, then, can represent the American Dream as an illusion promoted by culture, and the traumatized reality is the stark outcome at the failed poetic promise of the American West.
This is re-imagined frontier noir.

Conclusion

The journey west was one of American promise and colonial conquest. The mythic and optimistic dream stained by the removal of native
peoples also found its story an evolutionary but particularly American one
for traditional hero tales. The Western genre's mythic heroes would eventually ride into increasingly urban settings before finding their worlds
changed. Detectives became the urban cowboy in seedy and crime-ridden
environs. The West was claimed, and then World Wars introduced a new,
Atomic Frontier with a Cold War in its wake.[29] As America conquered the
nuclear frontier first, the trauma of it was still shared worldwide. This is
the environment of the film noir. This is the origin of re-imagined frontier narratives as they are regional narratives communicating aftermaths
of colonial conquest.

David Lynch's mysterious neo-noirs follow in this tradition. He is
neither a director of contemporary nor neo-westerns, but the traumas he

engages with his western-located fiction and characters have destinations that come with bills to be paid, representing the American's conflicted interiority at the terminus of geographic westward expansionism. In this context, his films are artistic extensions, a "new way of thinking" on the re-imagined frontier narrative as it evolved in California fiction of the '20s and '30s. These neo-noirs affirm and acknowledge their heritage to California fiction, where audiences can look for evidence of the evolution of western hero narratives and the traumatized American Dream.

Notes

1. Michael Craig Gibbs, "Frontier Re-imagined: The Mythic West in the Twentieth Century," MA thesis (University of South Carolina, 2018), 144, accessed June 2020, https://search-proquest-com.lib-e2.lib.ttu.edu/docview/2185956268?accountid=7098.

2. *Ibid.*, 86.

3. Alexandra Keller, "Historical Discourse and American Identity in Westerns since the Reagan Era," in *Hollywood's West: The American Frontier in Film, Television, and History*, eds. Peter C. Rollins and John E. O'Connor (Lexington: University Press of Kentucky, 2009), 239–260. Also noted by John G. Cawelti, *The Six-Gun Mystique Sequel* (Bowling Green: Bowling Green State University Popular Press, 1999), 2.

4. David Lynch and Kristine McKenna, *Room to Dream* (New York: Random House, 2018), 335.

5. Rob E. King, "The Horse is the White of the Eye: Pioneering and the American Southwest in *Twin Peaks*," *New American Notes Online*, 15 (February 2020), accessed June 2020, https://nanocrit.com/issues/issue15/The-Horse-is-the-White-of-the-Eye-Pioneering-and-the-American-Southwest-in-Twin-Peaks.

6. Josh Garrett-Davis, *What Is a Western?: Region, Genre, Imagination* (Norman: University of Oklahoma Press, 2019), Kindle, introduction, para. 1.

7. Lynch, *Room to Dream*, 119.

8. Martin Klepper, "'From Rags to Riches' and the Self-made Man," in *Approaches to American Cultural Studies*, eds. Antje Dallman, Eva Boesenberg, and Martin Klepper (London: Routledge, 2016), 111.

9. Nick Rose, "David Lynch Wants You to Meditate, Maybe Make a Lamp During Self-Isolation," *Vice*, April 9, 2020, accessed April 12, 2020, https://www.vice.com/en_ca/article/5dmvgq/david-lynch-wants-you-to-meditate-maybe-make-a-lamp-during-self-isolation.

10. Christopher Scheer, Sarah Victoria Turner, and James G. Mansell, *Enchanted Modernities: Theosophy, the Arts, and the American West* ([Logan, Utah]: Nora Eccles Harrison Museum of Art, Utah State University, 2019), 1.

11. William Michael Ashcraft, "'The Dawn of the New Cycle': Point Loma Theosophists and American Culture, 1896–1929" (PhD diss., University of Chicago, 2013), 99–100.

12. Gibbs, "Frontier Re-Imagined," 7–8.

13. Greg Grandon, *The End of the Myth: From the Frontier to the Border Wall in the Mind of America* (New York: Henry Holt and Company, 2019), 3.

14. David Fine, *Imagining Los Angeles: A City in Fiction* (Reno: University of Nevada Press, 2000), chap. 4, para. 2, Kindle.

15. Gibbs, "Frontier Re-Imagined," 83.

16. Douglas Keesey, *Neo-noir: Contemporary Film Noir from* Chinatown *to* The Dark Knight (Hapenden, Herts: Kamera Books, 2015), 14.

17. It is now well-cited in Lynch's biography *Room to Dream* in a quote by Tony Krantz that the initial concept for the series that would become *Mulholland Drive*, had *Twin Peaks*

Season 2 been successful, began with the concept of a *Twin Peaks* spin-off, wherein Audrey Horne would go to Hollywood.

18. Jane Tompkins, *West of Everything: The Inner Life of Westerns* (New York: Oxford University Press, 1992), 5.

19. the-numbers.com, "Number of Movies Released in North America from 1995 to 2019, by Genre," January 9, 2020, *Statista*, accessed April 12, 2020, https://www-statista-com.lib-e2.lib.ttu.edu/statistics/188672/movie-genres-in-north-america-by-number-of-releases-since-1995/.

20. "History of Hollywood, California," *U-S-History.com*, accessed February 18, 2020, https://u-s-history.com/pages/h3871.html.

21. Gary Krist, *The Mirage Factory: Illusion, Imagination, and the Invention of Los Angeles* (New York: Broadway Books, 2018), 59–60.

22. Fine, *Imagining Los Angeles*, preface and acknowledgments.

23. This author is taking the position that Fred Madison, in anguish over his murder, experiences dissociative or psychogenic fugue from his jail cell and projects himself into the life of Pete Dayton, a younger, hipper version of himself, in a dream. His dissociative fugue extends to the Mystery Man as well.

24. David Lynch and Barry Gifford, *Lost Highway* (London: Faber and Faber, 1997), 127.

25. Monica Montelongo Flores, "Cowboy Accommodations Plotting the Hotel in Western Film and Television," in *A Fistful of Icons: Essays on Frontier Fixtures of the American Western*, ed. Sue Matheson (Jefferson, North Carolina: McFarland & Company, Inc., 2017), 172.

26. *Ibid.*

27. Greg Olson, *David Lynch: Beautiful Dark* (Lanham: Scarecrow Press, 2008), 666.

28. Martha P. Nochimson, *David Lynch Swerves: Uncertainty from* Lost Highway *to* Inland Empire (Austin: University of Texas Press, 2013), introduction.

29. Rob E. King, "The Horse is the White of the Eye: Pioneering and the American Southwest in *Twin Peaks*," *New American Notes Online* 15 (February 2020), accessed June 2020, https://nanocrit.com/issues/issue15/The-Horse-is-the-White-of-the-Eye-Pioneering-and-the-American-Southwest-in-Twin-Peaks.

Works Cited

Ashcraft, William Michael. 2013. "'The Dawn of the New Cycle': Point Loma Theosophists and American Culture, 1896–1929" (PhD diss., University of Chicago), 99–100.

Cawelti, John G. 1999. *The Six-Gun Mystique Sequel.* Bowling Green, OH: Bowling Green State University Popular Press.

Donovan, Mia, dir. 2016. *Deprogrammed.* New York: FilmBuff. Prime Video (streaming online video).

Flores, Monica Montelongo. 2017. "Cowboy Accommodations Plotting the Hotel in Western Film and Television." In Sue Matheson (ed.), *A Fistful of Icons: Essays on Frontier Fixtures of the American Western.* 166–176. Jefferson, NC: McFarland.

Garrett-Davis, Josh. 2019. *What Is a Western?: Region, Genre, Imagination.* Norman: University of Oklahoma Press. Kindle, intro., para. 1.

Gibbs, Michael Craig. 2018. "Frontier Re-imagined: The Mythic West in the Twentieth Century." Order No. 10978380. Columbia: University of South Carolina. Accessed May 26, 2020. https://search-proquest-com.libe2.lib.ttu.edu/docview/2185956268?accountid=7098.

Grandon, Greg. 2019. *The End of the Myth: From the Frontier to the Border Wall in the Mind of America.* New York: Henry Holt and Company.

Keesey, Douglas. 2015. *Neo-noir: Contemporary Film Noir from* Chinatown *to* The Dark Knight. Harpenden, UK: Kamera Books.

Keller, Alexandra. 2009. "Historical Discourse and American Identity in Westerns since the Reagan Era." In Peter C. Rollins and John E. O'Connor (eds.), *Hollywood's West:*

The American Frontier in Film, Television, and History. 239–260. Lexington: University Press of Kentucky.

King, Rob E., "The Horse is the White of the Eye: Pioneering and the American Southwest in *Twin Peaks*," *New American Notes Online*, 15 (February 2020): https://nanocrit.com/issues/issue15/The-Horse-is-the-White-of-the-Eye-Pioneering-and-the-American-Southwest-in-Twin-Peaks.

Klepper, Martin. 2016. "'From rags to riches' and the Self-Made Man." In Antje Dallman, Eva Boesenberg, and Martin Klepper (eds.), *Approaches to American Cultural Studies.* 111–119. London: Routledge.

Krist, Gary. 2018. *The Mirage Factory: Illusion, Imagination, and the Invention of Los Angeles.* New York: Broadway Books.

Lynch, David, and Barry Gifford. 1997. *Lost Highway.* London: Faber and Faber.

Lynch, David, and Kristine McKenna. 2018. *Room to Dream.* New York: Random House.

McCoy, Horace. 2010. *They Shoot Horses, Don't They?* London: Serpent's Tail.

Nochimson, Martha P. 2013. *David Lynch Swerves: Uncertainty from* Lost Highway *to* Inland Empire. Austin: University of Texas Press.

Rose, Nick. "David Lynch Wants You to Meditate, Maybe Make a Lamp During Self-Isolation." *Vice*, April 9, 2020. Accessed April 12, 2020. https://www.vice.com/en_ca/article/5dmvgq/david-lynch-wants-you-to-meditate-maybe-make-a-lamp-during-self-isolation.

Tennessee State University. "Cults in America." Accessed May 26, 2020. https://www.arcgis.com/apps/Cascade/index.html?appid=7b33d5df643842a8875ff9f675ce6ae2.

The-numbers.com. "Number of movies released in North America from 1995 to 2019, by genre." Chart. January 9, 2020. *Statista*. Accessed April 12, 2020. https://www-statista-com.lib-e2.lib.ttu.edu/statistics/188672/movie-genres-in-north-america-by-number-of-releases-since-1995/.

Thompson, Hunter S. 1982. *Fear and Loathing in Las Vegas.* New York: Warner Books.

Tompkins, Jane. 1992. *West of Everything: The Inner Life of Westerns.* New York: Oxford University Press.

Toohill, Kathleen. "By the Decade: Notorious 20th Century American Cults." *Medium.* July 19, 2017. Accessed May 26, 2020. https://medium.com/s/how-to-cult/by-the-decade-notorious-20th-century-american-cults-d62939b065e5.

U-S-History.com. "History of Hollywood, California." Accessed February 18, 2020. https://u-s-history.com/pages/h3871.html.

Appendix

Character and Actor Guide for David Lynch Films in This Collection

The Cowboy and the Frenchman

Pierre the Frenchman—Frederic Golchan
Broken Feather—Michael Horse
Slim—Harry Dean Stanton

Eraserhead

Mrs. X—Jeanne Bates
The Boy—Thomas Coulson
Bill X—Allen Joseph
Pencil Machine Operator—Hal Landon, Jr.
Grandmother—Jean Lange
Henry Spencer—Jack Nance
Lady in the Radiator—Laurel Near
Beautiful Girl Across the Hall—Judith Roberts
Mary X—Charlotte Stewart

Elephant Man

Dr. Frederick Treves—Anthony Hopkins
Joseph Merrick—John Hurt
Bytes—Freddie Jones

Blue Velvet

Frank Booth—Dennis Hopper
Jeffrey Beaumont—Kyle MacLachlan
Dorothy Vallens—Isabella Rossellini

Twin Peaks (1990) and Twin Peaks: Fire Walk with Me (1992)

Ronette Pulaski—Phoebe Augustine
Bobby Briggs—Dana Ashbrook
Ben Horne—Richard Beymer
Donna Hayward—Lara Flynn Boyle
Josie Packard—Joan Chen
Log Lady/Margaret Lanterman—Catherine E. Coulson
Judge Clinton Sternwood—Royal Dano
Leo Johnson—Eric DaRe
Johnny Horne—Robert Davenport
Garland Briggs—Don S. Davis
Audrey Horne—Sherilyn Fenn
Albert Rosenfeld—Miguel Ferrer
Andy Brennan—Harry Goaz
Annie Blackburn—Heather Graham
Mike Nelson—Gary Hershberger
Tommy "Hawk" Hill—Michael Horse

Jerry Horne—David Patrick Kelly
Catherine Martell—Piper Laurie
Laura Palmer/Madeleine Ferguson—Sheryl Lee
Norma Jennings—Peggy Lipton
Gordon Cole—David Lynch
Dale Cooper—Kyle MacLachlan
James Hurley—James Marshall
Big Ed Hurley—Everett McGill
Pete Martell—Jack Nance
Andrew Packard—Dan O'Herlihy
Jacque Renault—Walter Olkewicz
Harry S. Truman—Michael Ontkean
Jean Renault—Michael Parks
Lucy Moran—Kimmy Robertson
Nadine Hurley—Wendie Robie
BOB—Frank Silva
Carl Rodd—Harry Dean Stanton
MIKE/Phillip Gerard—Al Strobel
Giant—Carl Struycken
Lawrence Jacoby—Russ Tamblyn
Joey Paulson—Brett Vadset
Windom Earle—Kenneth Walsh
Gwen Morton—Kathleen Wilhoite
Leland Palmer—Ray Wise
Dell Mibbler—Ed Wright
Sarah Palmer—Grace Zabriskie

Wild at Heart

Sailor Ripley—Nicolas Cage
Bobby Peru—Willem Dafoe
Lula Pace Fortune—Laura Dern
Uncle Pooch—Marvin Kaplan
Marietta Fortune—Diane Ladd

Lost Highway

Renee/Alice Wakefield—Patricia Arquette
Mystery Man—Robert Blake
Pete Dayton—Balthazar Getty
Mr. Eddy/Dick Laurent—Robert Loggia
Fred Madison—Bill Pullman

Mulholland Dr.

Mr. Roque—Michael J. Anderson
Rita/Camilla Rhodes—Laura Elena Harring
Cowboy—Lafayette Montgomery
Adam Kesher—Justin Theroux
Diane Selwyn/Betty Elms—Naomi Watts

Twin Peaks (2017)

Tamara Preston—Chrysta Bell
Bradley Mitchum—Jim Belushi
Buella—Kathleen Deming
Diane—Laura Dern
Richard Horne—Eamon Farren
Frank Truman—Robert Forster
Walter Lawford—Grant Goodeve
Ray Monroe—George Griffith
Rodney Mitchum—Robert Knepper
Carrie Page—Sheryl Lee
Chantal Hutchens—Jennifer Jason Leigh
Dale Cooper/Dougie Jones/Mr. C—Kyle MacLachlan
Bushnell Mullins—Don Murray
Naido—Nae
Lady Slot-Addict—Linda Porter
Candie—Amy Shiels
Fireman—Carl Struycken
Maggie (Dispatcher)—Jodie Thelen
Jade—Nafessa Williams
Lucy Brennan—Kimmy Robertson
Gary "Hutch" Hutchens—Tim Roth
Doctor Amp—Russ Tamblyn
Freddie Sykes—Jake Wardle
Janey-E Jones—Naomi Watts

About the Contributors

Geoff **Bil** is a historian of science and a visiting assistant professor in the Department of History at the University of Delaware, specializing in 19th- and 20th-century botany, anthropology, empire and Indigenous history. He is the author of numerous essays, including "Tensions in the World of Moon: *Twin Peaks*, Indigeneity, and Territoriality" for *Senses of Cinema* (2016). He is the author of *Indexing the Indigenous: Plants, Peoples and Empire*.

Franck **Boulègue** is a French film critic and author whose writing is published in a variety of books, journals and film magazines, including *Cahiers du Cinéma* and *Positif*. He is the author of Twin Peaks: *Unwrapping the Plastic* and Twin Peaks: *Squaring the Circle*, and a coeditor of *Fan Phenomena*: Twin Peaks.

Thomas **Britt** is a professor of film and video studies at George Mason University. He is the head of the department's screenwriting concentration and teaches courses on the ethics of film and video as well as global horror film. His previous writing on Lynch includes "There Are No Accidents on Mulholland Dr.," published in *PopMatters*, and "'Between Two Mysteries': Intermediacy in *Twin Peaks: The Return*," from *Critical Essays on* Twin Peaks: The Return.

Andrew T. **Burt** works in the English Department at Henderson State University where he teaches composition and literature courses. His research focuses on the interplay of true-crime narratives and fictional crime and horror texts. He specializes in crime studies, masculinity studies, and rock and roll studies. He has published chapters in the edited collections *Critical Essays on* Twin Peaks and *Music in* Twin Peaks.

Monica Montelongo **Flores** teaches multiethnic American literature at California State University, Stanislaus. She has given multiple presentations on Western elements in *Twin Peaks* and the films of David Lynch and includes the subject in her essay "Cowboy Accommodations: Plotting the Hotel in Western Film and Television," which appeared in *A Fistful of Icons: Essays on Frontier Fixtures of the American Western*.

Andy **Hageman** is an associate professor of English at Luther College, where he researches and teaches intersections of technology, ideology, and ecology in film and literature. He publishes academic essays and popular journalism on matters that range from Chinese science fiction and ecocinema critique to Gary Snyder's poetics and David Lynch's cinema.

Andréas **Halskov** holds an MA in film studies from Copenhagen University. He is a lecturer in media studies at Aarhus University, an editor of the scholarly film journal *16:9*, and a curator of film historical screenings at Cinemateket in Copenhagen. He has published articles in journals like *Kosmorama, Series*, and *Blue Rose Magazine* and has co-written four Danish anthologies on American television, the Oscars, and film and television comedy.

Marisa C. **Hayes** is a Franco-American scholar. Her research focuses on the intersections of moving images and the performing arts. Her writing on David Lynch and Mark Frost is featured in *The Women of David Lynch, The Supernatural Studies Journal* and a forthcoming research journal. She is coeditor, with Franck Boulègue, of *Fan Phenomena:* Twin Peaks. She is also the author of *Ju-on: The Grudge*.

Rebecca **Heimel** is an interdisciplinary artist and professor. An MFA graduate of Goddard College, she is a visiting lecturer and the Elizabeth J. McCormack Chair of Humanities at Cambridge College. Her academic research includes socially engaged art, public art, gender, adult education and multicultural education.

Mark **Henderson** earned his MA in English at the University of Louisiana at Monroe. He went on to earn his PhD in English at Auburn University with concentrations in American literature and psychoanalytic theory. His teaching and research interests include the American Gothic, American modernism, American film, and Afrofuturism.

Rob E. **King** is an associate librarian at Texas Tech University's Southwest Collection/Special Collections Library and a doctoral student in English at Texas Tech University with a dual concentration in literature, social justice, and environment and film and media studies. In addition to writing articles for *25YL* and contributing as a guest to *Blue Rose Magazine*, he has published articles in *New American Notes Online*, the *West Texas Historical Review*, and *AE*.

Marko **Lukić** is an associate professor in the English Department at the University of Zadar, Croatia. He teaches courses in American literature and cultural theory. His research interests include violence and trauma in American fiction, human spatiality and space in literature and film. He is the editor-in-chief of *[sic]—A Journal of Literature, Culture and Literary Translation*, and the cofounder of the Centre for Research in Social Sciences and Humanities.

Molly **O'Gorman** is a writer from Dublin, Ireland. Her work on posthumanism in Lewis Carroll's "Jabberwocky" was presented at the "Threshold, Boundary and Crossover in Fantasy" conference in 2020. Her short story "Dismember Me" features in the *fron//tera* literary journal. Her 2016 play *Broad Shadow* won the National Theatre New Views writing competition and was performed at the Dorfman Theatre.

Fernando Gabriel **Pagnoni Berns** is a professor at the Universidad de Buenos Aires. He teaches courses on international horror film and is director of the research group on horror cinema "Grite." He has authored a book about the Spanish horror TV series *Historias para no Dormir* and has edited a book on the Frankenstein bicentennial, one on director James Wan and one on the Italian *giallo* film.

Christine **Self** has worked in higher education for nearly 20 years. Her research interests include family involvement in higher education, the experiences of women in higher education, women's and gender studies, and sexual violence prevention in higher education. She serves as the Director for Family Outreach and Engagement at Texas Tech University, Parent & Family Relations.

David **Titterington** is a painter and teaches Native North American art at Haskell Indian Nations University, the largest all–Indigenous university in the United States, located in Lawrence, Kansas. He also researches American sites of tragedy, such as Japanese internment camps, nuclear test and toxic waste sites, and Indian and settler massacre sites.

John **Thorne** was, for thirteen years, the coeditor and co-producer of the magazine *Wrapped in Plastic*, where he wrote extensively about *Twin Peaks* and the films of David Lynch. He is the author of *The Essential* Wrapped in Plastic: *Pathways to* Twin Peaks and *Ominous Whoosh: A Wandering Mind Returns to* Twin Peaks, as well as coeditor and contributor to Twin Peaks *in the Rearview Mirror.*

Robert G. **Weaver** is the Manuscript Archivist of the Southwest Collection at Texas Tech University's Southwest Collection/Special Collections Library, where he coordinates the availability of both physical and digital archival collections. He served as editor of the *West Texas Historical Review* for the West Texas Historical Association.

Garrett Wayne **Wright** received his PhD from the University of North Carolina at Chapel Hill. His dissertation focused on Indigenous travelers who explored European and U.S. settlements in the eighteenth and nineteenth centuries. He is an independent scholar.

Index

Fictitious characters are listed by their first name.